CUBA by KORDA

Edited by Christophe Loviny

Text by Christophe Loviny and Alessandra Silvestri-Lévy

Preface by Jaime Sarusky

Translated by Nic Maclellan

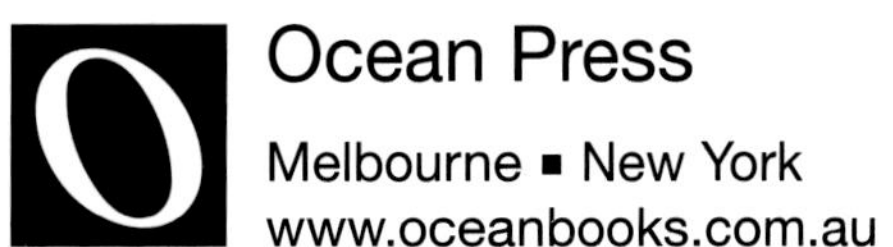
Ocean Press
Melbourne ▪ New York
www.oceanbooks.com.au

preface

Jaime Sarusky

I first met Alberto Díaz in 1941, within the austere walls of a Protestant college in the suburbs of Havana. That name probably means nothing to the reader, until I explain that the man was Alberto Korda, the photographer who took the picture of Che Guevara that is known around the world—the most reproduced image in the history of photography. At the time, we were students at the prestigious college where the Cuban author Alejo Carpentier had completed his studies some years before.

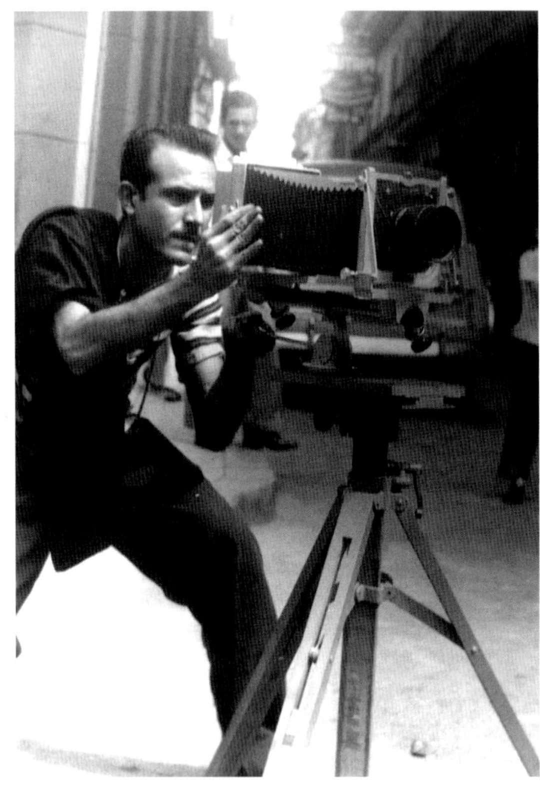

I still wonder whether it was in the chapel where, unaware, Korda developed his passion for women and feminine beauty. All of us witnessed the adoration for women he began to develop, contemplating those beautiful girls listening to the pastor's sermons.

Like a good number of his Cuban colleagues, Korda started out in photography as a *lambio*—someone who takes photos at banquets, baptisms, or weddings. He'd dash to his studio to develop the film, returning to the function to sell photos to people who wanted a souvenir of the event. In reality, the photo quality was very poor—the paper turned yellow after a few months and the images blurred. He later opened a studio with Luis Pierce, a resourceful fellow who cruised around Havana on a bicycle, doing bits and pieces to earn himself a bit of money. We gave Luis the nickname "Korda Senior," but many people called him "Hemingway" because he had an extraordinary resemblance to the famous writer. Their studio carried the name of two Hungarian directors, Alexander and Zoltan Korda, whose films were showing in Havana at the time. The name also evoked "Kodak," a term long associated with photography.

Alberto Korda was most interested in the world of fashion, which allowed him to combine his two passions, his two obsessions: photography and feminine beauty. He started to chase after up-and-coming models. This type of photography was unknown in Cuba. But Korda managed to find a regular spot in a Havana weekly where elegant, beautiful young women posed, all suggestively erotic, with dresses, perfume, and soap. Korda became the pioneer of fashion photography and advertising in Cuba. This was without doubt his real vocation, but as they say, fate has a tendency to intervene. History erupted and there was a turning point in Korda's professional career and his life in general. His plans were radically altered by

CUBA by KORDA

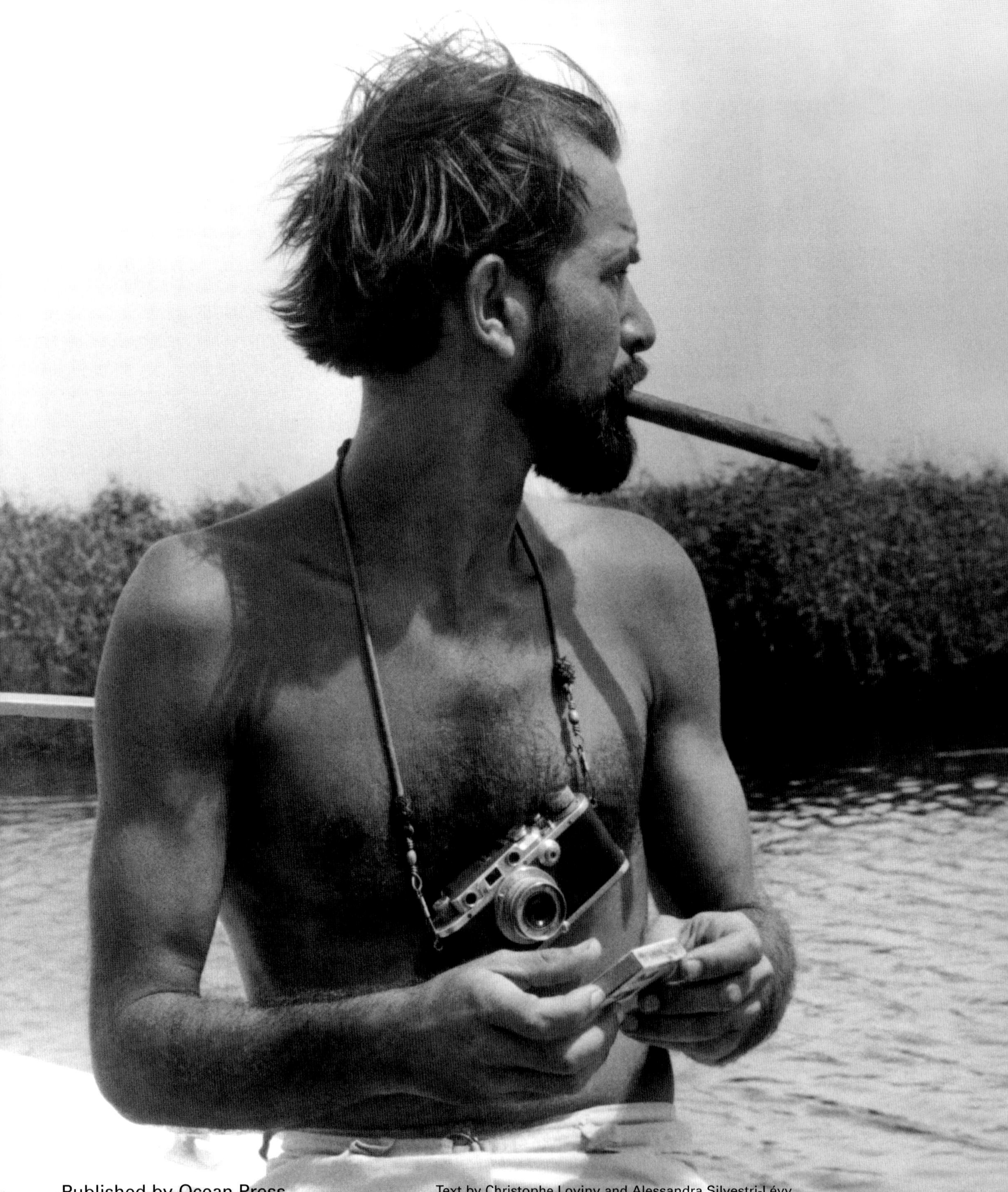

Published by Ocean Press

First published in French as *Cuba par Korda*

ISBN 10: 1-920888-64-0
ISBN 13: 978-1-920888-64-0
Library of Congress Control No: 2006923940

First printed 2006

Text by Christophe Loviny and Alessandra Silvestri-Lévy
Preface by Jaime Sarusky
Translated by Nic Maclellan

Graphic design and layout by Paula Holme and
::maybe, www.maybe.com.au

the victory of the revolutionaries, the *barbudos* (bearded ones) who came down from the mountains to take over the cities.

Korda was called on to join the staff of the newly created newspaper *Revolución*. We were in the first weeks of 1959 and Cuba was a world turned upside down. The newspaper offered vast space for photography; giant headlines were like posters calling on the population to mobilize. They published a photo supplement three times a week. When Fidel Castro visited the United States in April 1959, Korda was part of the team sent to cover the trip. He was swept up in this extraordinary event, photographing the Cuban leader day by day. He captured activities such as Castro's visit to the Lincoln Memorial in Washington, producing a striking image of the event. He then accompanied Castro on his tours around Cuba and overseas, including the *comandante*'s visits to the Soviet Union in 1963 and 1964. He shared intimate moments with Nikita Khrushchev and his family, in a casual atmosphere, which he recorded for posterity. These photos reveal, or appear to reveal, the rapprochement between the two leaders, ending a breach created by their diverging policies during the Cuban Missile Crisis of October 1962.

In New York, Korda contacted Richard Avedon who welcomed the Cuban to his studio. Korda showed Avedon photos of Norka, his favorite model, his muse, and his wife. The famous US photographer suggested that Korda should photograph models in the midst of revolutionary events, which Korda tried to do on different occasions: during the 1960s, *Paris Match* published a long photo essay where Norka appeared in a blue work shirt and olive green pants, the uniform of the Cuban militia.

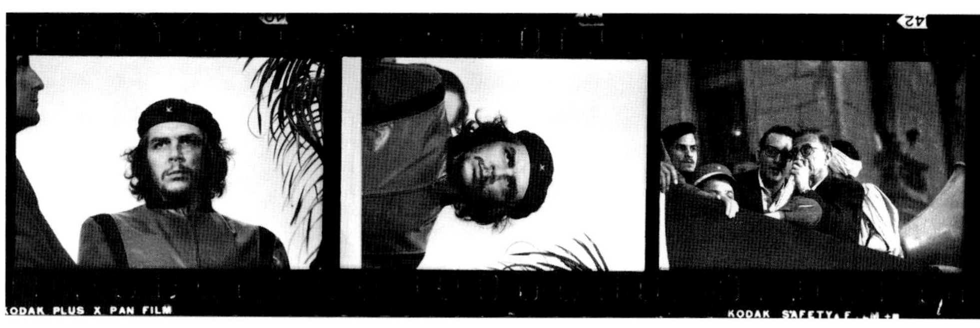

I had lost contact with Alberto Díaz for almost 20 years, but I encountered him again as Alberto Korda. He was a photographer; I was a journalist with *Revolución*. On March 5, 1960, the day Korda took his famous photo of Che Guevara, I was on the platform working as an interpreter for Jean-Paul Sartre and Simone de Beauvoir. It was during the funeral ceremony for victims of the sabotage of the French freighter *La Coubre* in Havana's port. Korda was taking photos less than a dozen steps from the platform where Fidel Castro was addressing the crowd. Che came forward to the barrier to look over the crowd. At that moment Korda's lynx-like eye focused on Che through his camera's telephoto lens. The contrast between the momentary nature of that snapshot and the durability of the image in our time is striking. This photograph has become a universal symbol, to which everyone can give their own interpretation.

At the time, photographers were not really conscious that in photographing the dynamic of a revolution and starting to write the history of Cuban photography, they were extraordinary witnesses to the events underway on the island. The fate of the photo itself was not remarkable until after Che's assassination in Bolivia, when it became a cultish object of veneration. In Italy, the publisher Feltrinelli sold hundreds of thousands of posters after Korda had given him a print of the photo, for which Korda nevertheless possessed the copyright.

Let us stop for a moment to look at this photo of Che and his appearance. It was a cool and cloudy Havana morning in March, filled with pain, anger, and suppressed violence. Che was wearing a bright green and black leather jacket, closed at the neck, highlighting his stern, severe face. It was the ideal image with which to create a legend, which may not have flourished from other photos of him. The almost religious fervor which greeted this image of Che was very surprising—anyone who is familiar with Che's beliefs knows that he would be the first to reject this adoration. Paradoxically, the more this icon of Che is reproduced, the farther it drifts from Che's essence.

That night, spread across the layout table at *Revolución*, there were dozens of photos from the funeral service for the victims of the attack. But Korda's photo of Che, which lay among them, was not chosen. Instead, the daily paper published images of Fidel Castro and of the crowd, as he addressed it holding two explosives [the same as those used in the sabotage]. Korda's photo of Che was only published a year later on April 15, 1961, (on the eve of the Bay of Pigs invasion). It accompanied a brief paragraph announcing a televised interview which Che was giving as minister of industry.

Korda left a vast body of work. Nevertheless, he was known and recognized throughout the world for this one photo. Korda had the privilege to live and work intensely. His vocation was to be an aesthete and a hedonist, and he always did what he wanted to do. He could have lived as he wished no matter where he was in the world. But he preferred to stay in his own country, in his apartment by the sea, surrounded by friends and the young, beautiful women he loved in his way, filled with the tranquility of someone who knows he has achieved what he set out to do.

Jaime Sarusky

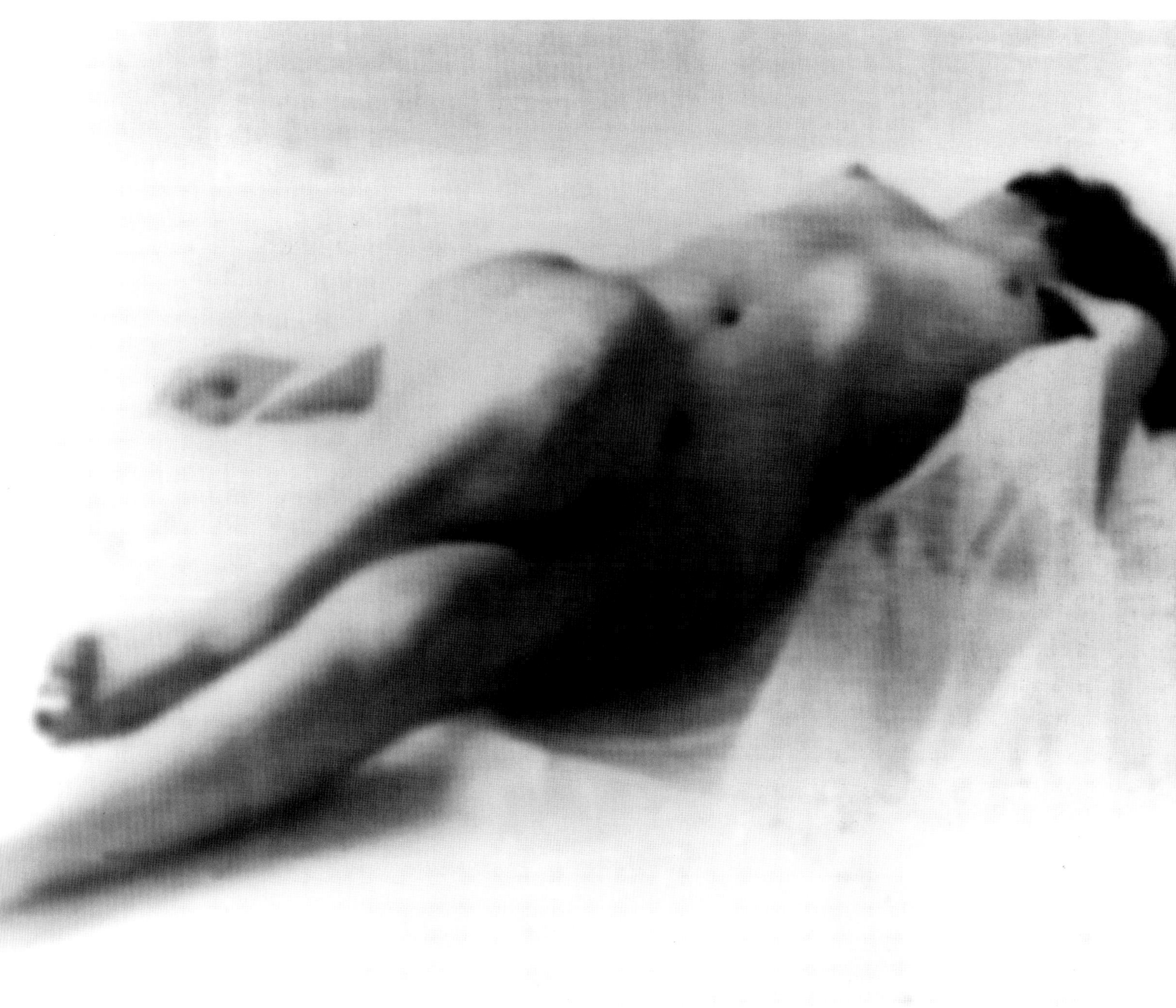

Above: Korda's first nude, circa 1950.

Following double page: Nudes for the Cuban magazine Carteles, *circa 1955. Recent prints taken from copies.*

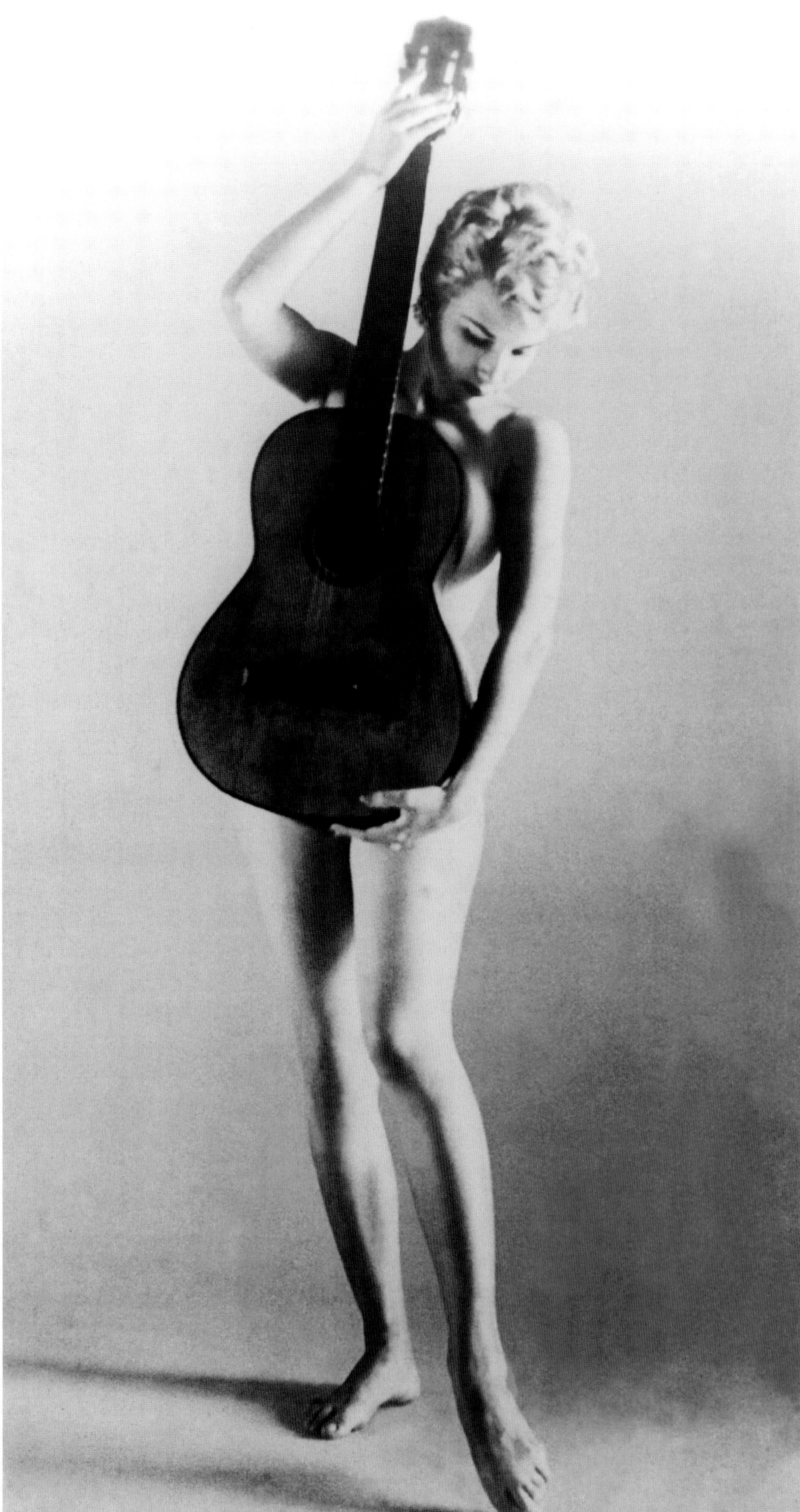

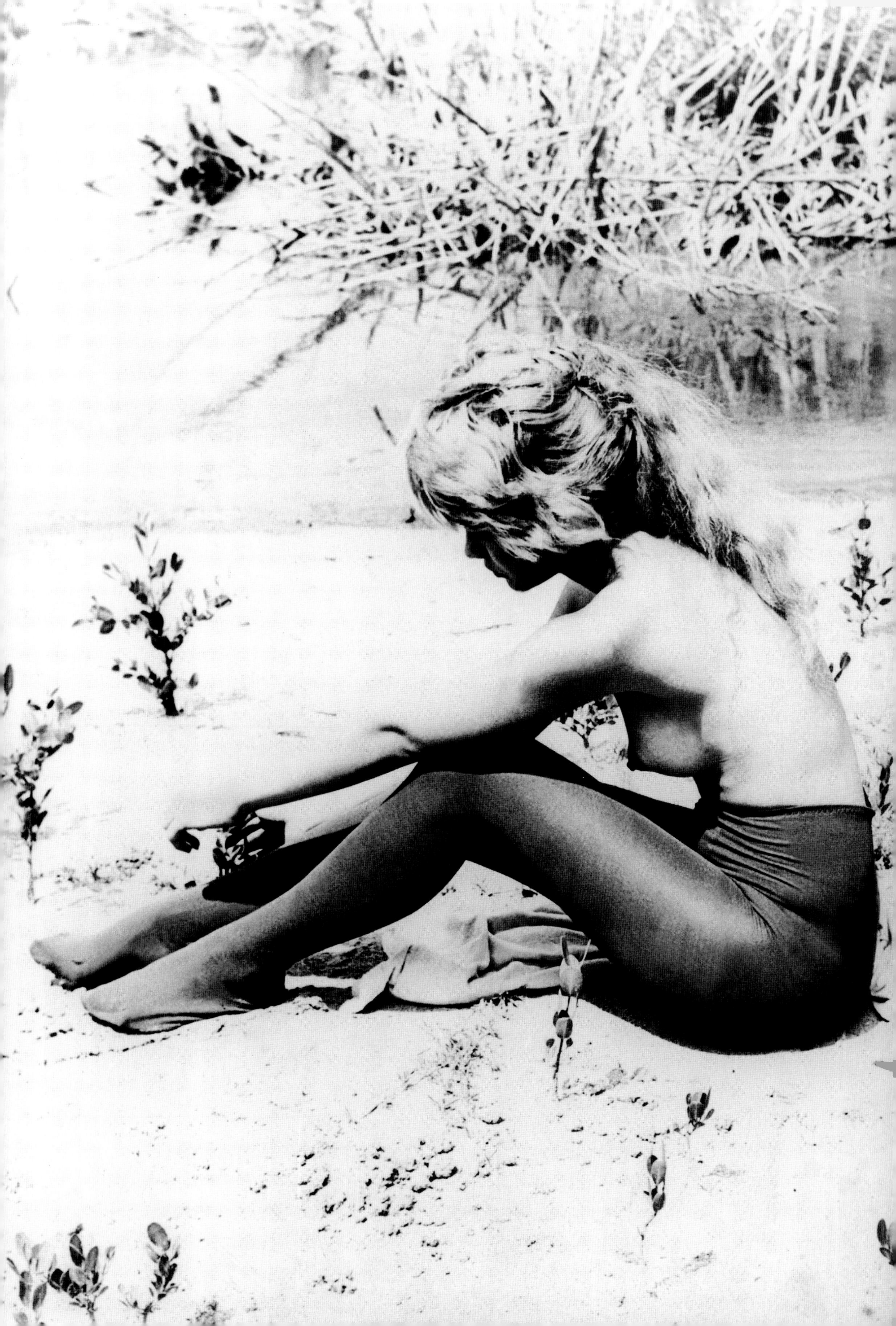

"My first studio, the Metropolitana, was located in Old Havana. In 1953, I was able to move it opposite the Hotel Capri. This became Korda Studios. I was working with another photographer, my friend Luis Pierce. He was Korda Senior and I was Korda Junior! To make a living, I started doing advertisements, photographing sausage wrappers and packets of coffee. And then I became the first fashion photographer in Cuba."

Norka, by Korda. Advertising photo for a line of lingerie. Recent print taken from copy.

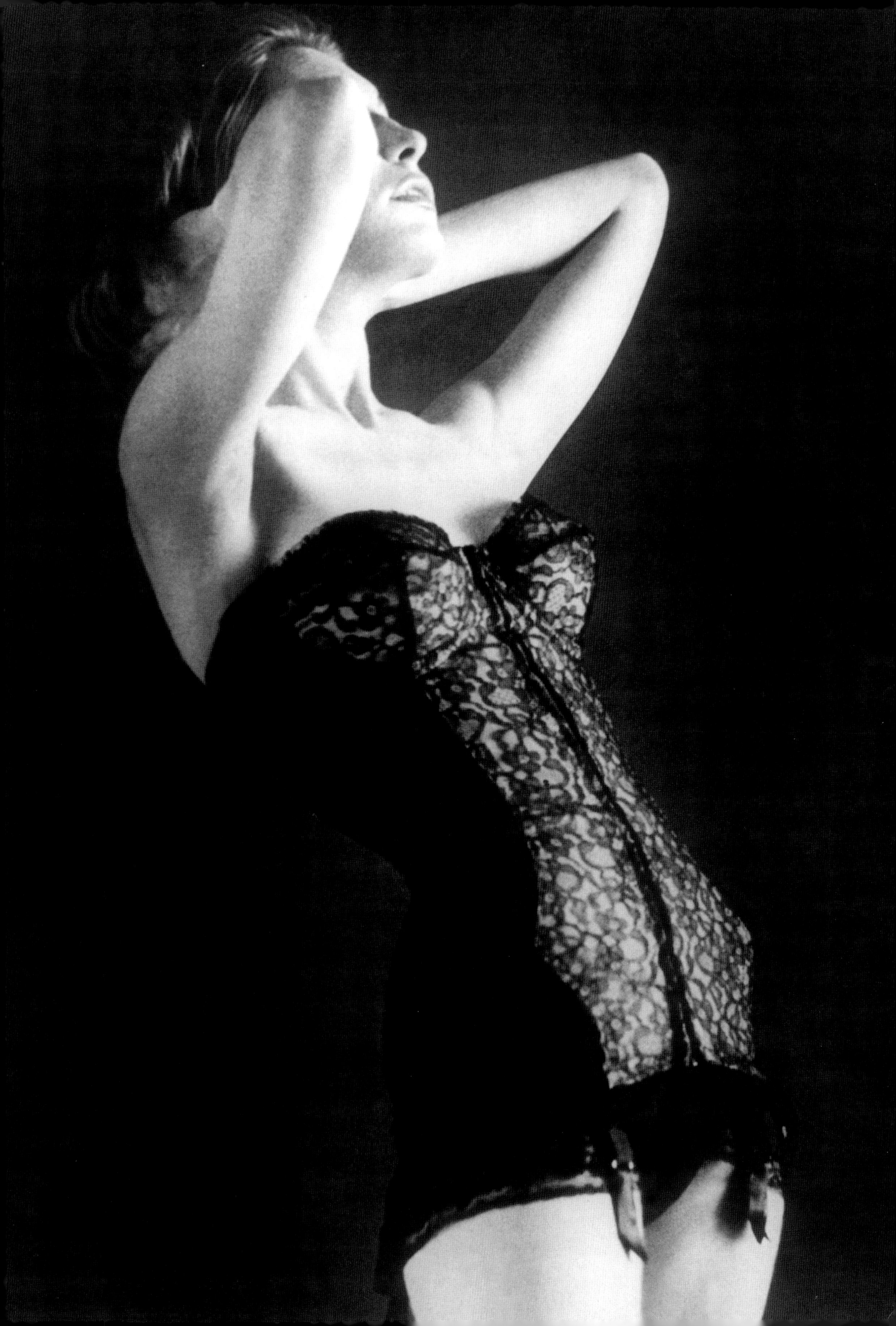

"Until that time, models had been small, well-rounded, with large hips and busts. I had great difficulty finding a woman with classic lines, capable of impressing other women. Because it's women who buy the clothes we photograph. Finally, I met Norka..."

Norka, by Korda.
Personal work.
Original print restored.

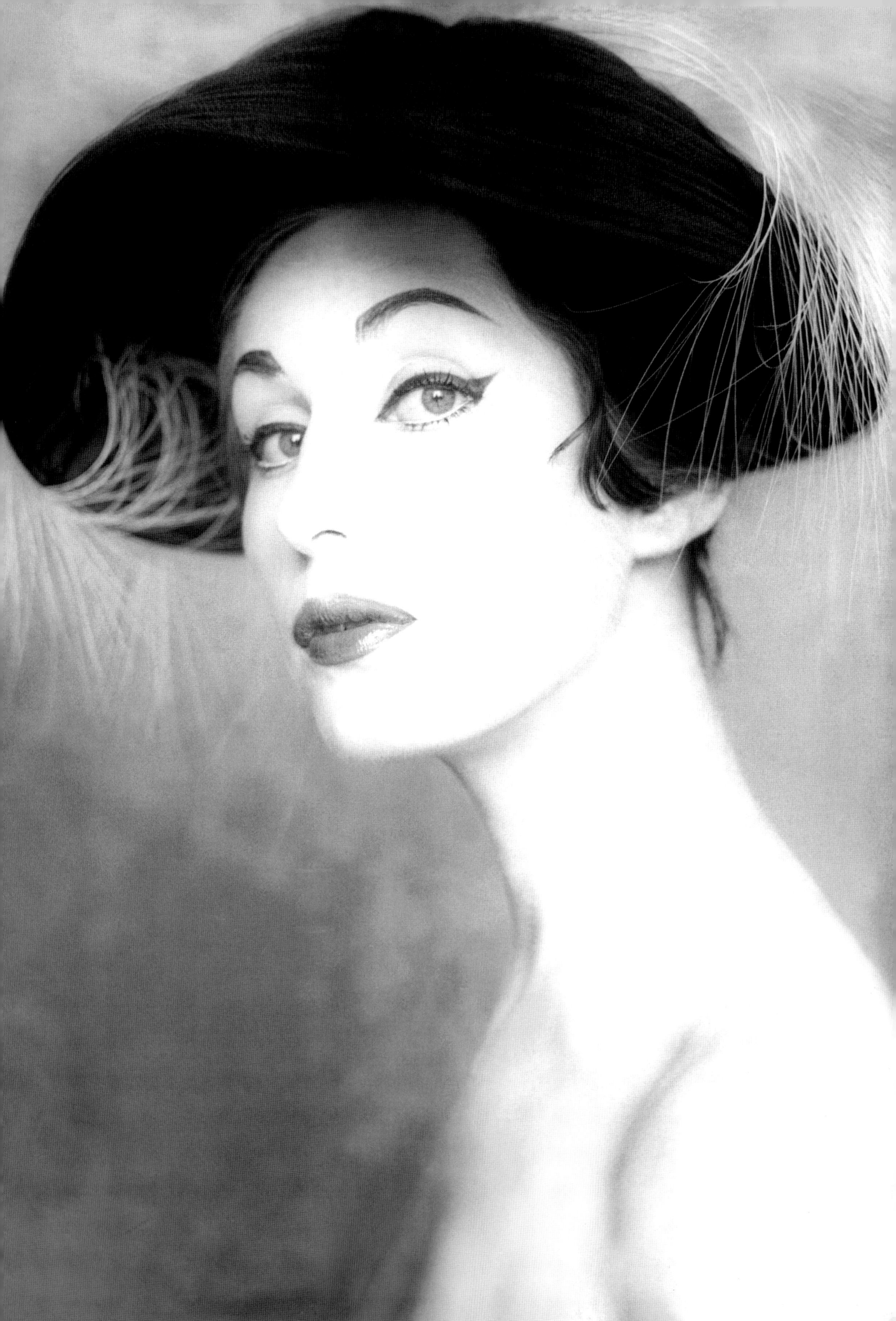

"Norka's real name was Natalia Mendez. She was my favorite model, my muse, then my wife. Of Sioux Indian heritage, she possessed an uncontrollable, expressive power... She was the most famous model in Cuba and had been a catwalk model for Dior in Paris."

Norka, by Korda. Advertising photo for a dress designer. Original print.

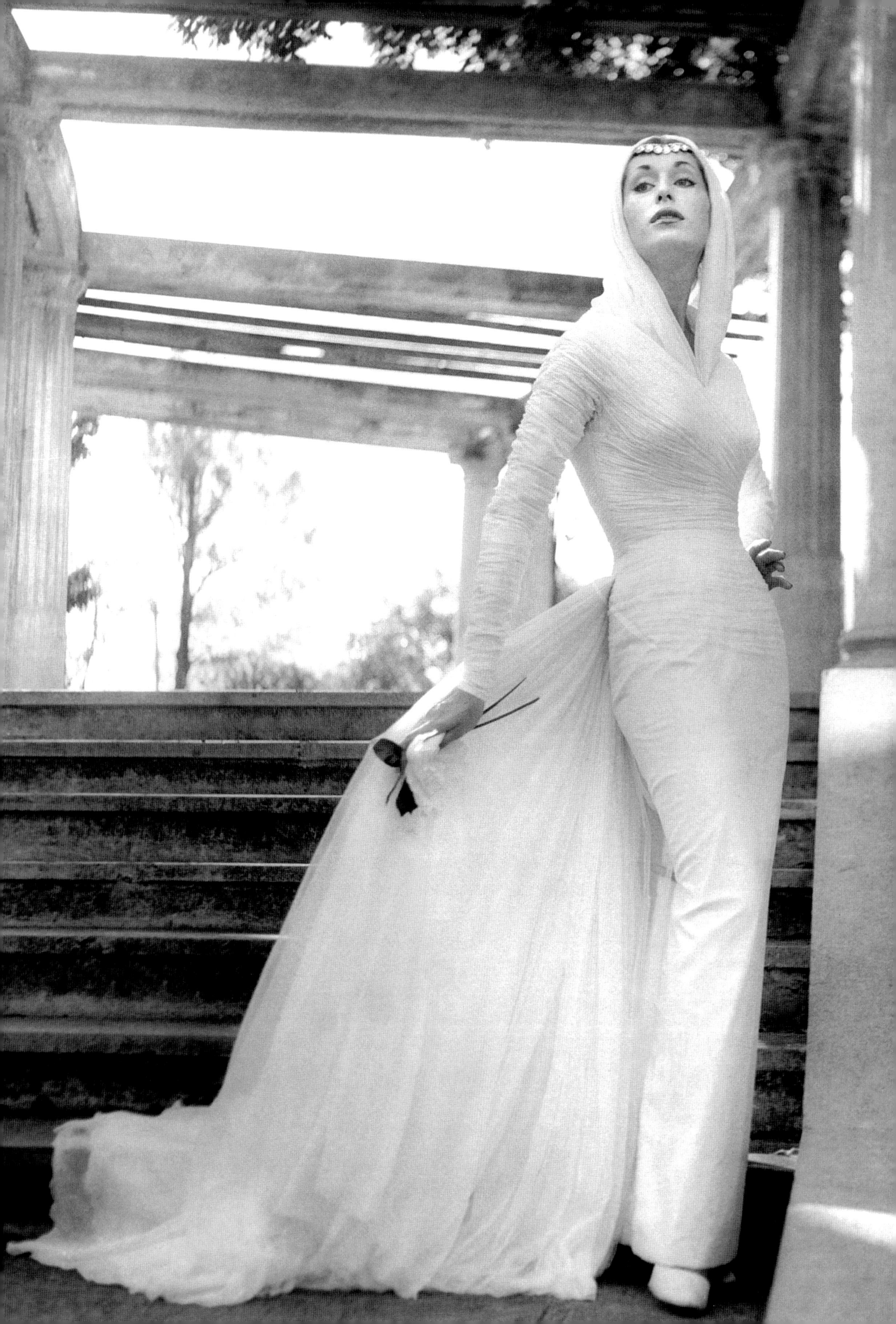

"I only like using natural light. Artificial lighting is a travesty of reality. The windows of my studios always faced north to avoid direct sunlight. At the beginning, I made reflectors with the shiny packaging of photo paper. My mentor was Richard Avedon..."

Norka, by Korda.
Personal work.
Original print restored.

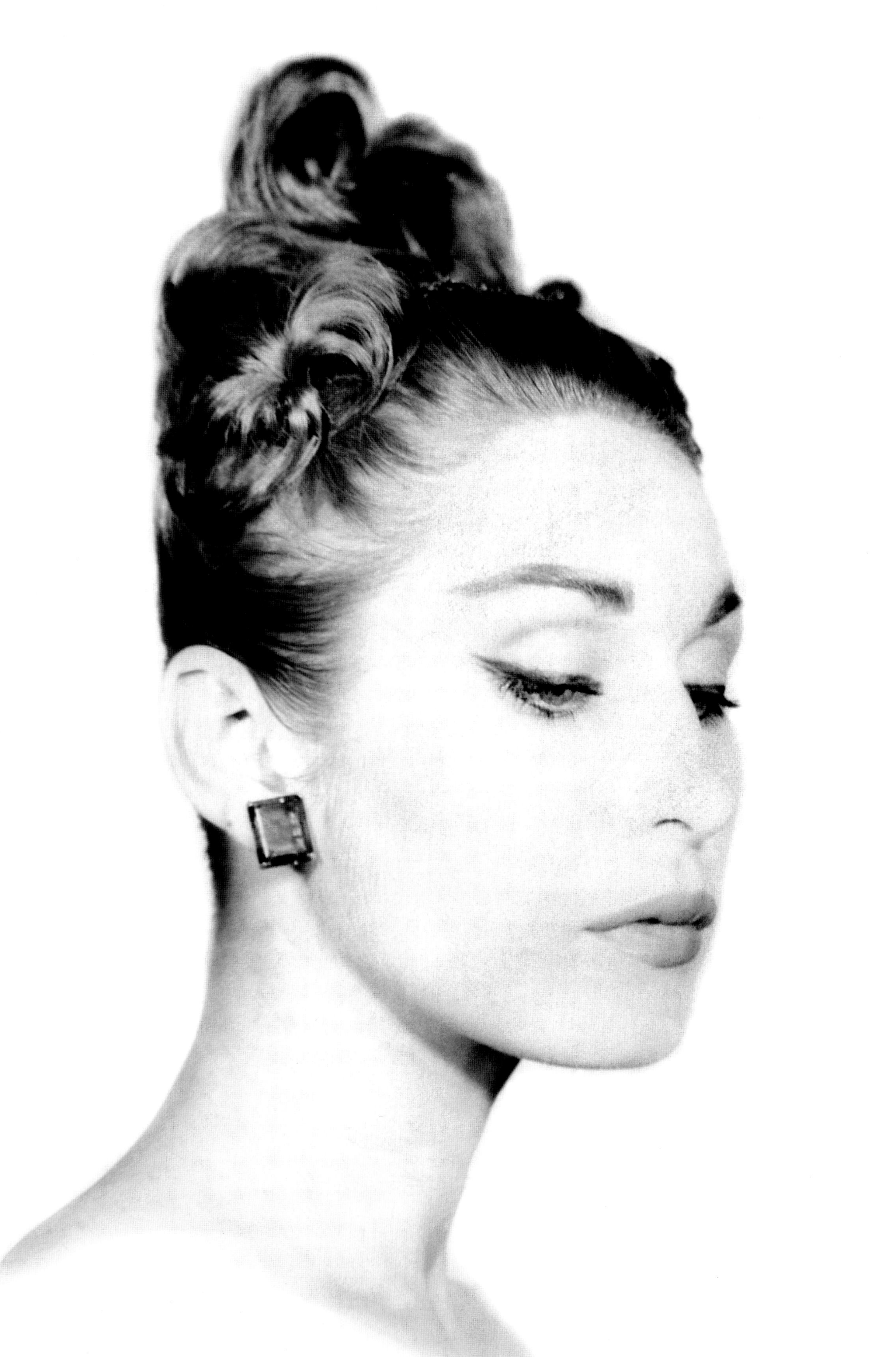

"One day, some idiot was talking about me on TV. He called me Kodak—he didn't even get my name right—and asked: 'Why does this fellow always photograph Cuban women in the nude to show their beauty?' I was really annoyed. So I asked my secretary, who was very pretty, to put on a black dress with no neckline and I took her to the cemetery to photograph her..."

*Personal work.
Recent print taken
from copy.*

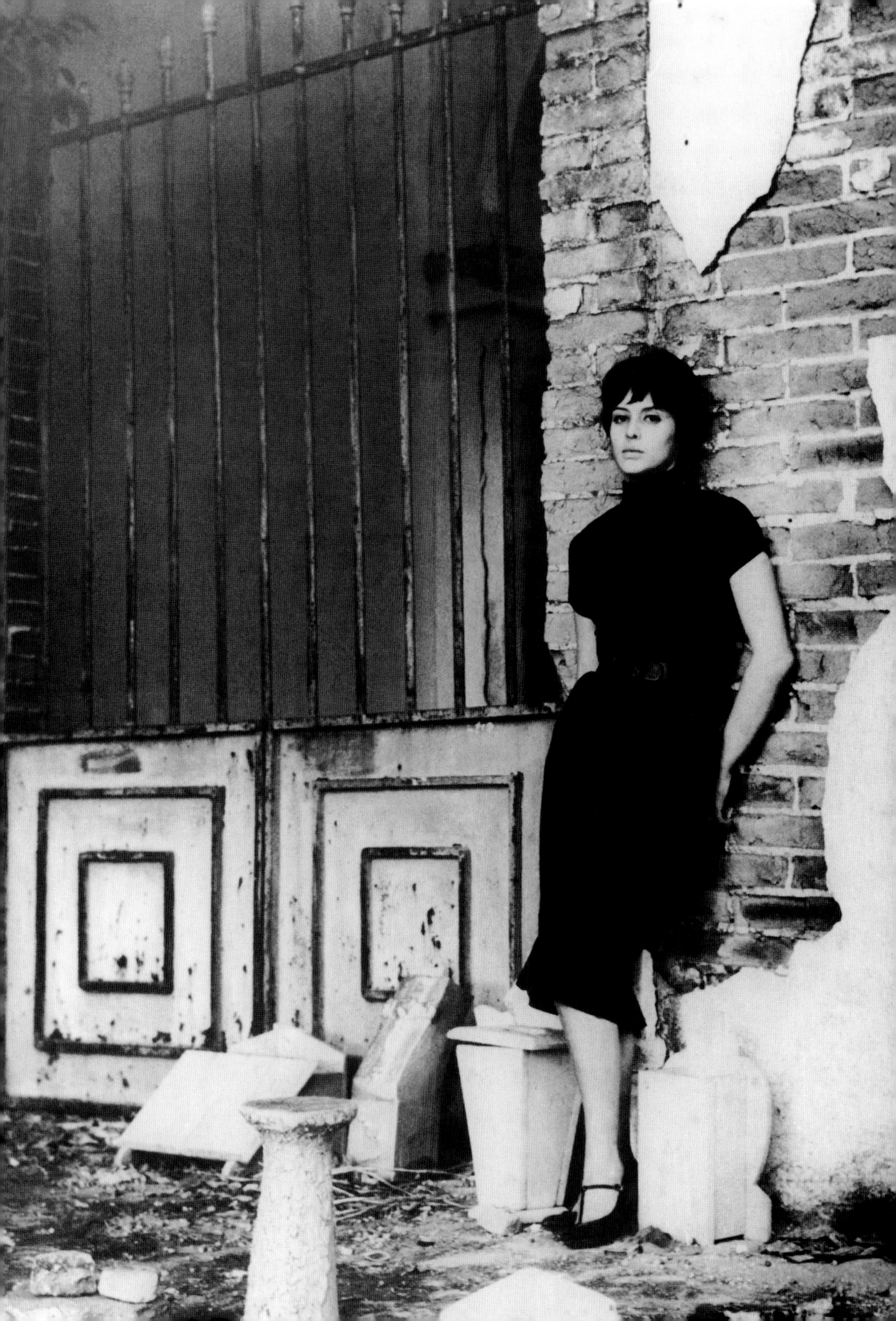

Norka, by Korda.
Advertising photo for a
bathing suit company.
Original print.

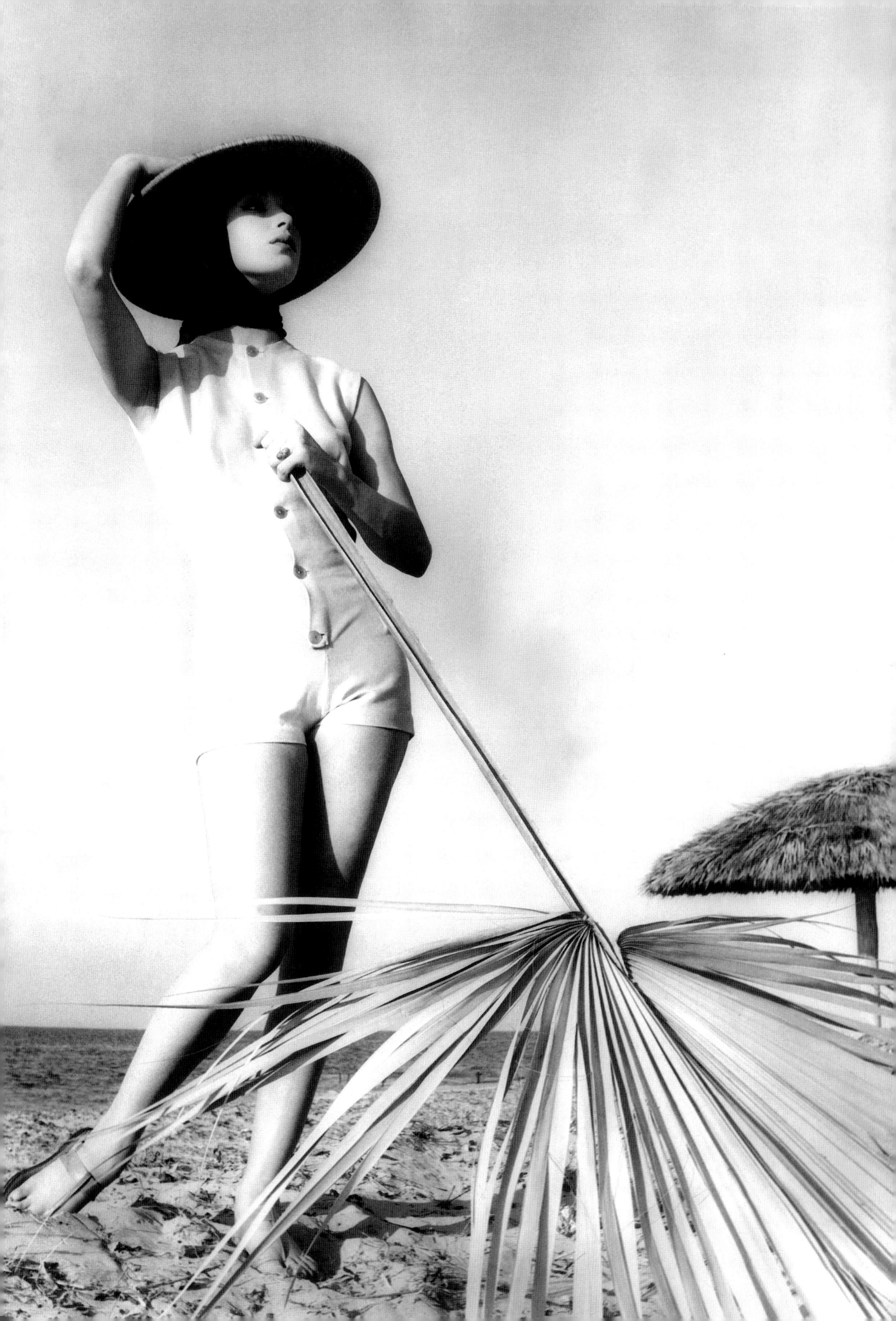

Norka, by Korda.
Personal work.
Original print restored.

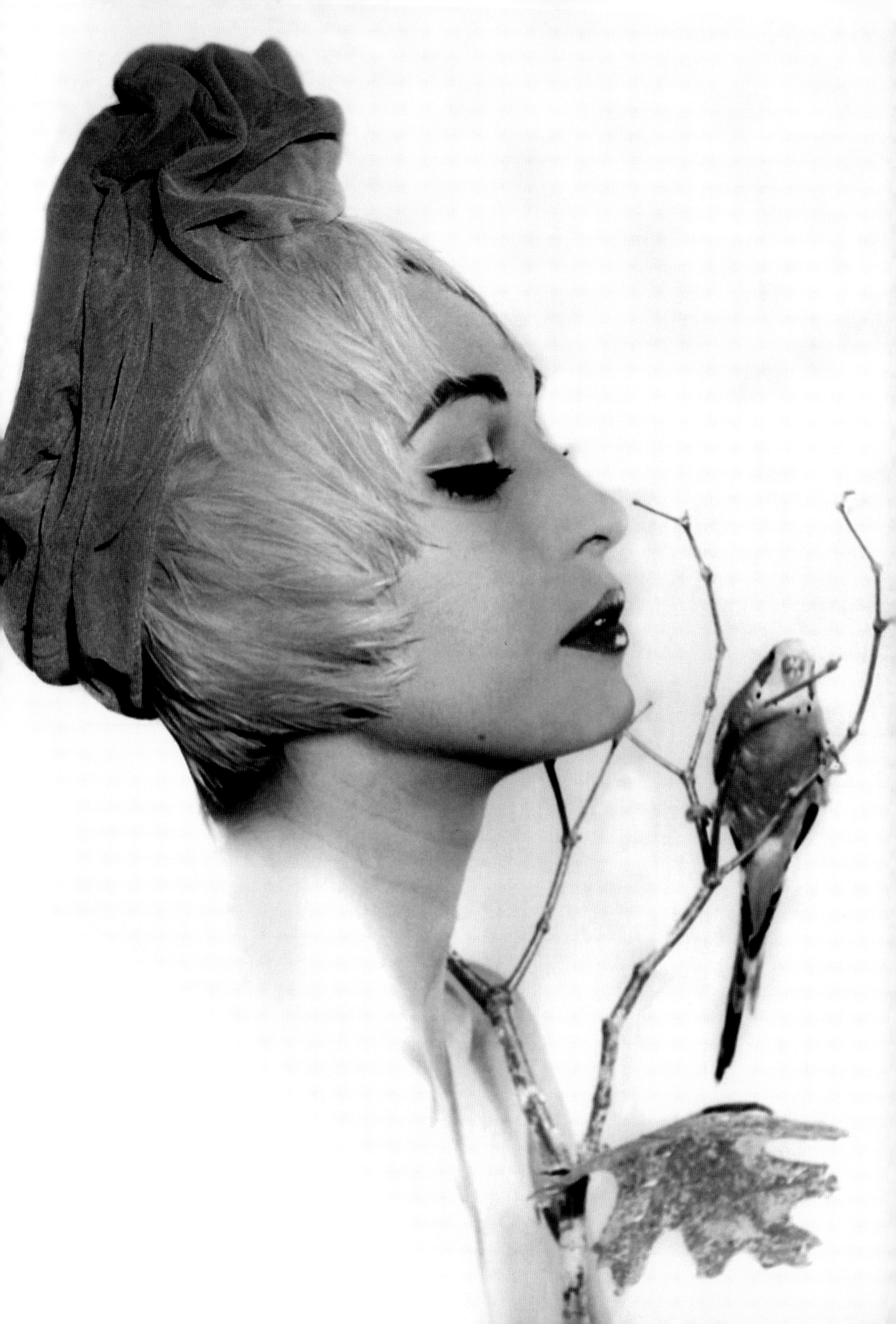

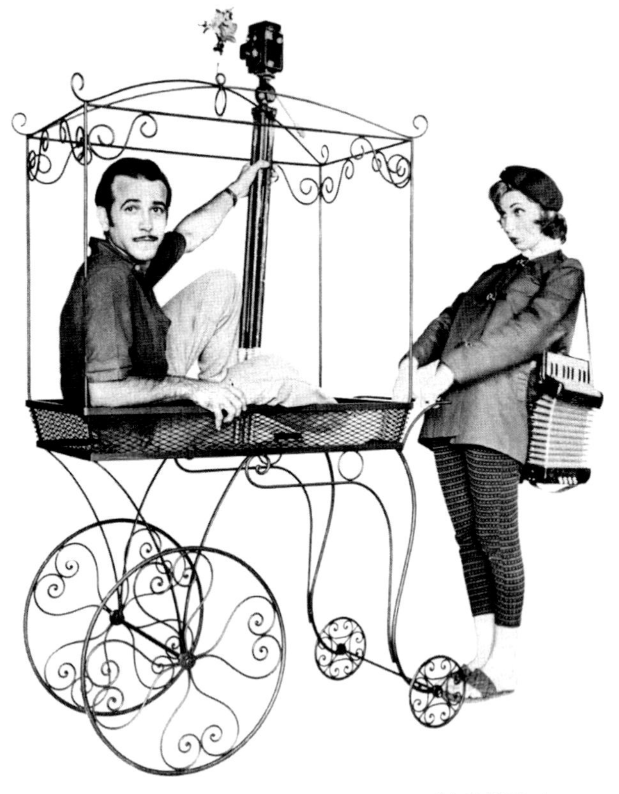

Above: Self-portrait with Norka. Advertisement for Korda Studios.

Right: Norka by Korda. Publicity photo for a fashion designer. Reproduction from a printed advertisement.

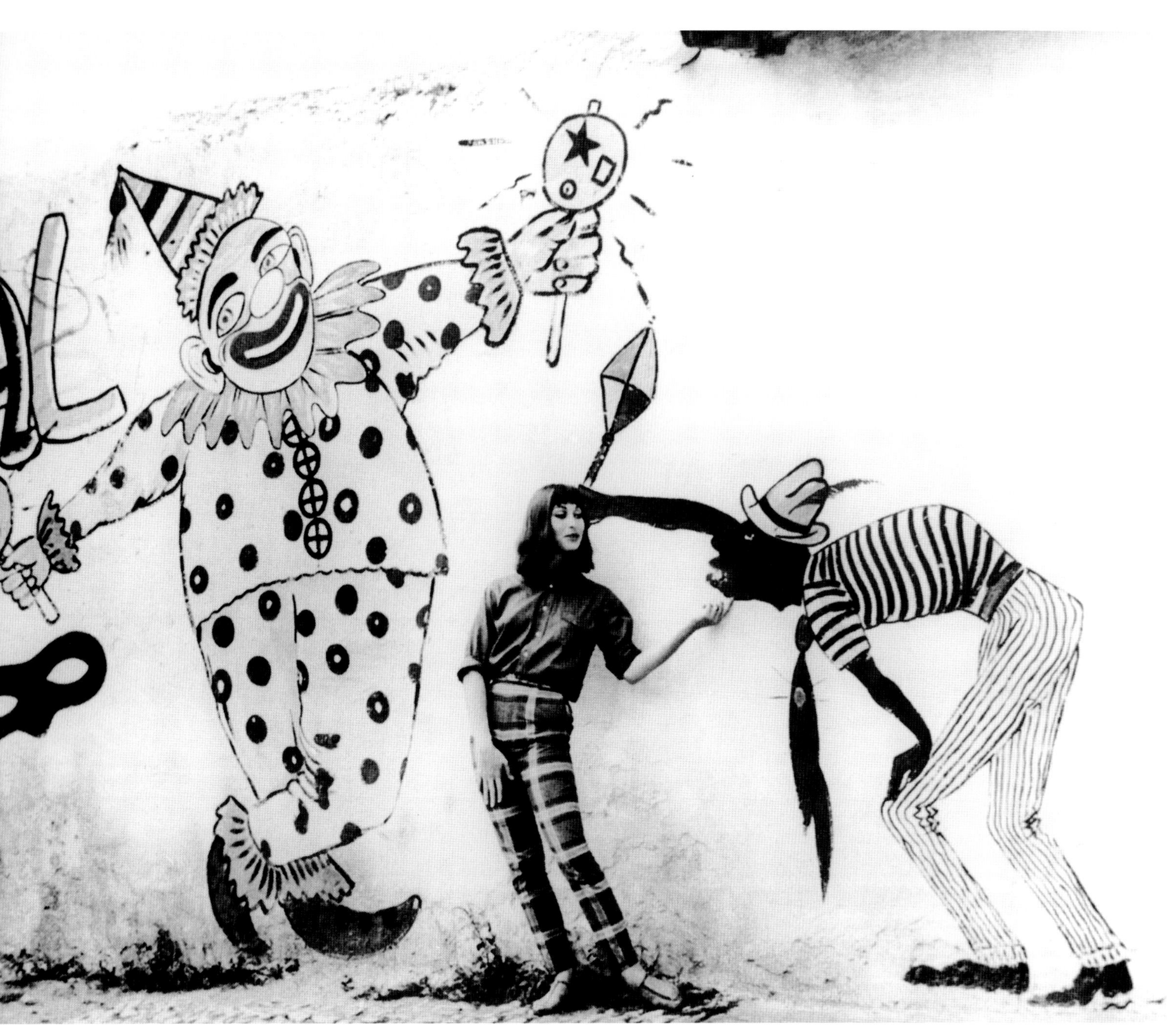

"Nearing 30, I was heading toward a frivolous life when an exceptional event transformed my life: the Cuban Revolution. It was at this time that I took this photo of a little girl, who was clutching a piece of wood for a doll. I came to understand that it was worth dedicating my work to a revolution which aimed to remove these inequalities."

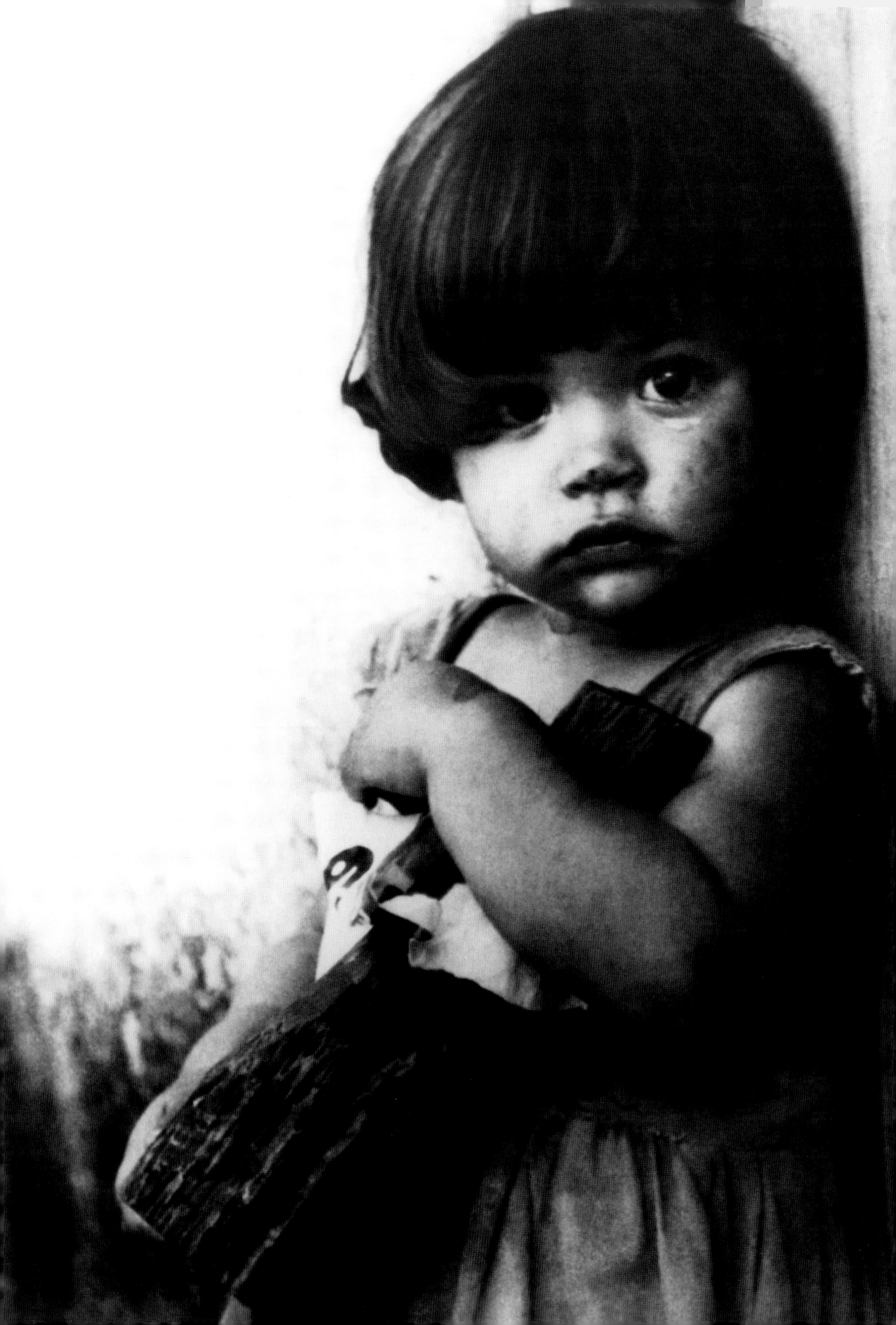

On November 25, 1956, 82 men set off from Tuxpan in Mexico aboard the *Granma*, a small 12-meter yacht. They were mostly Cubans and their leader was a young exiled lawyer, Fidel Castro. In the group there was also an Italian, a Dominican, a Mexican, and an Argentine doctor, Ernesto Guevara, known as "Che." Writing about the crossing, which was undertaken in bad weather, Che said: "The boat assumed a ridiculous, tragic appearance: men clutching their stomachs,

"'A landing? It was a shipwreck!' Che said later with his wry humor..."

anguish written in their faces, some with their heads in buckets, others lying immobile on the deck in strange positions, their clothes covered in vomit." The boat was damaged, the pumps wouldn't work and they had to bail the water with buckets. On December 2, the boat finally ran aground in the mud near a mangrove swamp on Cuba's southeast coast. They had to abandon nearly all their equipment and supplies. Immediately spotted by soldiers of the dictator Batista's army, the small group of rebels was decimated in the first ambush. The survivors scattered. Fidel Castro found himself with Universo Sánchez and Faustino Pérez: "For a moment," he recalled later on, "I was commander-in-chief of two men." In small dispersed groups they made their way toward the mountainous Sierra Maestra, with the support of local peasants. When Raúl Castro joined his brother on December 18, with five companions, Fidel asked: "How many rifles do you have?" On hearing that they had five, Fidel cried with his typical optimism: "With mine, that makes seven. We have won this war!"

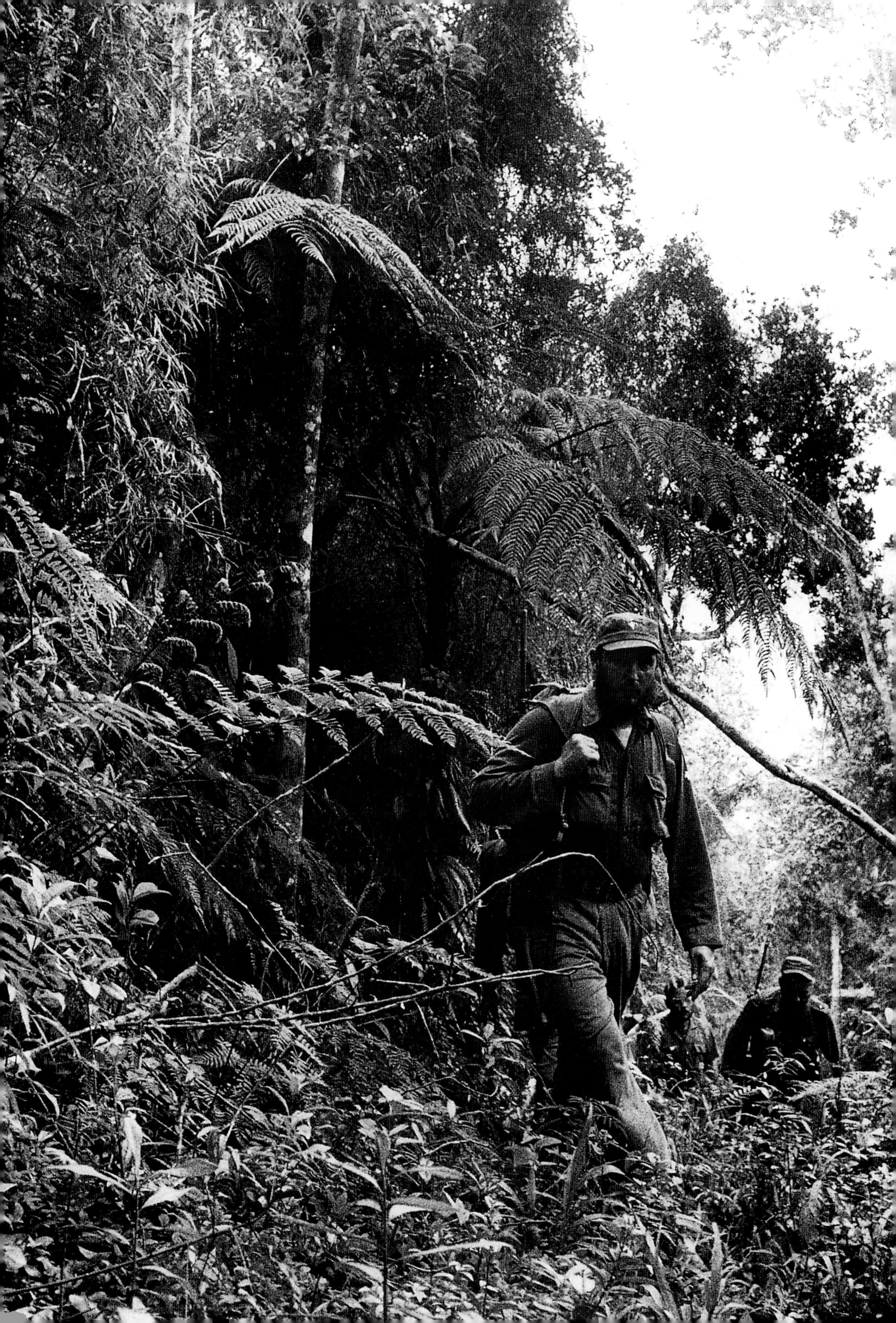

In early December 1956, Fidel Castro and his small group of survivors took refuge in the Sierra Maestra. In Cuba's southeast, this mountainous range stretches 150 kilometers in length and is 50 kilometers wide. It reaches 2,000 meters at Turquino Peak, the highest point on the island. The few tracks are difficult to traverse, strewn with sharp stones known as "dog-tooth rocks" which shred shoe leather. From this citadel the rebels intended to overthrow Fulgencio

"I took these photos for a report for the daily newspaper *Revolución* in 1962. It was called 'Fidel returns to the Sierra,' and the title came from him..."

Batista's regime. In March 1952 this former sergeant took power in Havana in a bloody coup, supported by the land-owning bourgeoisie and the United States. It was then that the young lawyer Fidel Castro turned to armed struggle. On July 26, 1953, he attacked the Moncada garrison in Santiago, but the attack failed. Six men were killed during the assault and another 45 were captured, tortured, and later summarily executed. Fidel himself fled, but was soon captured as well. It was only the intercession of the archbishop of Santiago that saved him from execution. The trial provided the opportunity for him to be heard far and wide. For five hours, he addressed the judges in a closing speech against the dictatorship which would become historic: "History Will Absolve Me." Condemned to 15 years in jail together with his brother Raúl, he took advantage of an amnesty in 1955 to go into exile in Mexico.

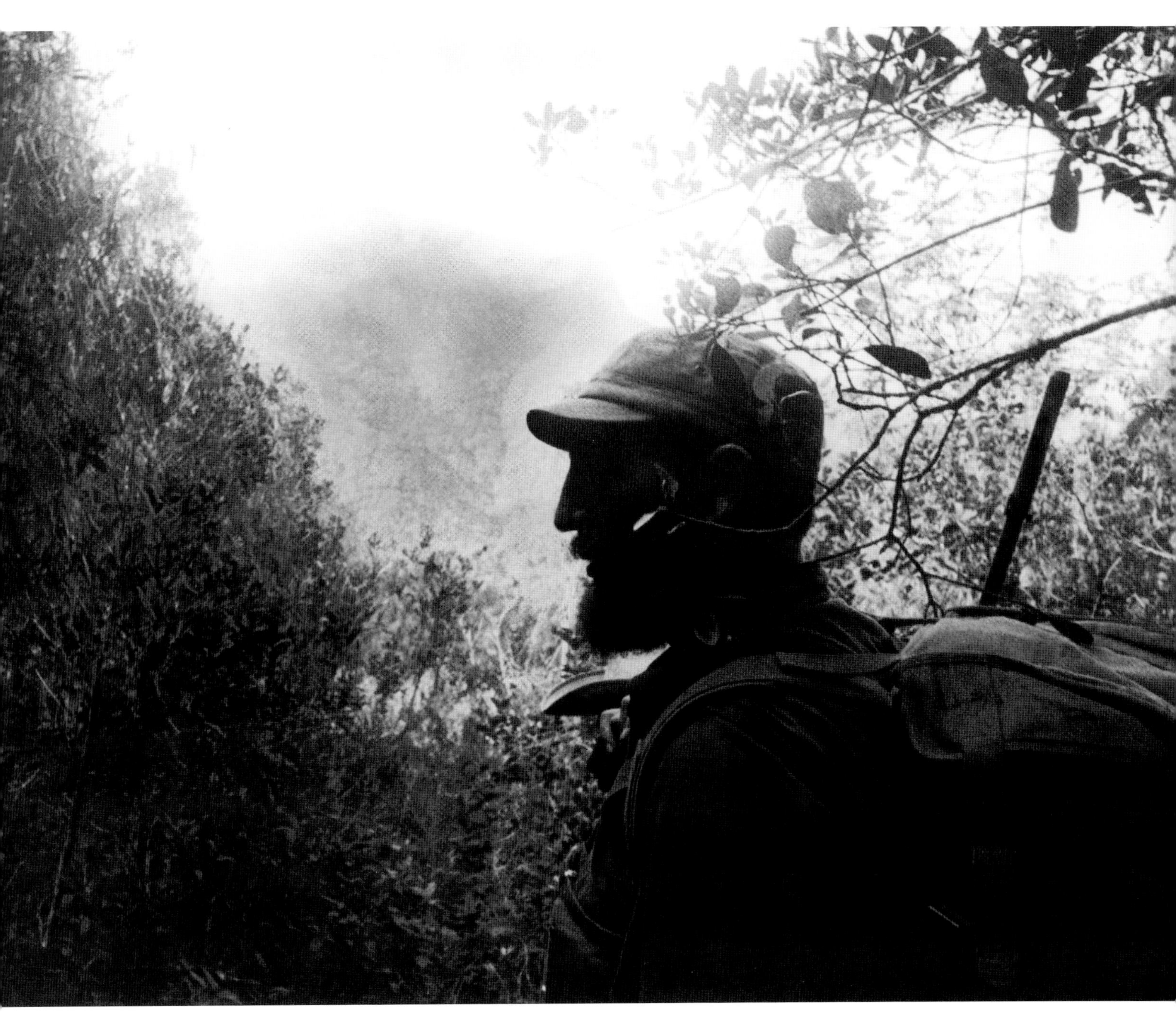

"I always moved to the front of the column in order to take photos. His doctor René Vallejo had joined Castro with a small escort, and Fidel joked to him: 'Look, this scrawny fellow is tireless!' When I returned home to Havana, my eldest daughter Diana was scared when she saw me arrive. I was so dirty and unshaven that she didn't recognize me!"

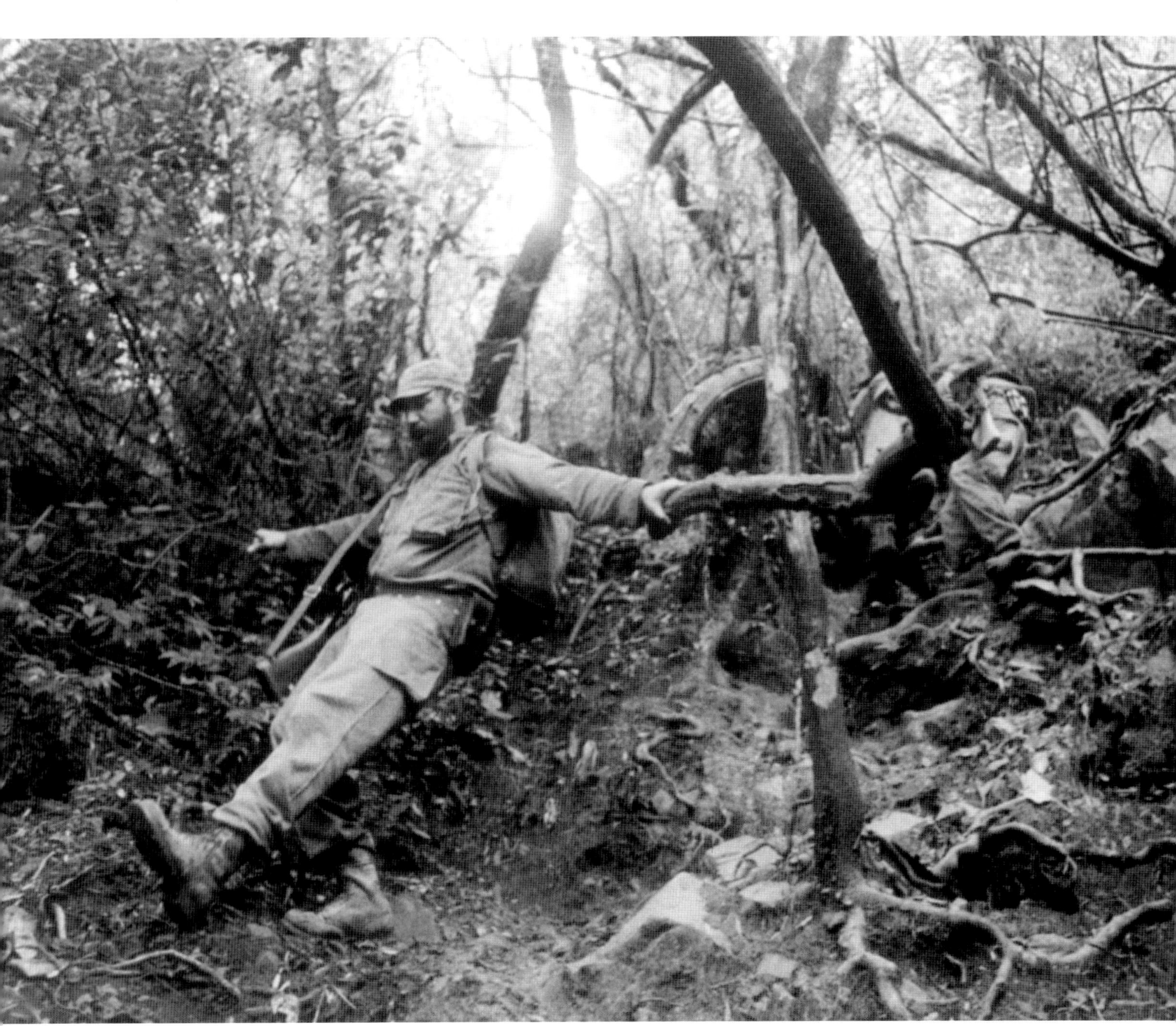

The *campesinos* or peasants of the Sierra Maestra had been pushed up into the inhospitable heights because of the growing population in the valleys. In semi-autonomy, they grew coffee and raised a few head of cattle. But to survive, they had to come down to the plains each summer for the sugarcane harvest, the *zafra*. Wages were a dollar a day for back-breaking work. There were no schools or hospitals nearby. In spite of their fear of persecution, the peasants turned

"They needed a photographer who was also able to write. Fidel asked me if I'd had any articles published. I said 'yes'—a huge lie, but there was no way in the world that I was going to miss this expedition."

naturally to the rebels, who were being chased by the government forces. The small band of guerrillas did not act as occupiers. They established the practice of paying for their food and of respecting the peasant women. After a local teacher pretended to be Dr. Guevara in an attempt to rape a local girl seeking medical treatment, he was tried and shot. Fidel Castro never forgot this region, and later said that it was the place where he'd passed the best days of his life. After taking power, he returned there often to rejuvenate, and for exercise! A tall man, he was an accomplished athlete who always wanted to be the best at everything: he was a champion runner, a ping-pong champion, a good baseball pitcher, and captain of his law school's basketball team.

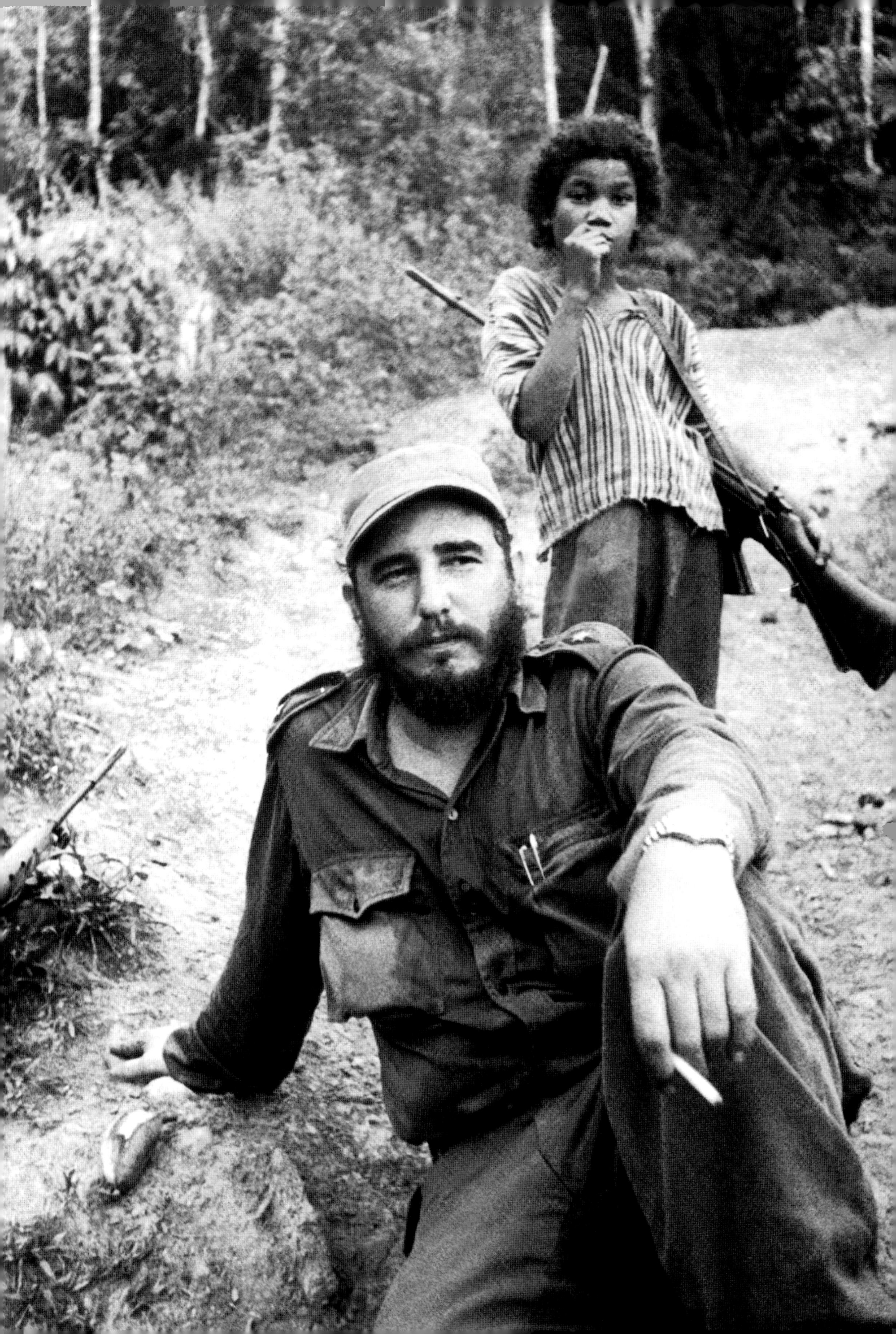

"'This woman and her son are the image of the kindness of our peasants,' said Fidel, as he asked me to take a photo of these two *guajiros* from a family that had aided him. For several days, we had marched from a place known as Las Mercedes to Turquino Peak. Fidel spoke with all the peasants we met on the way, putting his arm around their shoulders. One asked for vaccines for his pigs, another for an extra teacher at the school. On each occasion, he turned to me and said, 'Take note of this...'"

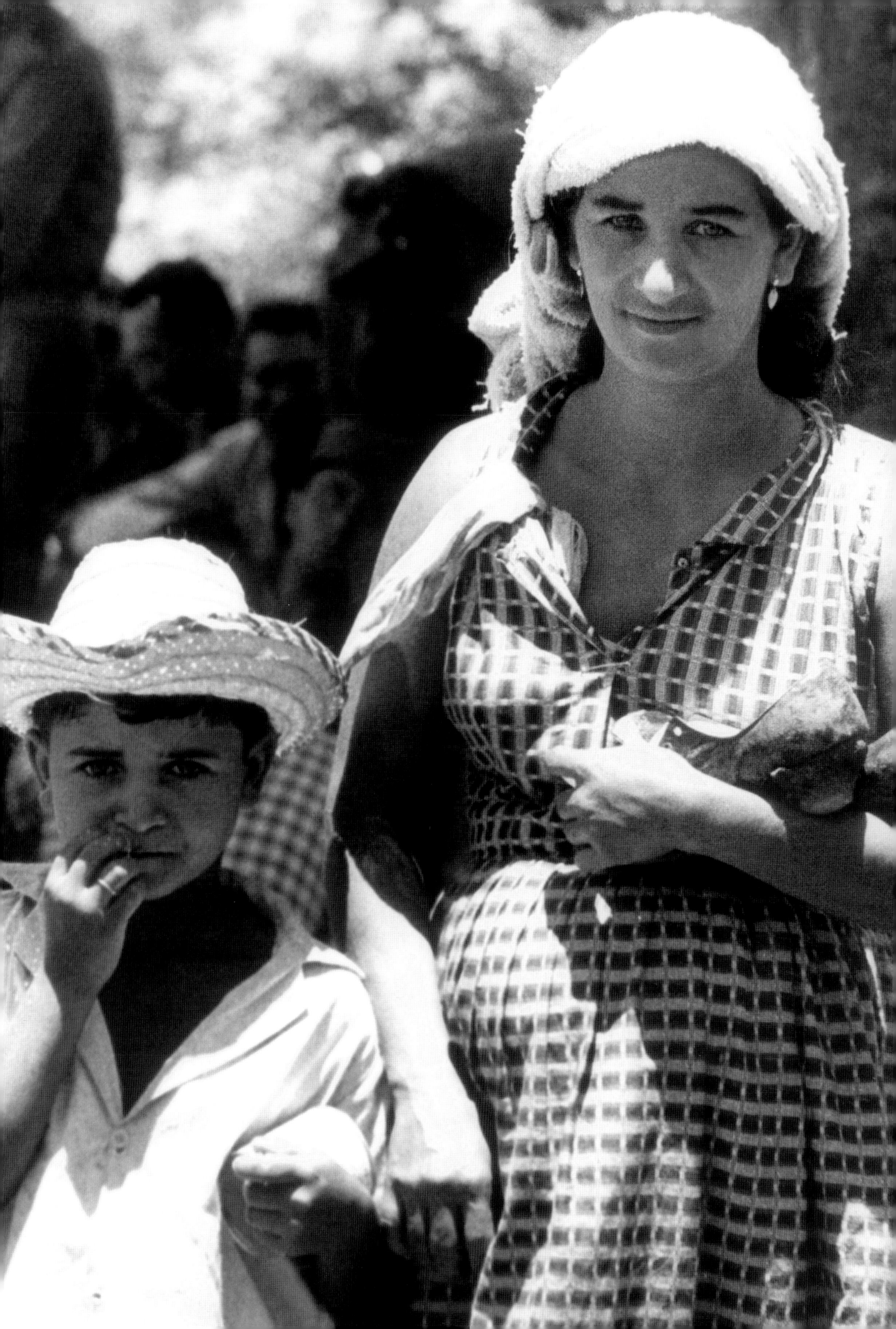

His glasses perched on his nose, always ready to take aim, Fidel strode through the Sierra with giant steps. One of the rebels remembered: "He always went so fast that when we wanted to slow down, we got him to sit on a mule..." To the rhythm of his enormous stride, the small band of guerrillas ran across the mountains, digging holes everywhere to protect themselves from aerial bombardment and simply hanging a hammock for the night. No matter how long

"In the Sierra, his men called him 'The Horse,' for his endurance and his courage..."

the march had been, Fidel would explain at each stop, "what had happened during the day, both to the enemy and ourselves. In this way, the men were always up-to-date with what was happening around them. They spoke with extraordinary devotion about their commander-in-chief." As early as January 17, 1957, just six weeks after the landing, Castro took the offensive and captured the small barracks at La Plata, at the head of just 25 men. It wasn't a great feat of arms, but it was a psychological coup, carried out in order that news about the rebels would spread. A month later, he had another such victory. Fidel welcomed *New York Times* reporter Herbert Matthews on to the mountain, without allowing him to see that the rebel numbers were still so few. The journalist was seduced by the young leader's personality: "It was easy to see that his men adored him and also to see why he has caught the imagination of Cuban youth over the island. Here was an educated, dedicated fanatic, a man of ideals, of courage, and of remarkable qualities of leadership."

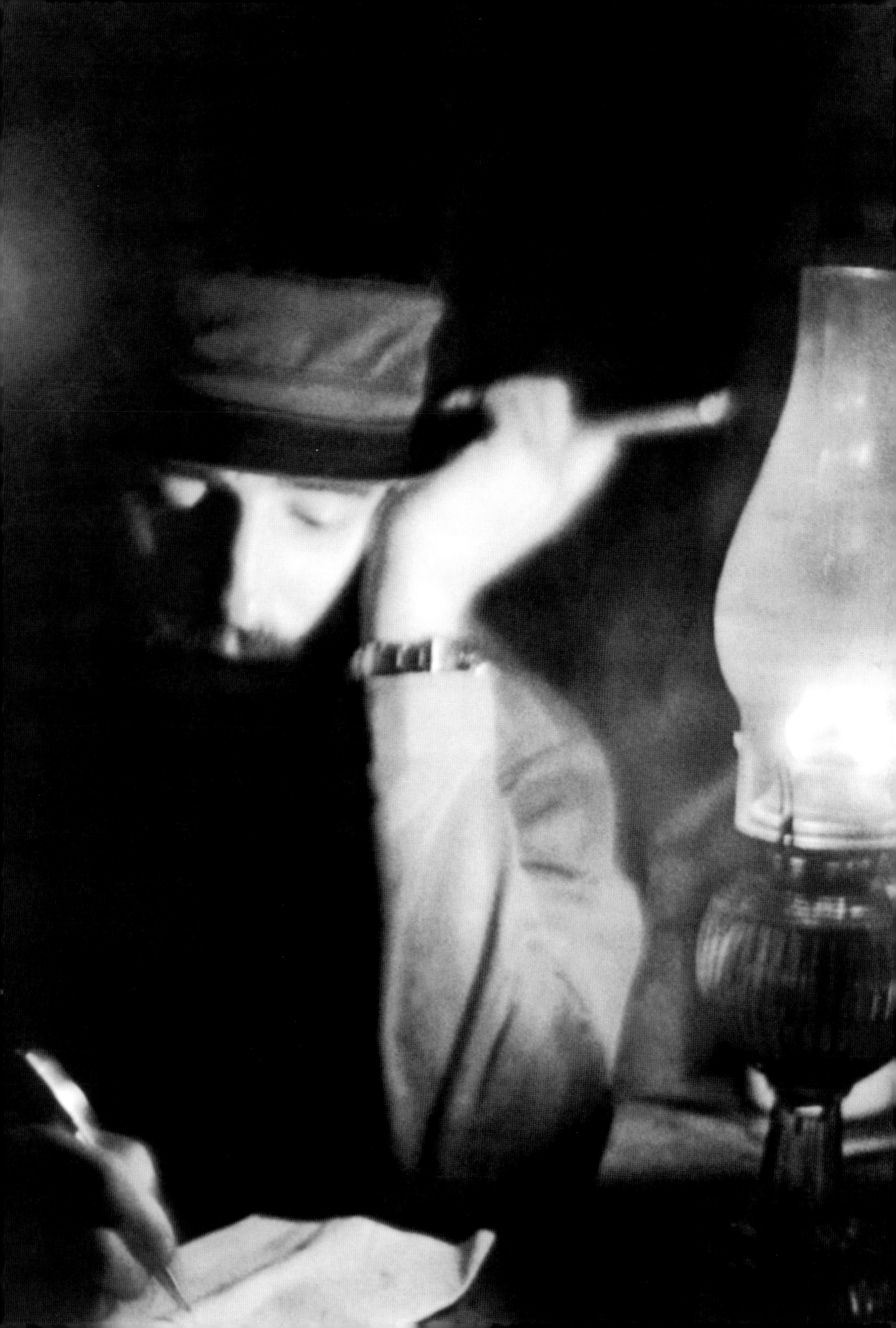

From mid-1957, people began to talk of "liberated territory," an embryonic state of a few dozen, then hundreds of square kilometers in the Sierra Maestra. The zone was administered by the rebels who established the first schools and health clinics. Between ambushes, Che Guevara cared for the wounded and sick. Fidel said: "The doctor is *cojonudo*, he's a real fighter." He awarded the 29-year-old Argentine the star of *comandante*, the highest rank in

"All through the Sierra, Fidel knew everyone's names and all the paths across the mountains. He has an incredible memory and is capable of reciting whole books..."

the Rebel Army. And Fidel knew what he was talking about, because he himself often led his men into battle. From the start of 1958, the guerrilla force numbered 200 men and started to move around freely. Che established his group at El Hombrito, creating an armory, a bakery, a butcher, a shoe repair shop, and other supply depots. He published a small roneoed newsletter, *El Cubano Libre*. As for Fidel, he established his first permanent headquarters at La Plata, one of the most inaccessible areas of the Sierra Maestra. The fortified camp was surrounded by trenches, bristling with anti-aircraft shelters, and protected by radio-controlled mines. In June, when the rebels had suffered setbacks from the government forces, the guerrillas counterattacked, inflicting crushing defeats on the army at San Domingo and then in July at El Jigüe. A monk, Father Sardiñas, joined the "liberated" zone with the permission of his bishop, and baptized the children of the Sierra. On each occasion, Fidel served as godfather.

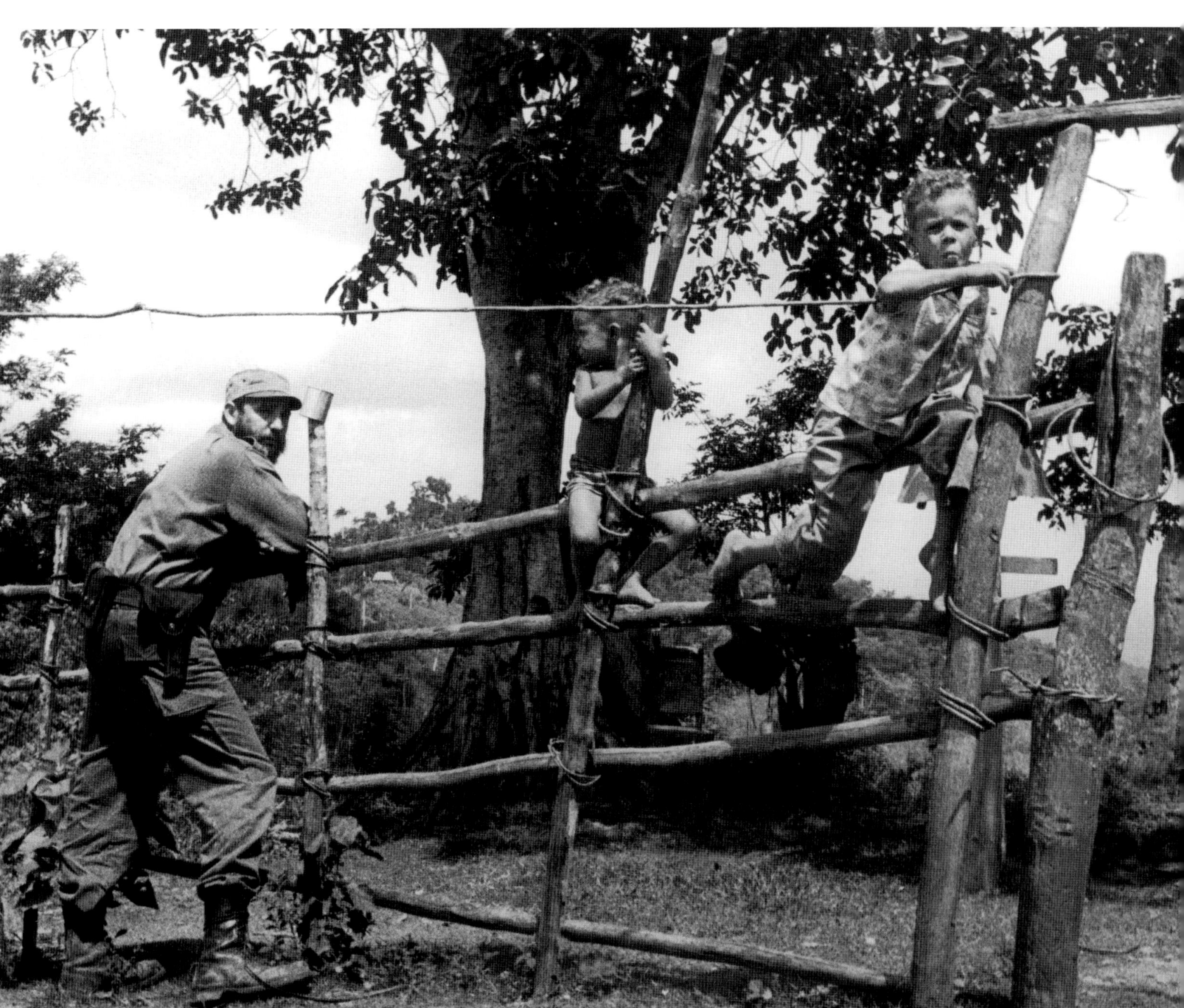

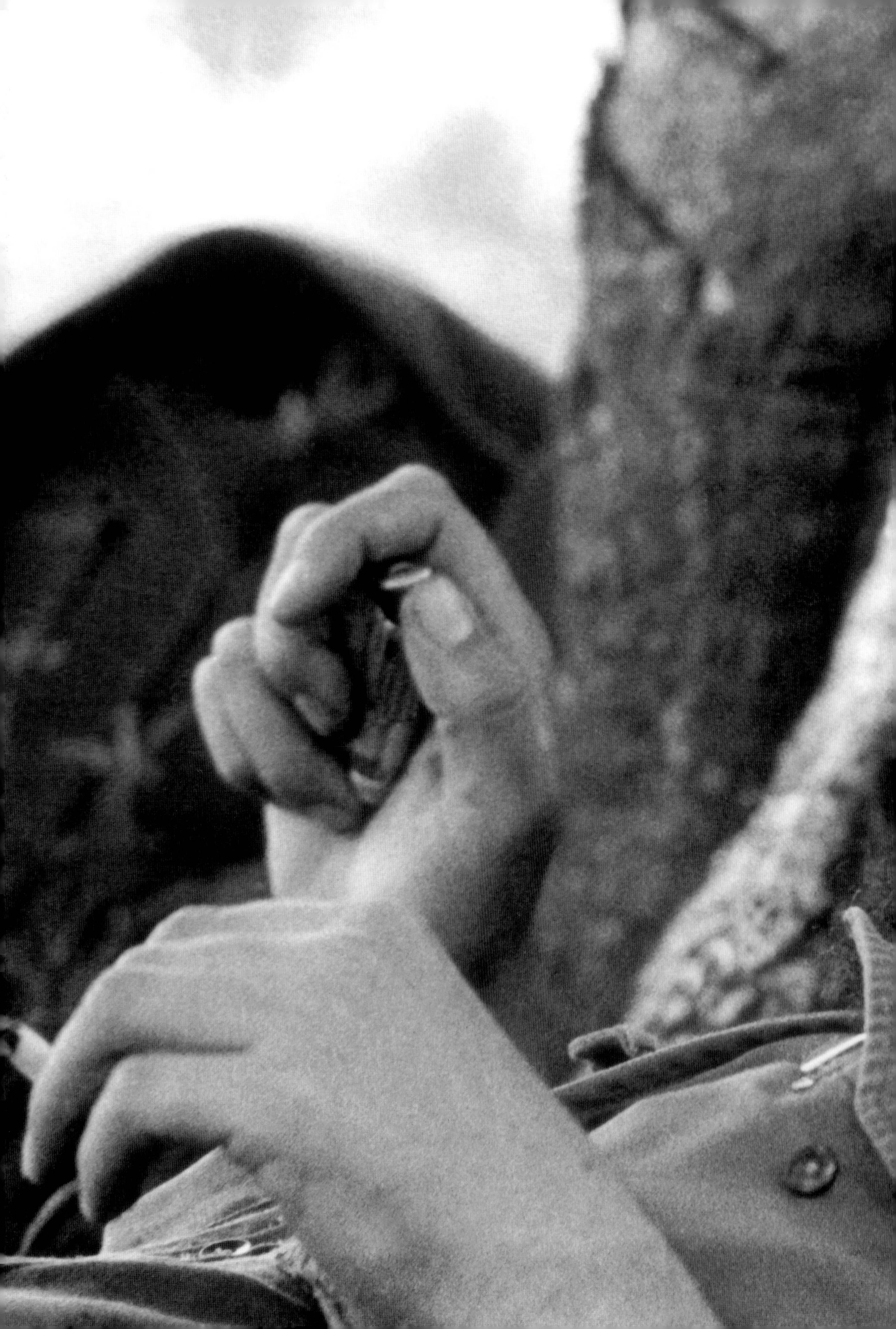

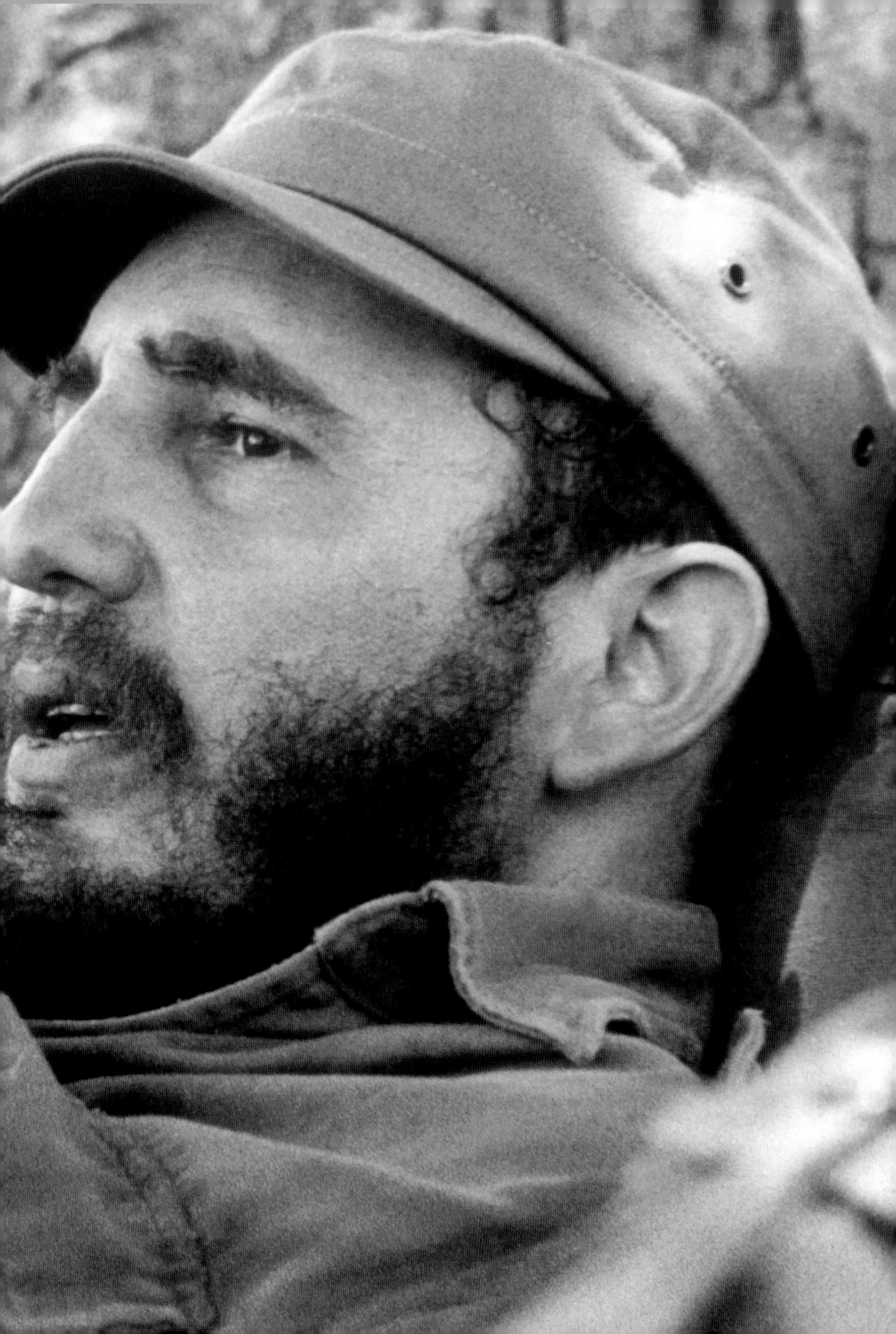

On February 16, 1957, Fidel Castro met Celia Sánchez. It was the start of an exceptional relationship which was to last for 23 years, until Celia's death from cancer. One of five daughters of a local doctor, Celia organized the first contacts in the Sierra before the rebels landed. Raised like a boy, this 36-year-old woman was searching for a task that matched her willpower and intelligence. Henceforth, she was to consecrate her life to Castro's fight. Fascinated by Fidel, both as a man

"Without question, the most important woman in Fidel's life was Celia Sánchez..."

and as a revolutionary, neither bombs nor forced marches could stop her following him like his shadow, through his struggles and dreams. Secretary and friend, mother and nurse, she cooked for him, passed on his orders, organized his papers. Celia was also an expert in drilling with weapons and was the first woman to fight with the guerrillas. After serving as the liaison between the Sierra and the rest of the island, she was forced to remain in the mountains from the end of 1957, as Batista's police were trying to arrest her. After the rebels' victory, this exceptional woman would be the right-hand person to Fidel Castro, the only person with authority to give orders in his absence and, for reasons of security, one of the few people who knew where Fidel was sleeping every night.

Each evening, she went through the pockets of his olive green battle dress, gathering small scraps of paper—ideas the revolutionary had jotted down during the day which were to be put into practice.

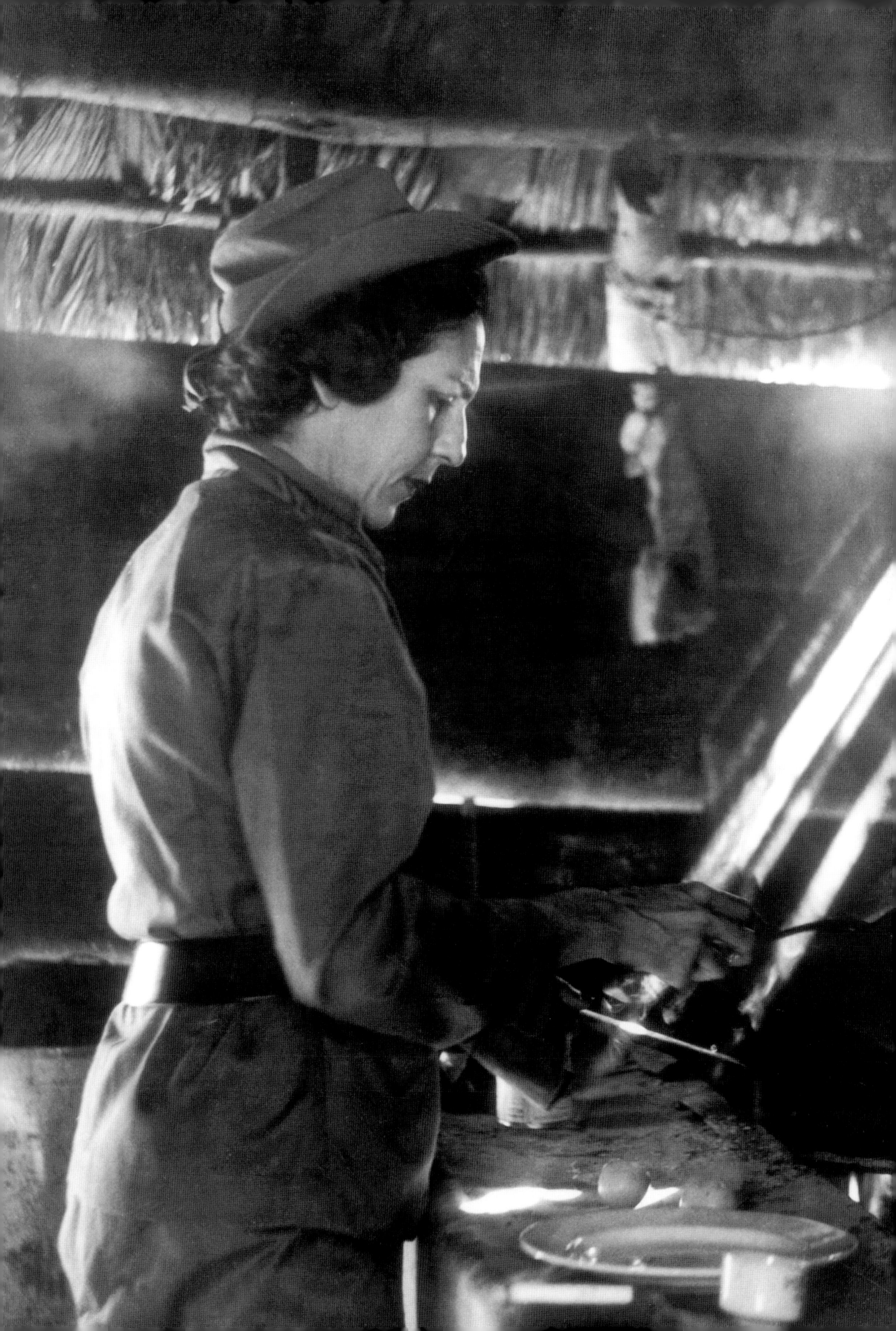

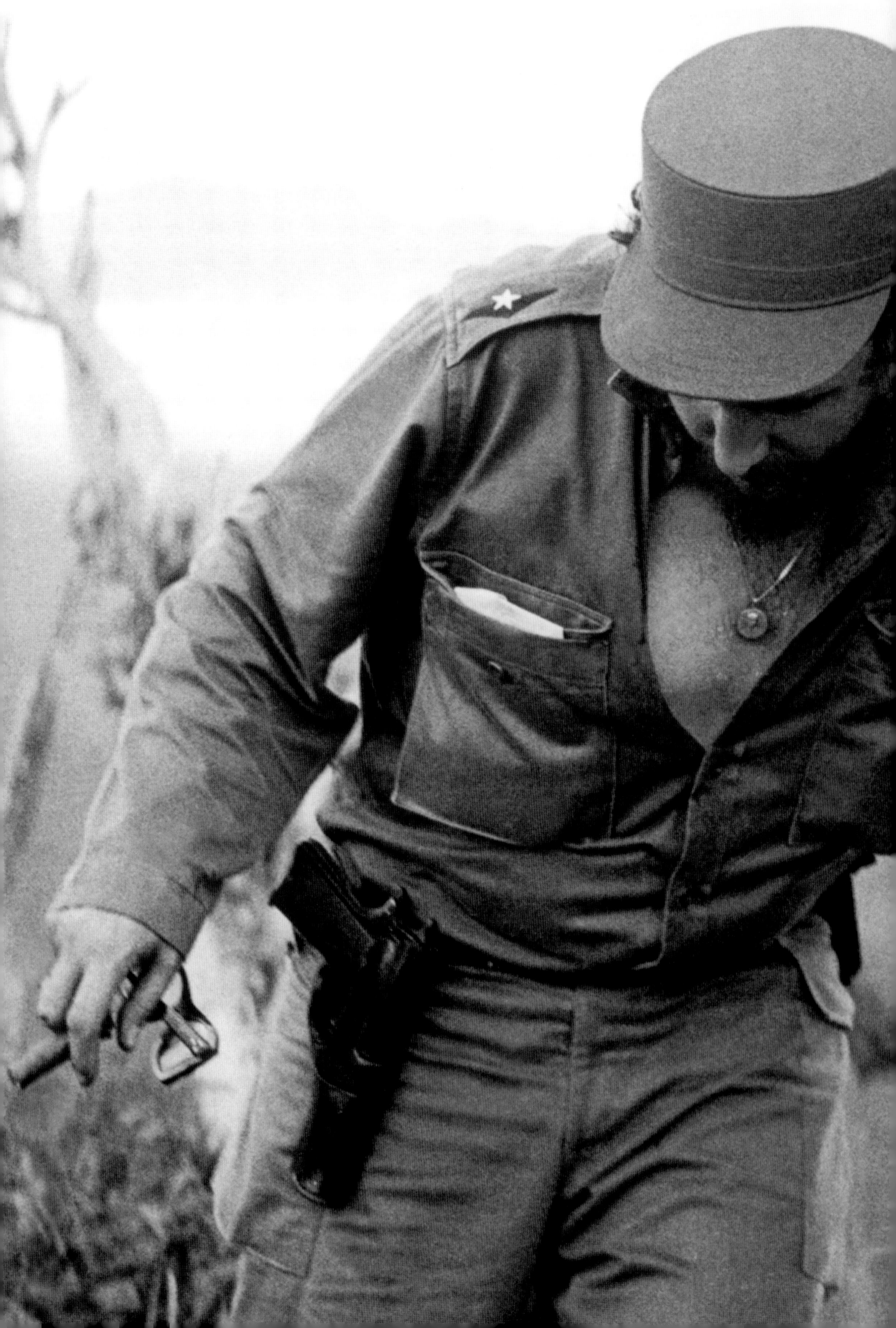

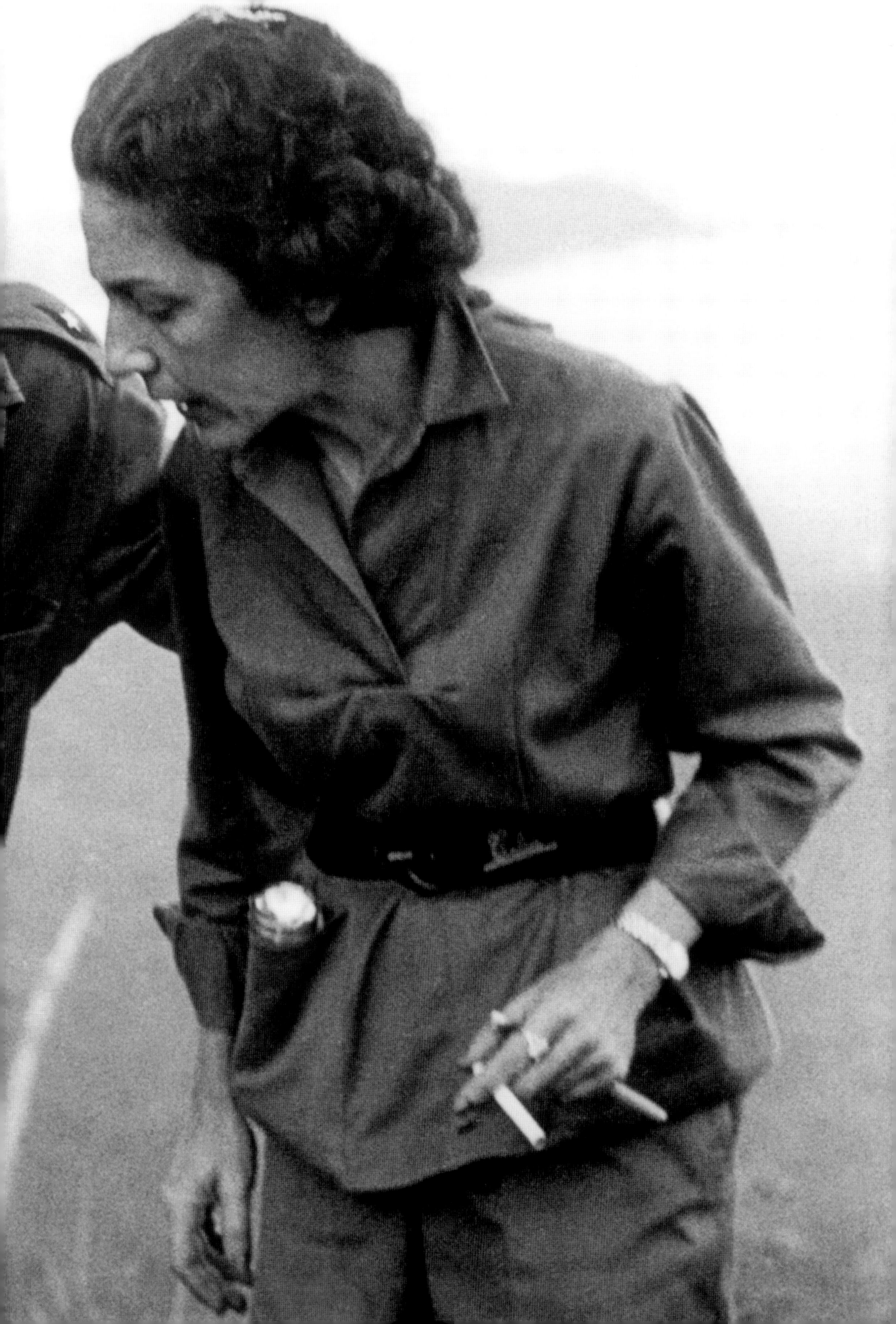

On August 21, 1958, Fidel Castro used Radio Rebelde to relay his orders for the advance into the rest of the island. Across mountains and swamps, braving aerial bombardment and also two cyclones, the armed columns led by Che and *comandante* Camilo Cienfuegos covered several hundred kilometers on foot. On October 3, marching with his men in appalling conditions, Che wrote: "I wanted to open my wrists to offer them something warm to drink, as they've had

"The Cuban people first came to know Fidel through his broadcasts, like the French with General de Gaulle. He had quite a peculiar voice, a bit high-pitched but with a hypnotic quality..."

nothing to eat or drink for the past three days." Fortunately, Batista's army had lost the will to fight, and hardly even left its barracks. Batista's officers were rarely seen at the front and, sensing the turning tide, began to plot against him. The whole country and even the powerful US neighbor turned against the dictator. The key to control of Havana was the town of Santa Clara—located in the center of the island, it hosted Batista's last fortress with 2,500 men. The dictator sent his troops to Santa Clara, playing his last card, an armored train. But with audacity and 364 guerrillas, Che derailed the train and attacked it with Molotov cocktails. The armor plating transformed the train into a giant oven for the soldiers. The officers offered to surrender, knowing they would be well treated by the rebels. On January 1, 1959, the last garrison at Santa Clara surrendered its weapons. The previous night in Havana, the dictator had opted to quietly flee to Santo Domingo.

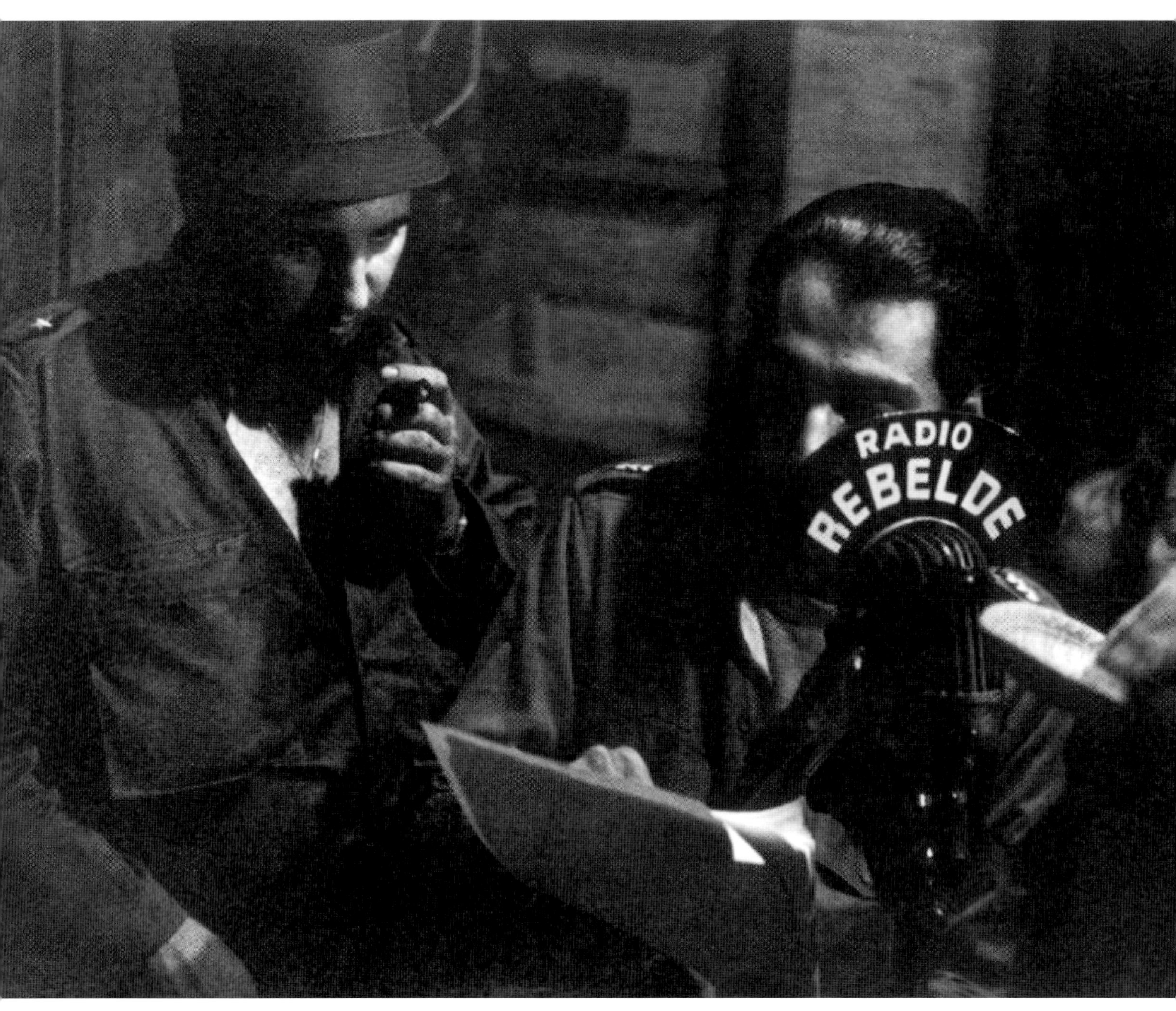
RADIO
REBELDE

The young guerrillas entered Havana on January 2, 1959, which gave them the chance for an extended New Year's celebration, a fantastic wild party, a carnival. Only two years and one month had passed since the catastrophic landing of the *Granma*. While Che Guevara and Camilo Cienfuegos took control of the two military camps in the capital, their commander-in-chief Fidel Castro entered Santiago de Cuba, in the far east of the country.

"In the streets, some young guys smashed open parking meters with a baseball bat. But there was no anarchy. I remember above all an enormous joy in people having regained their freedom and dignity…"

Once he was assured that Batista's army was neutralized, Fidel set off for Havana.

This triumphal procession across the island lasted a week. With the passing kilometers and the first of his endless speeches, several thousand men with newly grown beards joined the ranks of the real *barbudos* who had defeated Batista. On January 8 the people of Havana gave a delirious welcome to the central leader of the revolution. Church bells rang out, factory and ship sirens howled. That night as Fidel Castro addressed a vast crowd, his victory speech was broadcast in full for the first time on TV. Shifting between humor and passion, discussion and polemic, the bewitching orator of the Caribbean created a truly collective euphoria. At one point, a white dove landed on the shoulder of the rebel chief. For the dumbfounded Cubans, it was a sign from the Afro-Cuban god Obatala—Fidel had the gift of spiritualism.

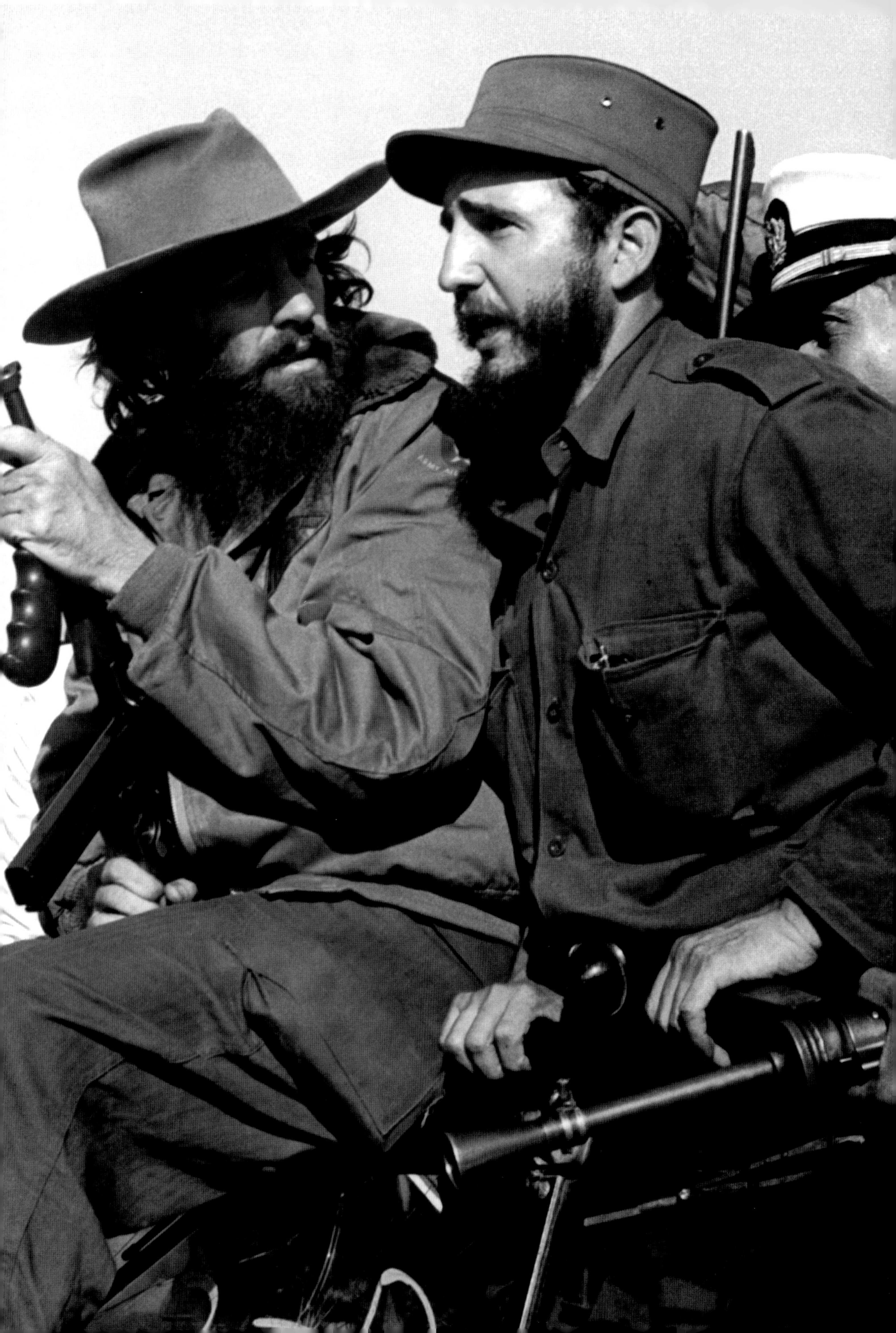

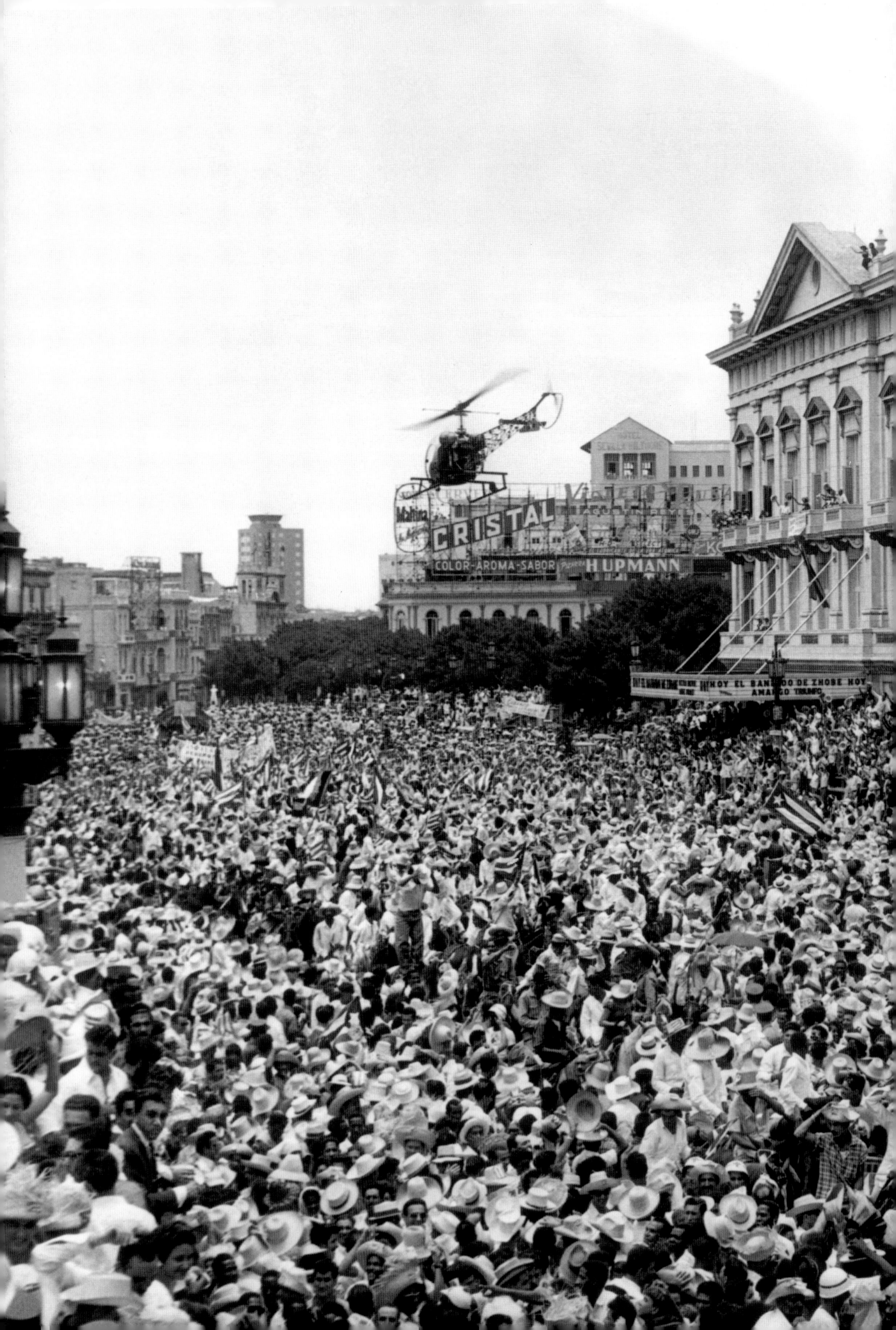
CRISTAL
COLOR-AROMA-SABOR
HUPMANN

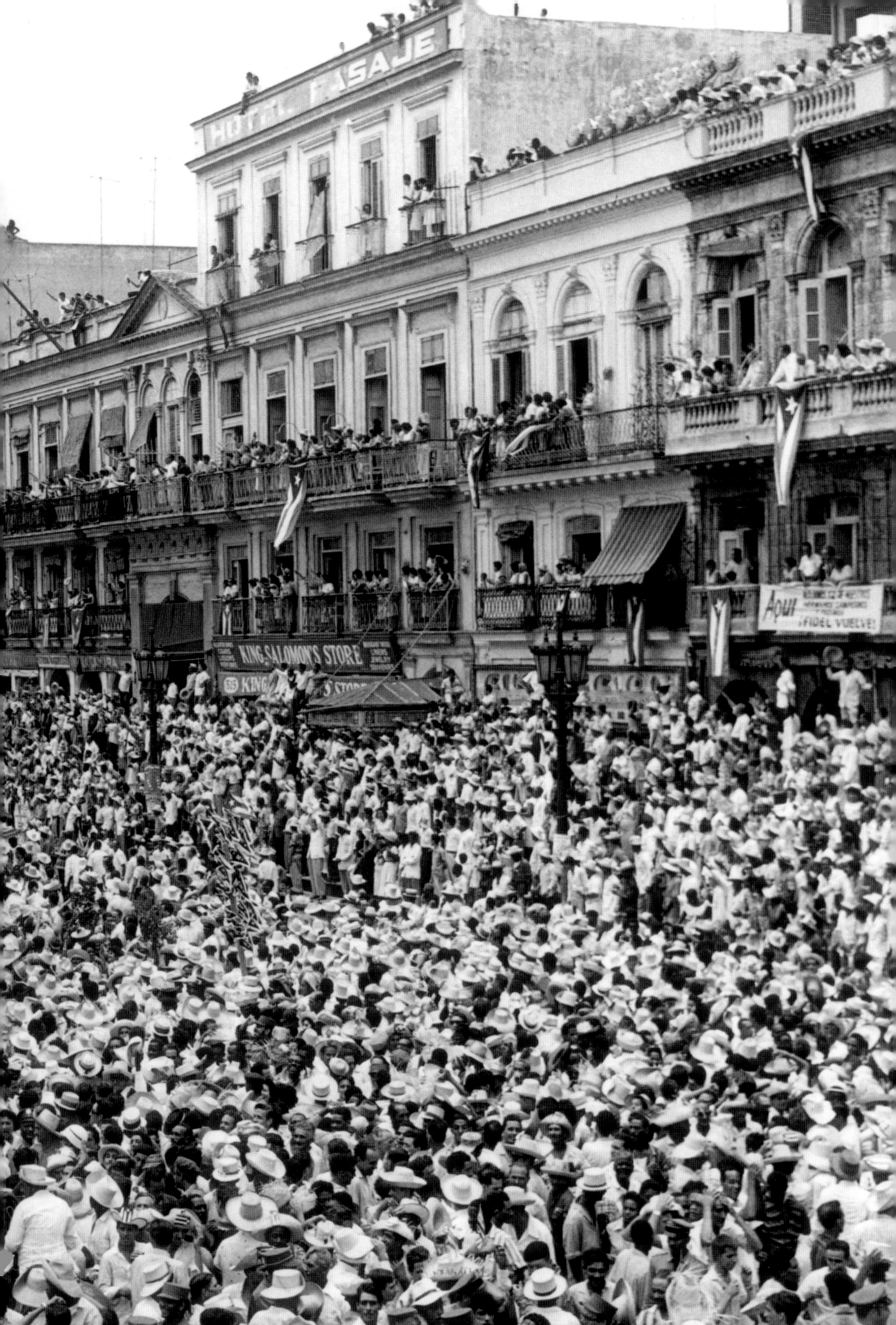
PASAJE
HOTEL
KING SALOMON'S STORE
Aqui
¡FIDEL VUELVE!

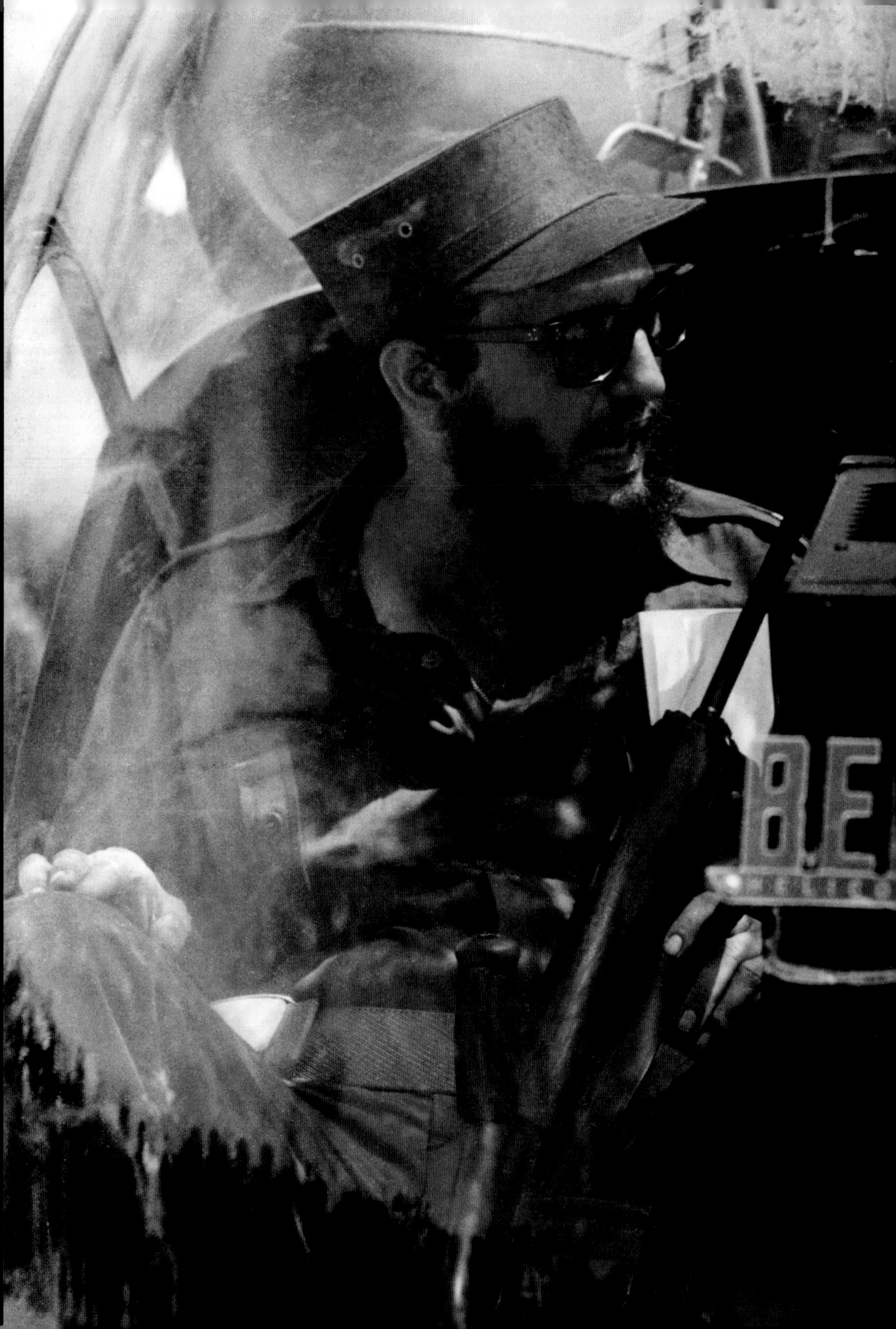

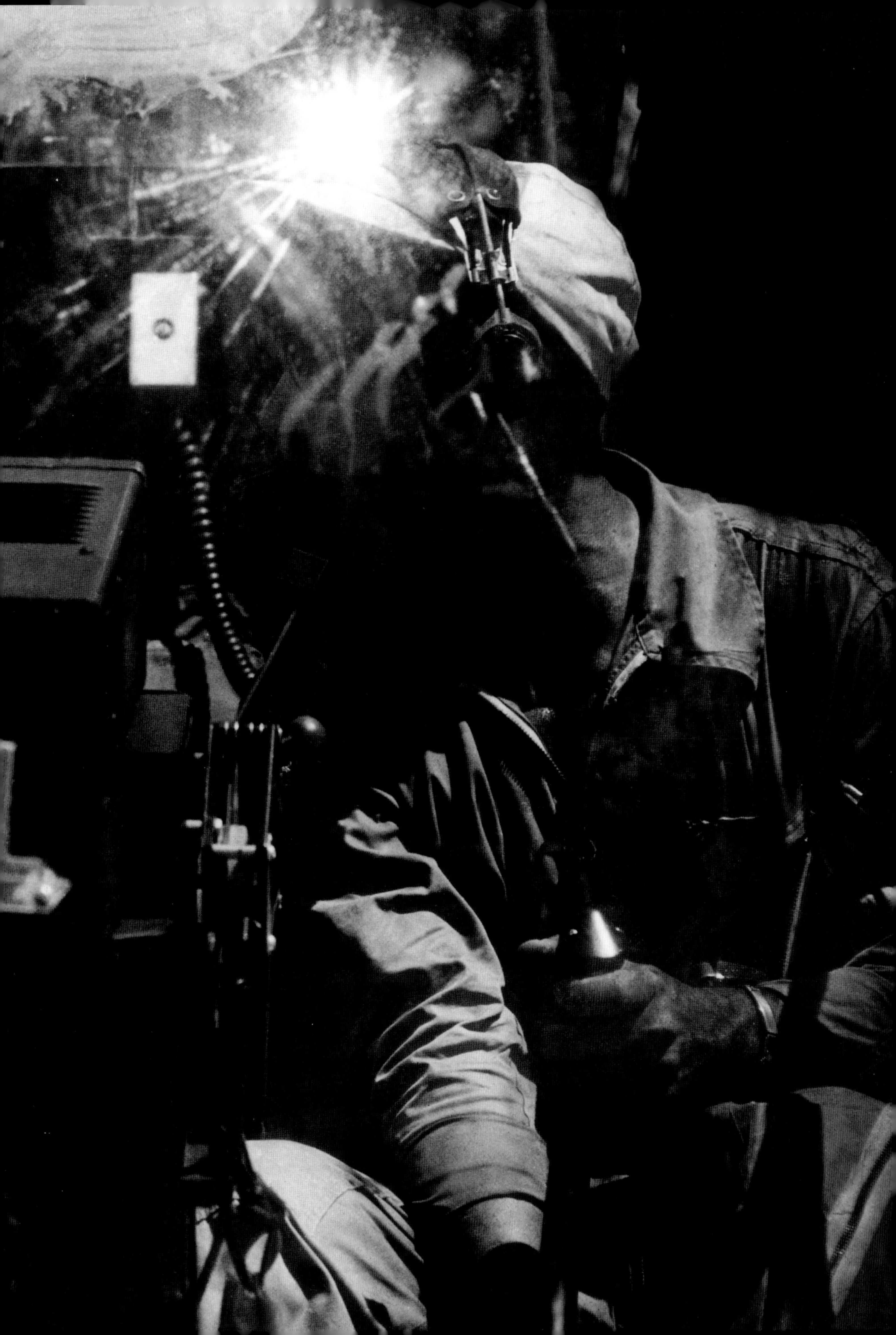

Fidel took his first overseas trip just three weeks after taking power. But breaking with Washington's established protocol, he traveled to a Latin American country rather than the United States. On January 23, 1959, he flew to Caracas for celebrations to mark the first anniversary of the fall of the dictator Pérez Jiménez. He wanted to thank Admiral Larrazabal and the Venezuelan army for the weapons they had provided during the last months of the guerrilla

"I was chosen as the photographer for the delegation which traveled to Caracas. It was the first time I found myself in direct contact with him..."

struggle. He visited the President-elect Romulo Betancourt, in spite of the scorn he felt and the president's anti-revolutionary attitudes. The two men didn't hit it off. In contrast, the welcome of ordinary Venezuelans was overwhelming, with people praising the man as much as his revolution. In Havana, the revolutionary government granted Cuban nationality to the Argentine Ernesto Che Guevara. The *comandante* was first appointed military governor of La Cabaña fortress, where revolutionary tribunals were held. Batista's torturers were tried and often condemned to death. Guevara was then named minister of industry and president of the National Bank. This led to a joke that spread throughout the island. Fidel asked his assembled team: "Is there an economist in the room?" Che lifted his hand, and Castro replied: "OK, you will be president of the National Bank!" But Che had thought the question was: "Is there a communist in the room?" With pointed irony, Guevara signed the new banknotes with his nickname "Che."

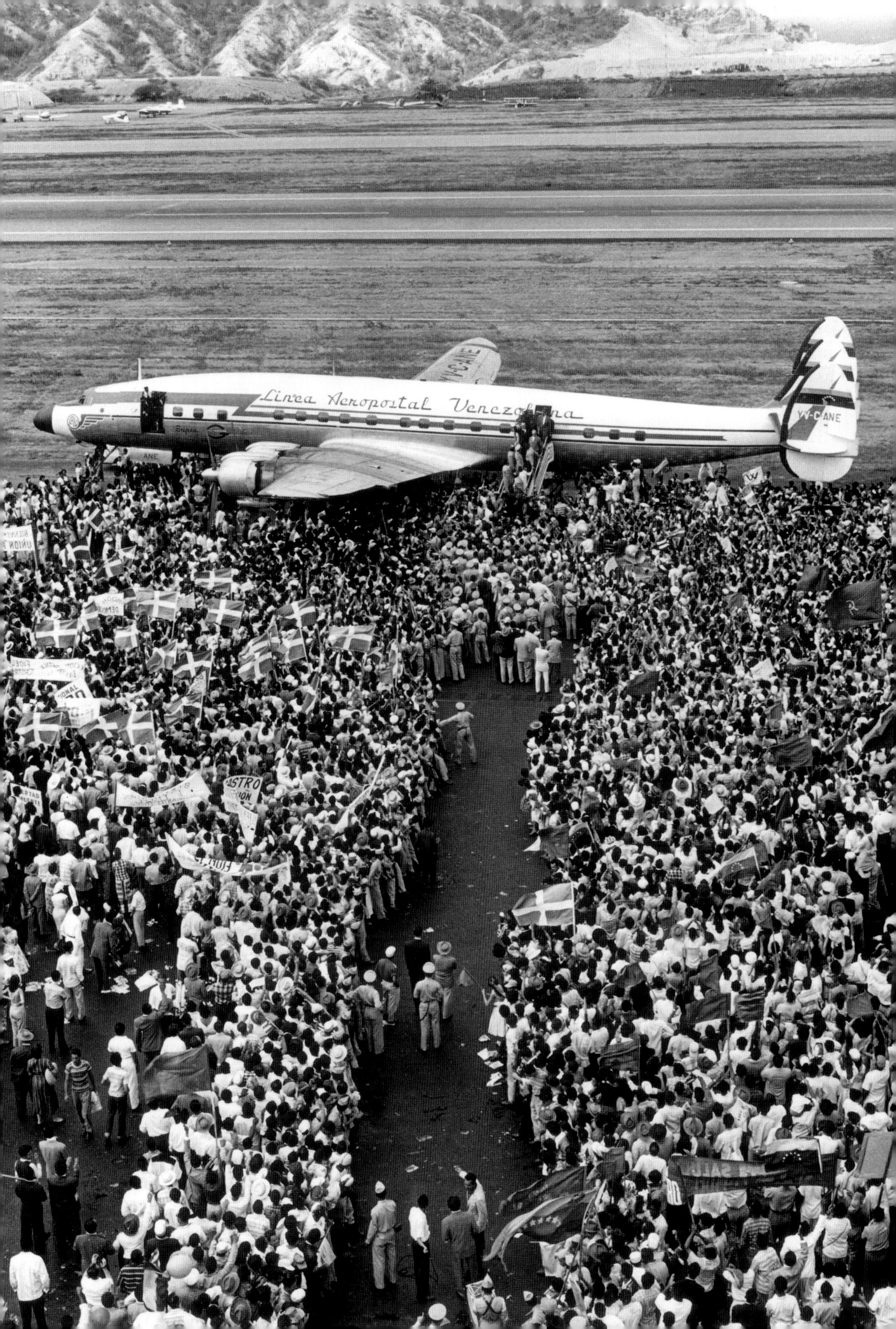
Linea Aeropostal
YV-C-ANE

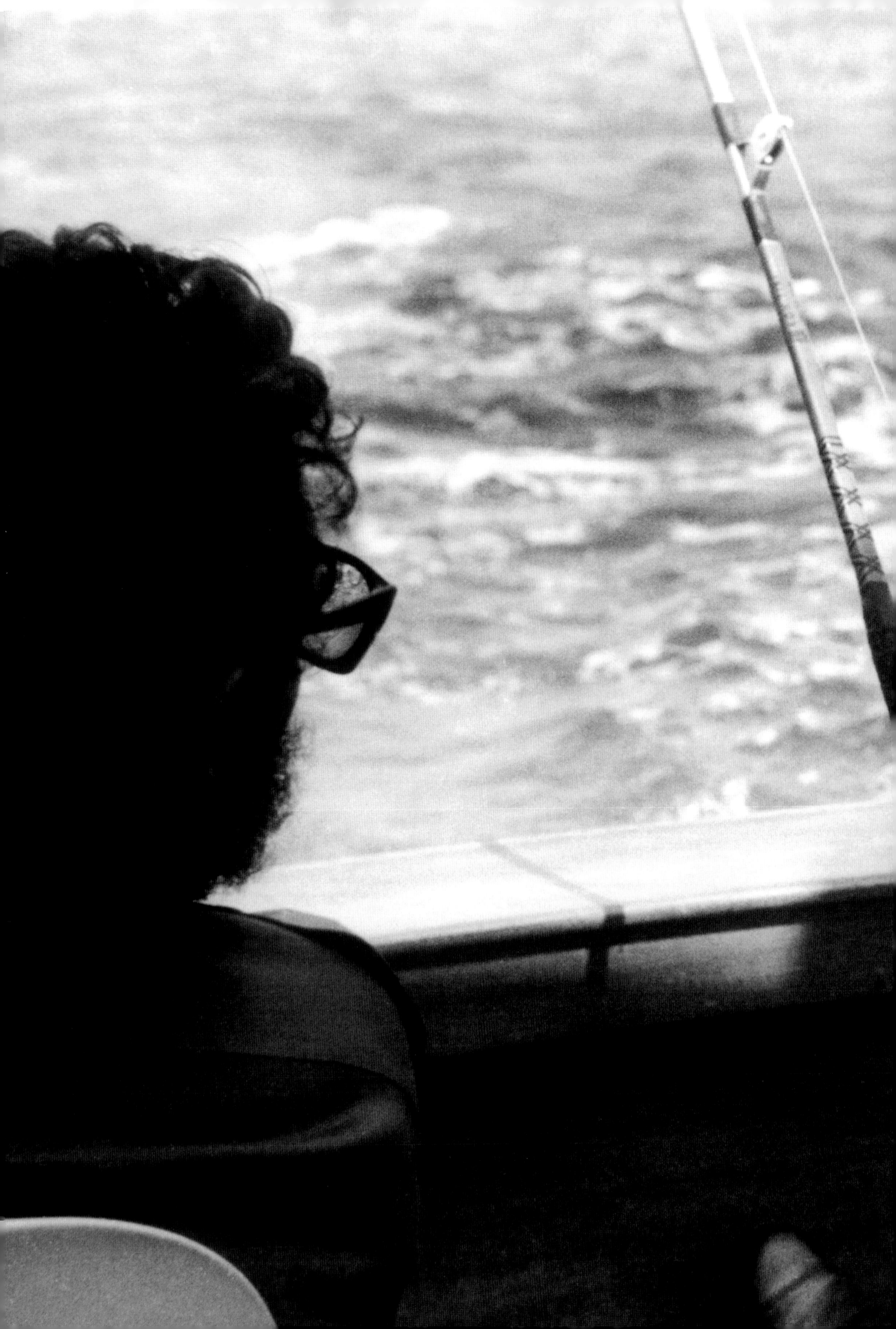

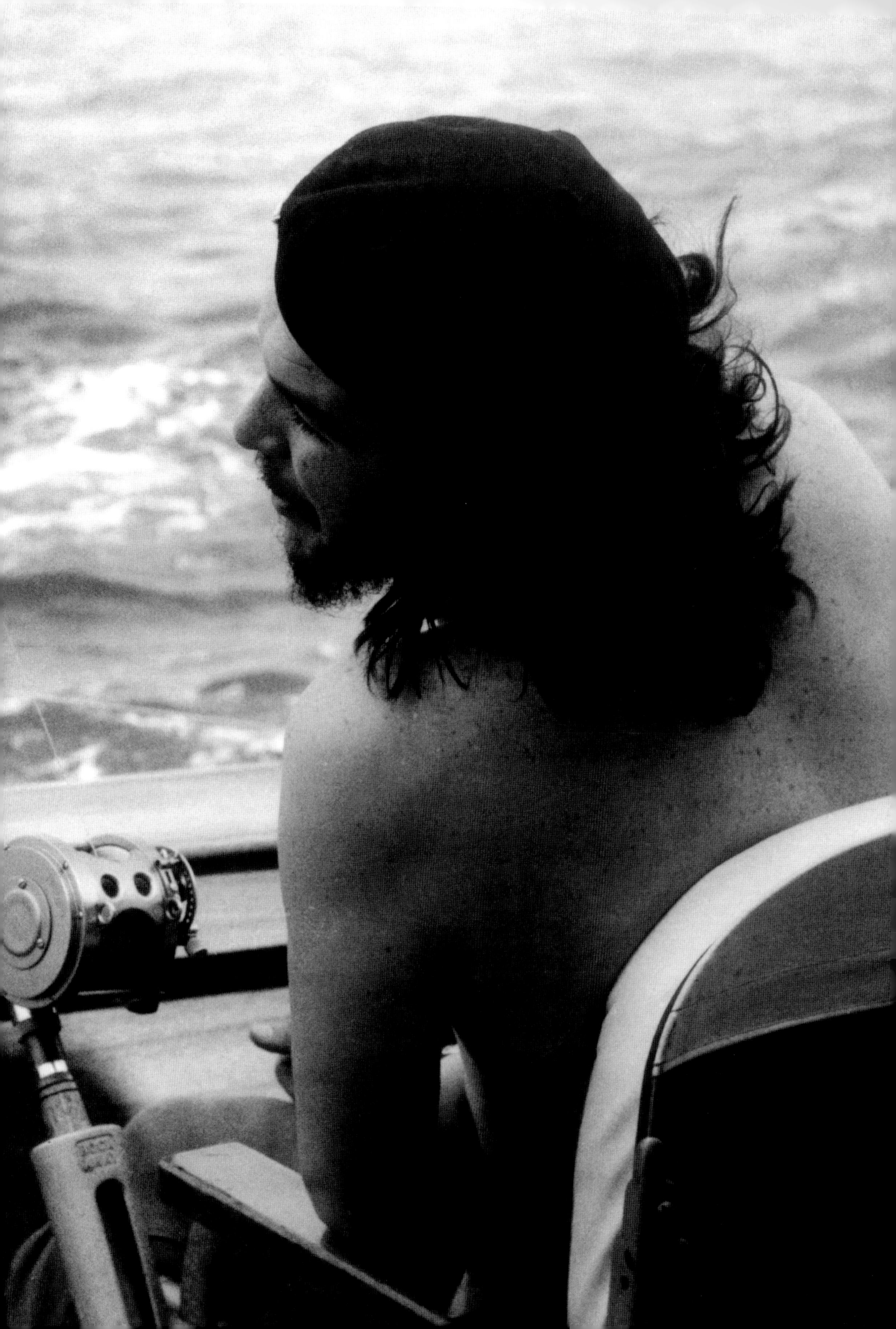

After the triumph of the *barbudos*, Che Guevara's parents flew from Buenos Aires to find their oldest son in Havana. Six years earlier, the young medical graduate had left them in Argentina. With his degree, Ernesto took to the roads to "take the political pulse" of the Latin American continent, which he'd already traversed by motorcycle in his youth. A "Doctor without Borders" before his time, he traveled through Peru, Bolivia, Ecuador, and Costa Rica. In Guatemala,

"Fidel invited Che and his mother to go fishing when Hemingway organized a fishing tournament. The Guevaras seemed very close. I overheard them speaking in French..."

he saw mercenaries trained by the United States try to overthrow the regime of President Árbenz, which was judged too progressive. With Hilda Gadea, the woman who was to become his first wife, he joined the resistance but had to flee to Mexico. He survived there by taking photographic portraits of lovers in the parks and was even employed by the Latina press agency to cover the Pan-American Games. But in 1955, he had a meeting that transformed the rest of his life. He wrote to his parents: "A young Cuban leader invited me to join his movement, a movement which sought the armed liberation of his country. Of course, I accepted... From now on, I wouldn't consider my death a frustration, but, like Hikmet, 'I will take to my grave only the regret of an unfinished song.'" Arriving in Havana at the beginning of 1959, the Guevaras found their son was a warrior hero, celebrated by a whole people.

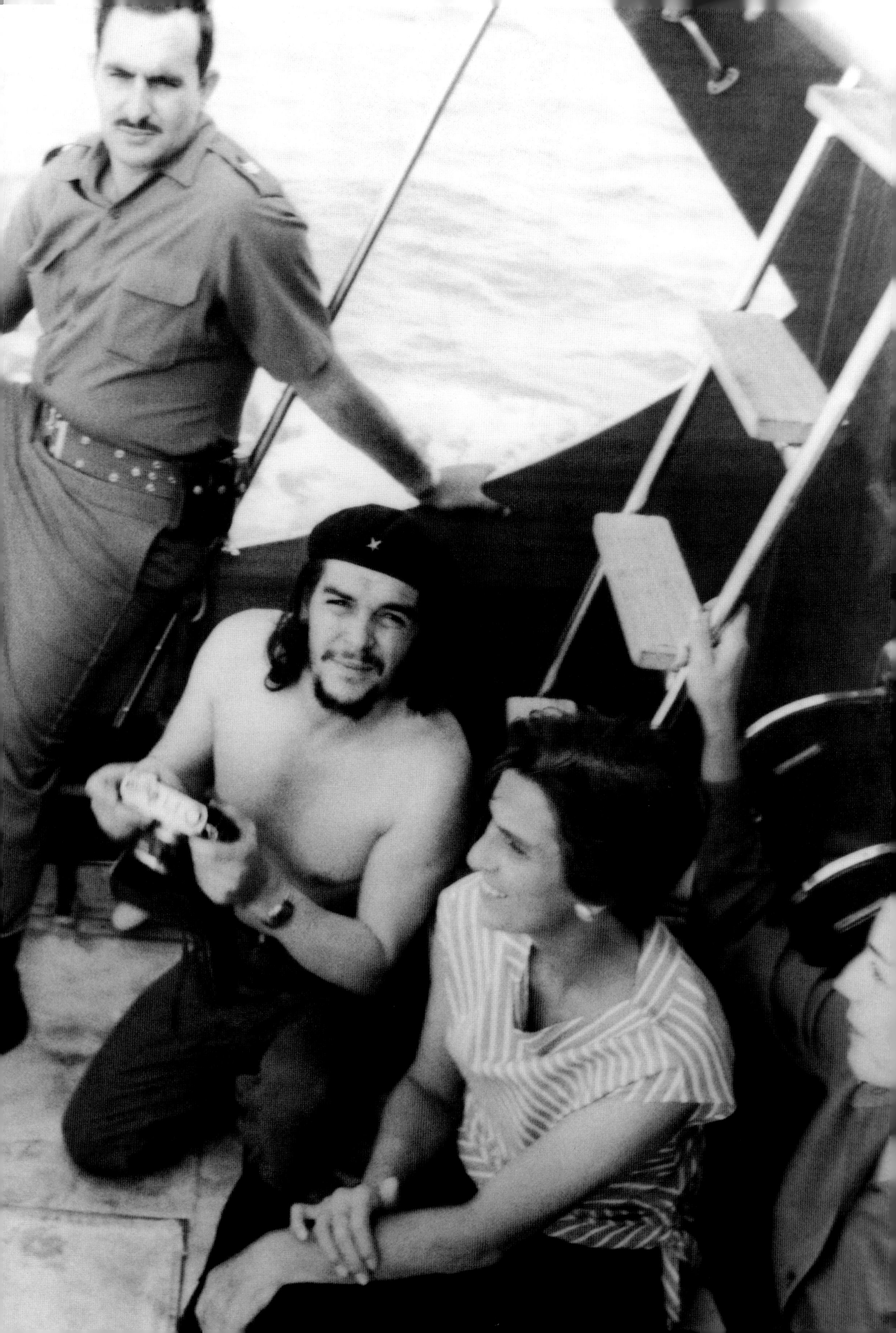

Since 1939, Ernest Hemingway had often lived at his estate, Finca Vigia, southeast of Havana. He wasn't in Cuba when the *barbudos* took power, but he wrote to a journalist in New York: "...Castro's going to run up against a huge pile of money... If he can govern without compromises, he'll be tremendous..." Strangely, the only meeting between the Nobel Prize winner and the young leader took place at the prize giving for the fishing tournament that took

"The prize giver for the fishing competition was none other than Hemingway. And the winner of the contest that day was Fidel..."

Hemingway's name. However, according to Gabriel García Márquez (another Nobel Prize laureate and friend of Fidel), Castro knew Hemingway's work "in depth, he liked to talk about it, and could discuss it in a convincing manner." He was particularly impressed by the novel *For Whom the Bell Tolls*, about the republican guerrilla struggle against the Spanish nationalist forces. He even went so far as to tell foreign visitors that he learned the art of guerrilla warfare from the book. For the biographer Tad Szulc: "It was without doubt the only time Fidel hesitated in imposing himself on someone, meeting a man he considered a genius." The following year, the writer returned to Idaho and was hospitalized to treat his liver and blood pressure. Unable to accept the idea of his physical decline, Hemingway killed himself with a shotgun blast to the head on July 2, 1961. He left a note: "My body has betrayed me, so I am doing away with my body."

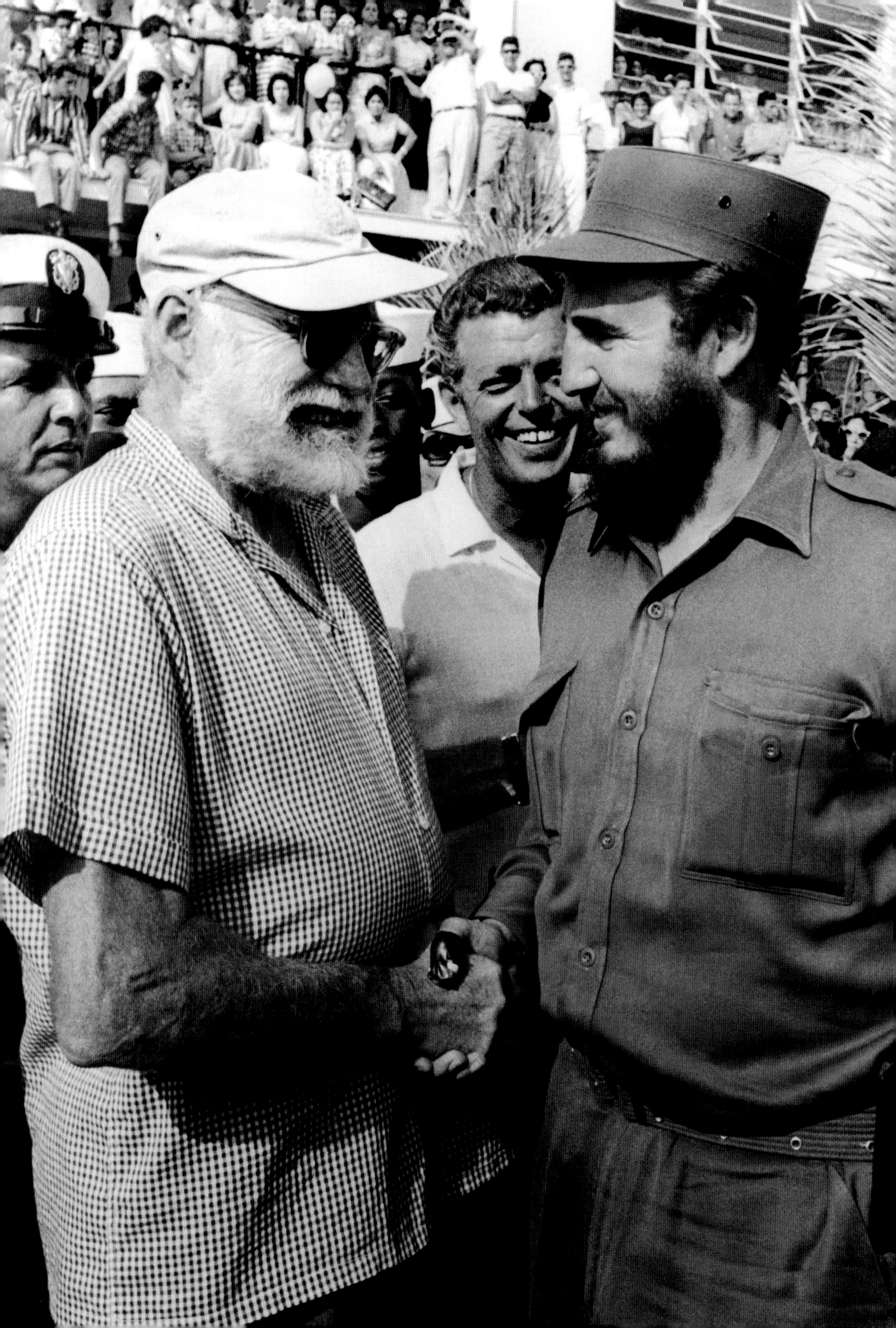

"On July 26, 1959, the anniversary of the assault on the Moncada and a new national holiday, Fidel invited *guajiros* from all over the island to Havana. They arrived in their thousands with palm leaves in their hats and machetes in their belts. Camilo Cienfuegos, the Rebel Army's chief of staff, rode at the head of the horsemen. With his easy smile and looking like Jesus out for a good time, he became the darling of Havana's women. After Fidel, he was the most popular leader, but unfortunately, in October 1959, he disappeared while flying alone in a Cessna from Camagüey to Havana. Fidel organized a week-long search, but they never found a trace..."

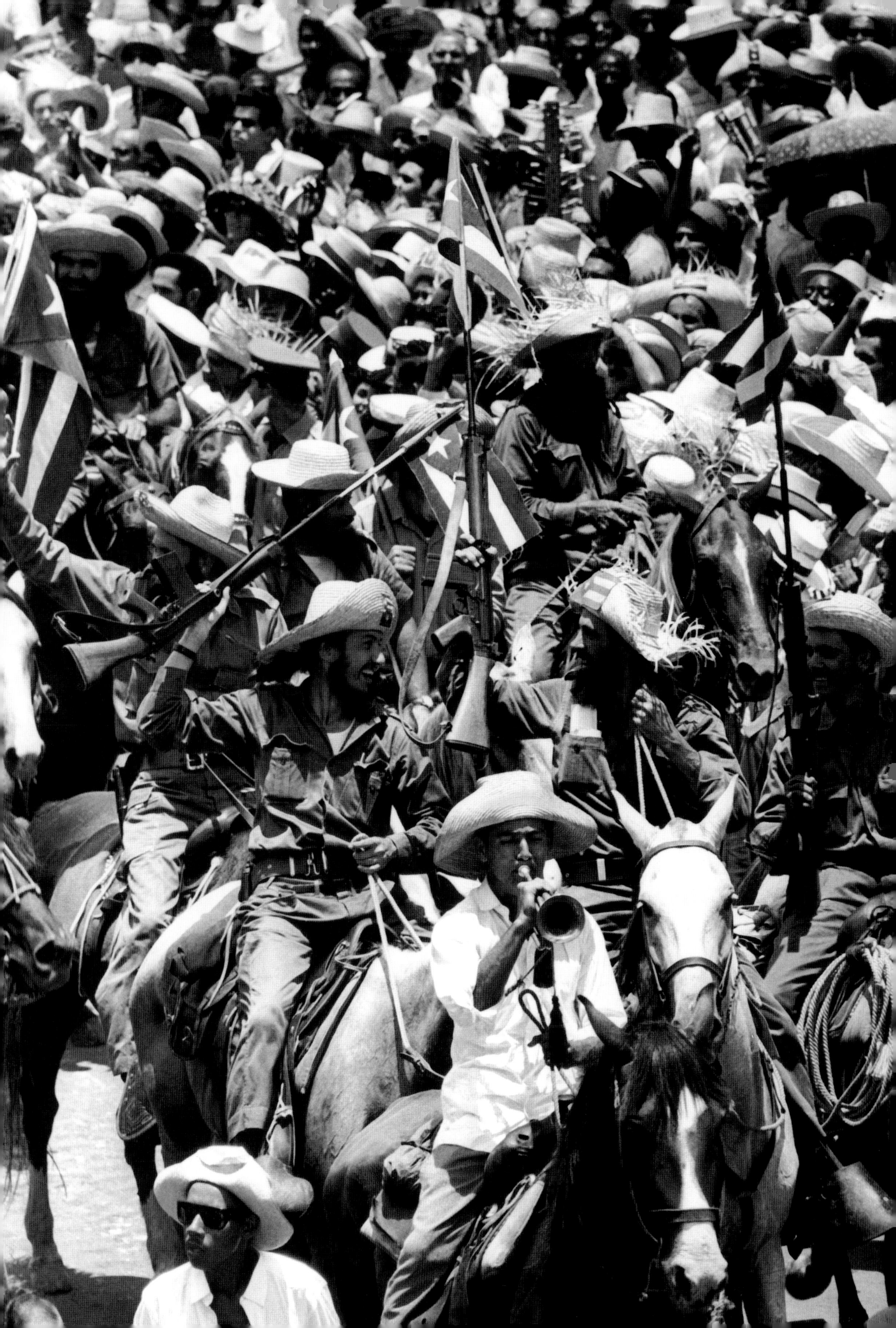

In the euphoria of the first months of the revolution, the new government introduced a series of social policies. Setting their own salaries at the level of the basic wage, the members of Castro's government lowered the price of meat, medicine, housing, telephones, electricity, and transport. They abolished past policies of racial discrimination against Afro-Cubans and opened the best beaches to the whole population. But the first truly revolutionary

"While Fidel was making his speech, this fellow scrambled up the street light like a cat, then settled astride the lights and calmly lit a cigarette. I called him 'Don Quixote of the Lamp Post.'"

legislation focused on agrarian reform. The *guajiro*, the Cuban peasant with a fringed straw hat, was presented as the man of the hour. On May 17, 1959, the ministers signed the reforms into law at a highly symbolic location—a village near Fidel Castro's former headquarters in the Sierra Maestra. The key provision limited landholdings to 400 hectares, ending the epoch of *latifundias* and large landholdings by US interests such as the United Fruit Company. However, the focus was on collectivization of land rather than redistribution to individual farmers. For Castro: "From this date, there was a true break between the revolution and the wealthiest, privileged sectors of society, a rupture with the United States and the multinationals."

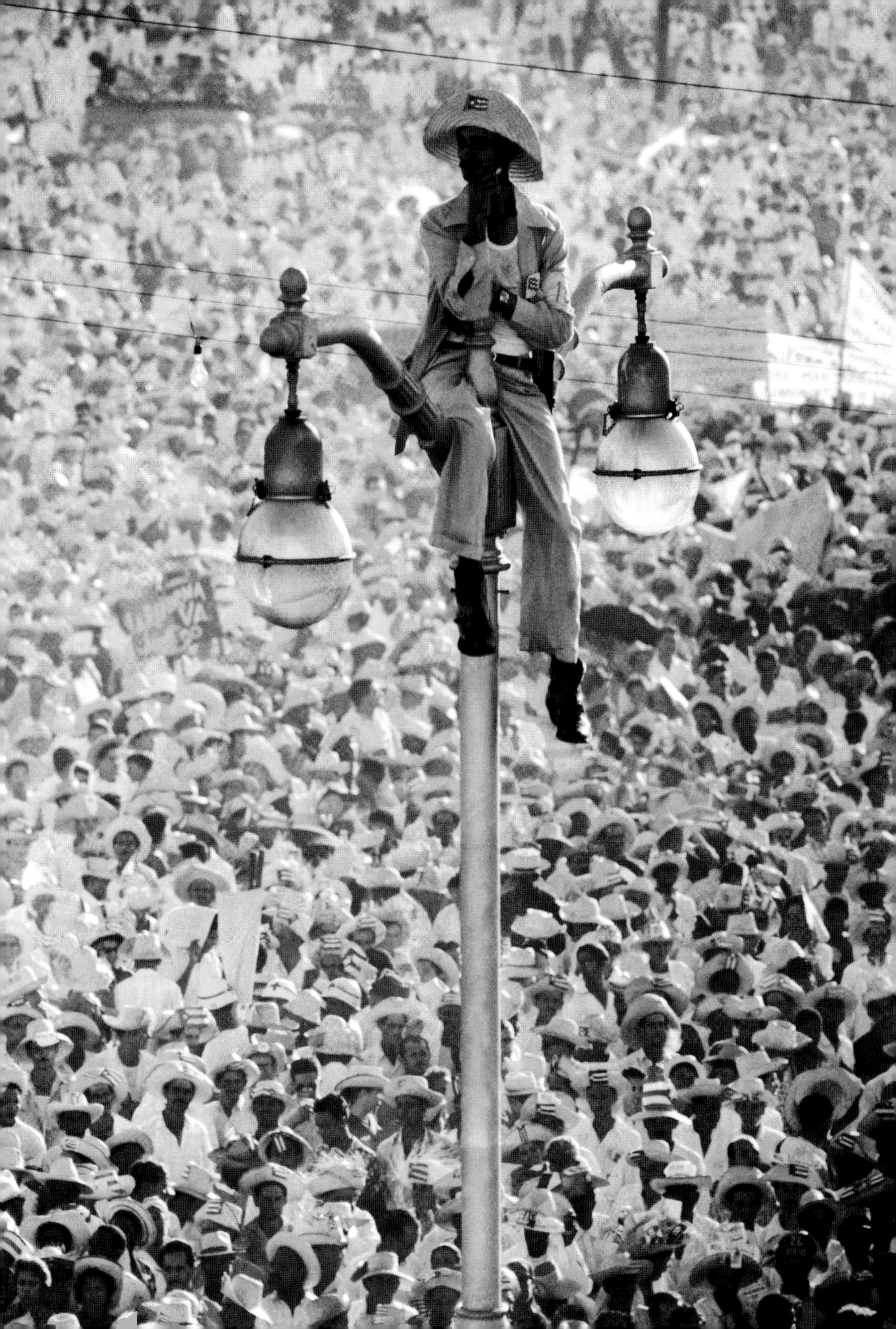

From March 1959, well before Fidel Castro had declared the socialist character of the Cuban Revolution, the Eisenhower administration was studying the best method to get rid of him. On March 10, a meeting of the US National Security Council focused on the means "to bring another regime to power in Cuba." Castro in turn was obsessed by one idea, as detailed by Manuel Vázquez Montalbán—that the United States should not steal the revolution as

"For the US public at that time, Fidel was still the handsome and romantic Robin Hood who had defeated the evil Batista..."

they had done in 1898 with Cuban independence. The new leader in Havana took advantage of an invitation from the Association of Newspaper Editors to visit the United States and launch a public relations campaign. But Castro didn't arrive in Washington with his hand extended like a beggar, as happened with all new Latin American leaders seeking urgent economic aid. This was unimaginable for the bureaucrats of the State Department. Rather than a visit to the US government, Fidel used the occasion to meet with the US people, calling for a policy of friendship and mutual respect. During his previous visit to the United States four years earlier, Castro was just a young exile seeking funds from the Cuban diaspora to maintain his struggle. He had to humbly apply to the US immigration authorities for an extension to his tourist visa. This time he arrived as the kind of star Americans love. He was pursued by the media and given an extraordinary welcome by the US public.

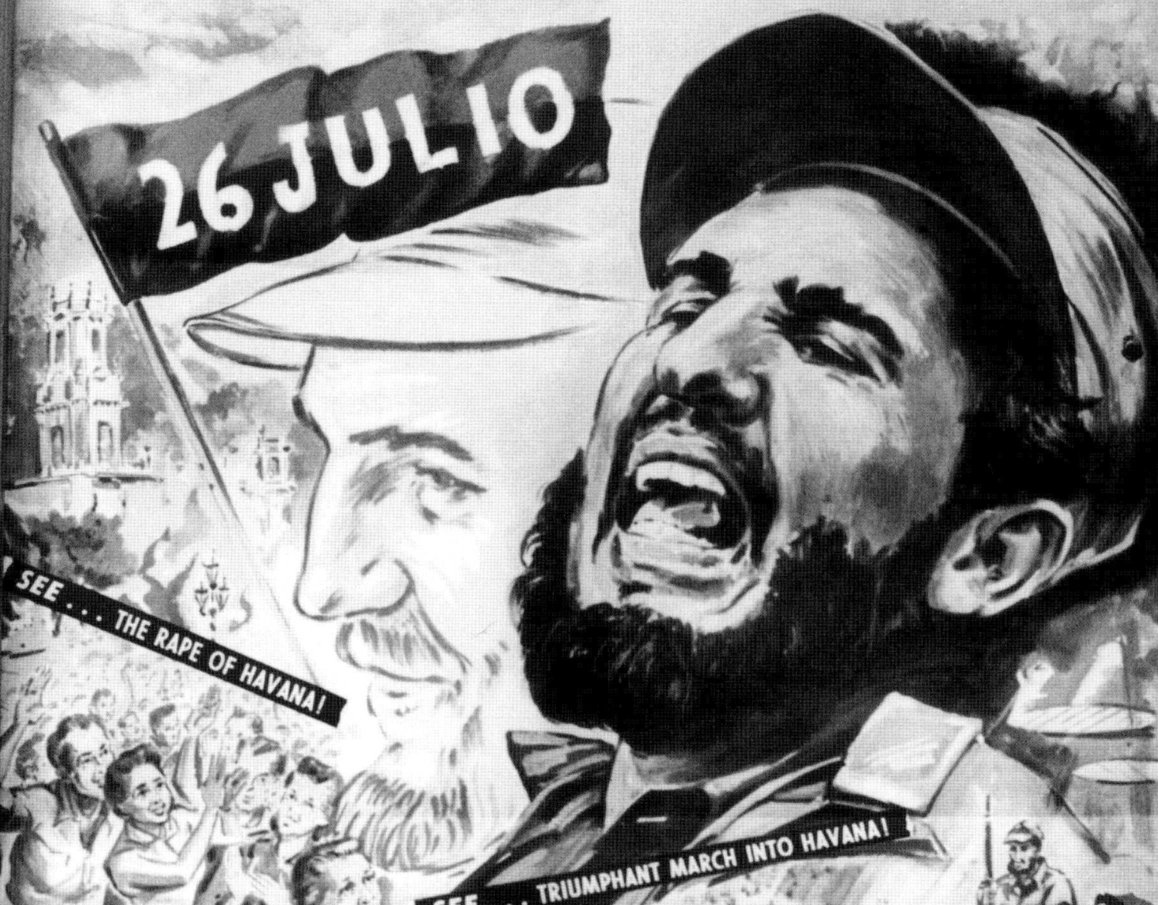
NOW PLAYING
MAN OF ACTION—IN ACTION!
26 JULIO
SEE . . . THE RAPE OF HAVANA!
SEE . . . TRIUMPHANT MARCH INTO HAVANA!
THE
REBEL
CASTRO
FROM OUTLAW TO PRIME MINISTER!!
SEE . . . THE WAR TRIALS!

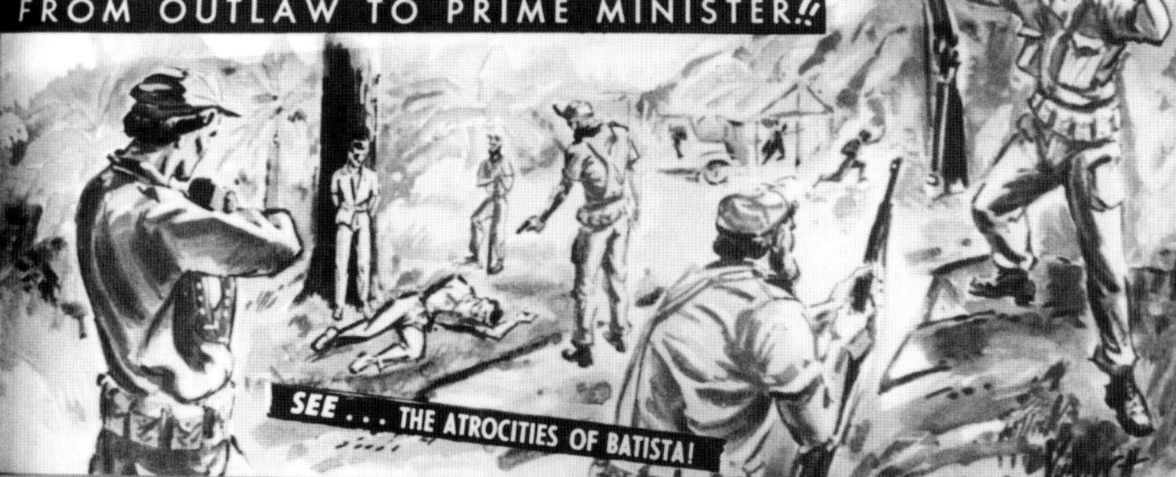
SEE . . . THE ATROCITIES OF BATISTA!

While the new Cuban head of state was visiting Washington, President Eisenhower was playing golf. Fidel Castro met for two and a half hours with Vice-President Richard Nixon, but they didn't hit it off. Nixon saw Castro as "intelligent and insightful" but "incredibly naive about communism or living under its influence." In contrast, the bearded giant was the darling of the media. He responded to questions in English during a luncheon at the National Press Club,

"Fidel amused himself by playing tricks on the Secret Service..."

and joined in the TV program "Meet the Press." On each occasion, he hammered home the point that the era of the Platt Amendment was over—the Cuban people would no longer accept this provision in the 1902 Cuban constitution that the United States had added, giving a legal basis to intervention in Cuban affairs at the whim of Washington. Everyone wanted to meet the famous guerrilla, but Fidel also found some time for tourism. He visited the icons of US democracy: the Lincoln and Jefferson Memorials. One evening, he even slipped away from his security detail to drive around incognito. He went to eat in a Chinese restaurant and chatted to some students. After Washington, Castro left for New York. It was a city he already knew, as he'd spent a good part of his honeymoon there with Mirta Díaz-Balart in 1958. With his son Fidelito, he toured the Bronx Zoo and was so entranced by the animals that he expanded Havana's zoo as soon as he returned home. In Central Park, he addressed a crowd of 30,000 people.

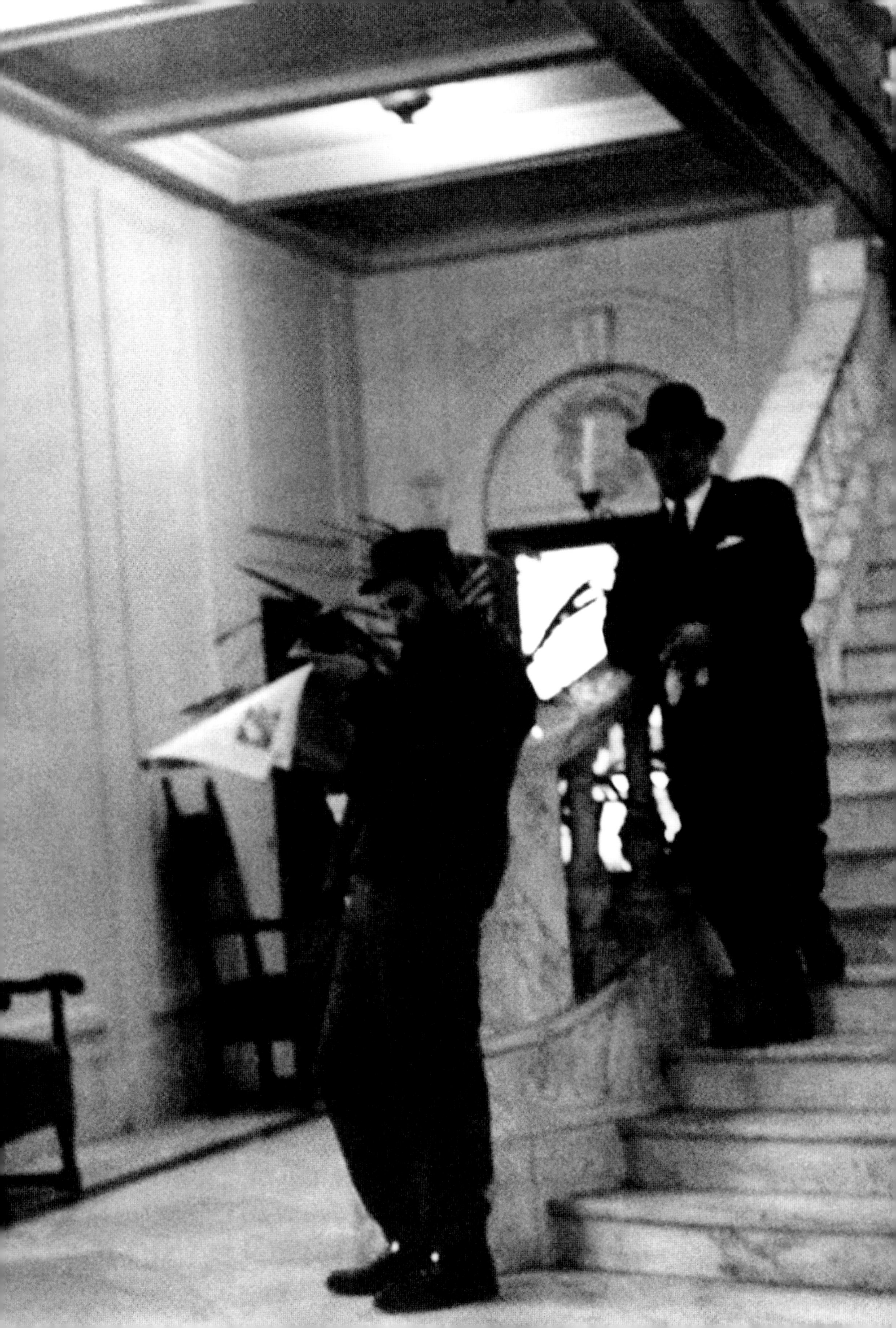

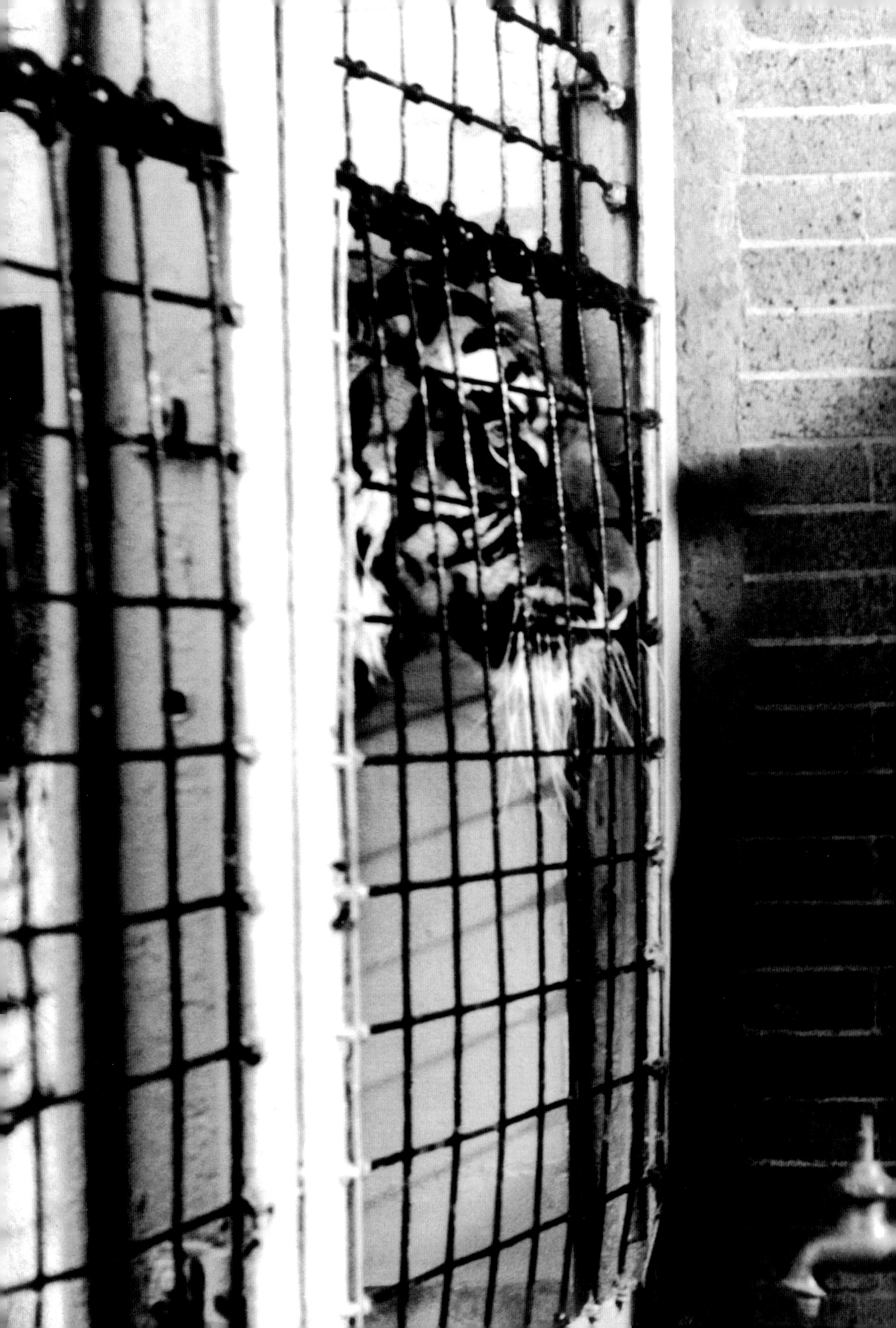

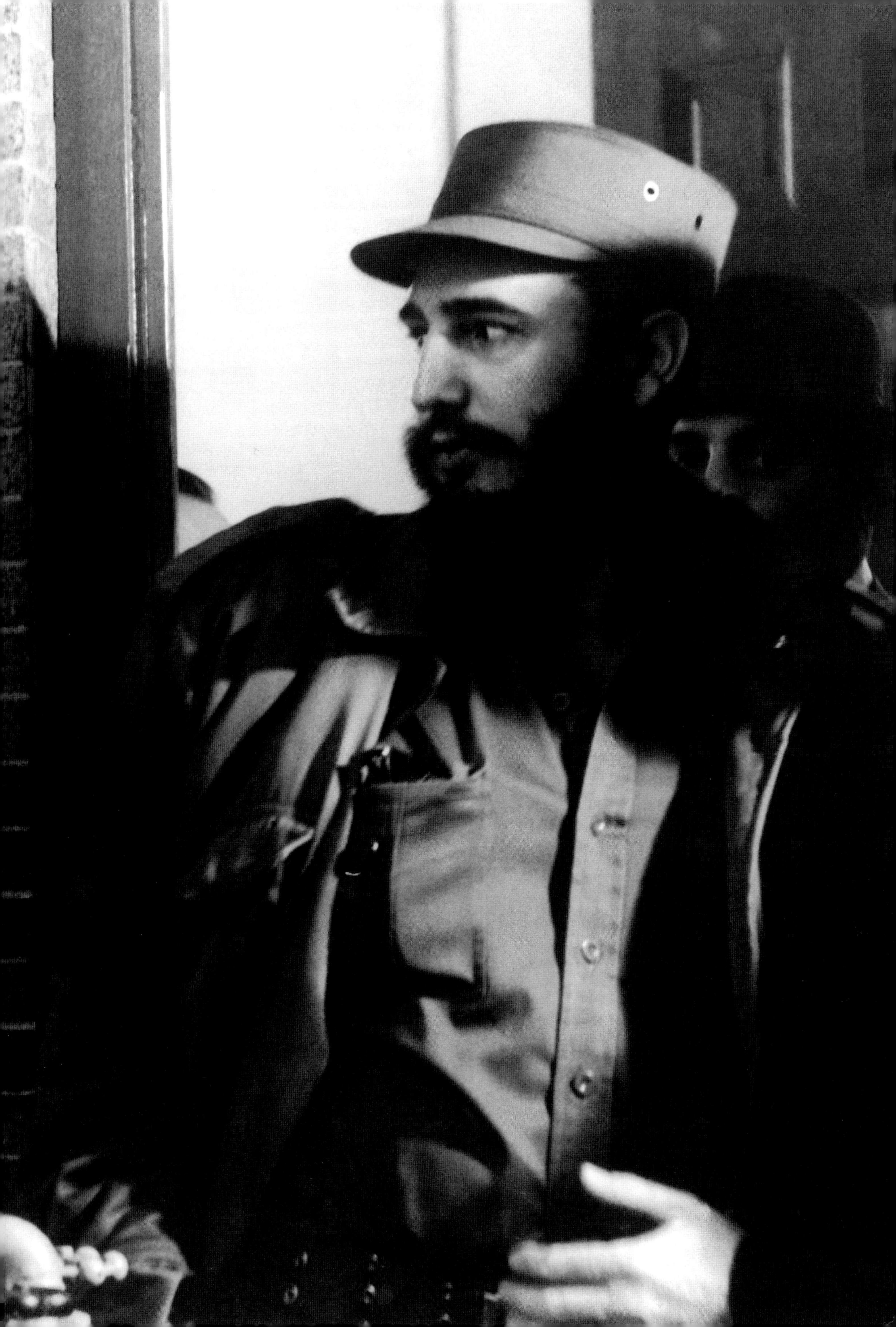

“I called this photo ‘David and Goliath.’ From the day I gave a copy to Fidel, he never contacted me at the newspaper but rang me directly. I didn’t become his official photographer; no, I became his personal photographer. I never had a title or a salary. We were like friends. From then on, it wasn’t the leader giving orders I tried to photograph, but a relaxed man, very human, interested in everything and everyone…”

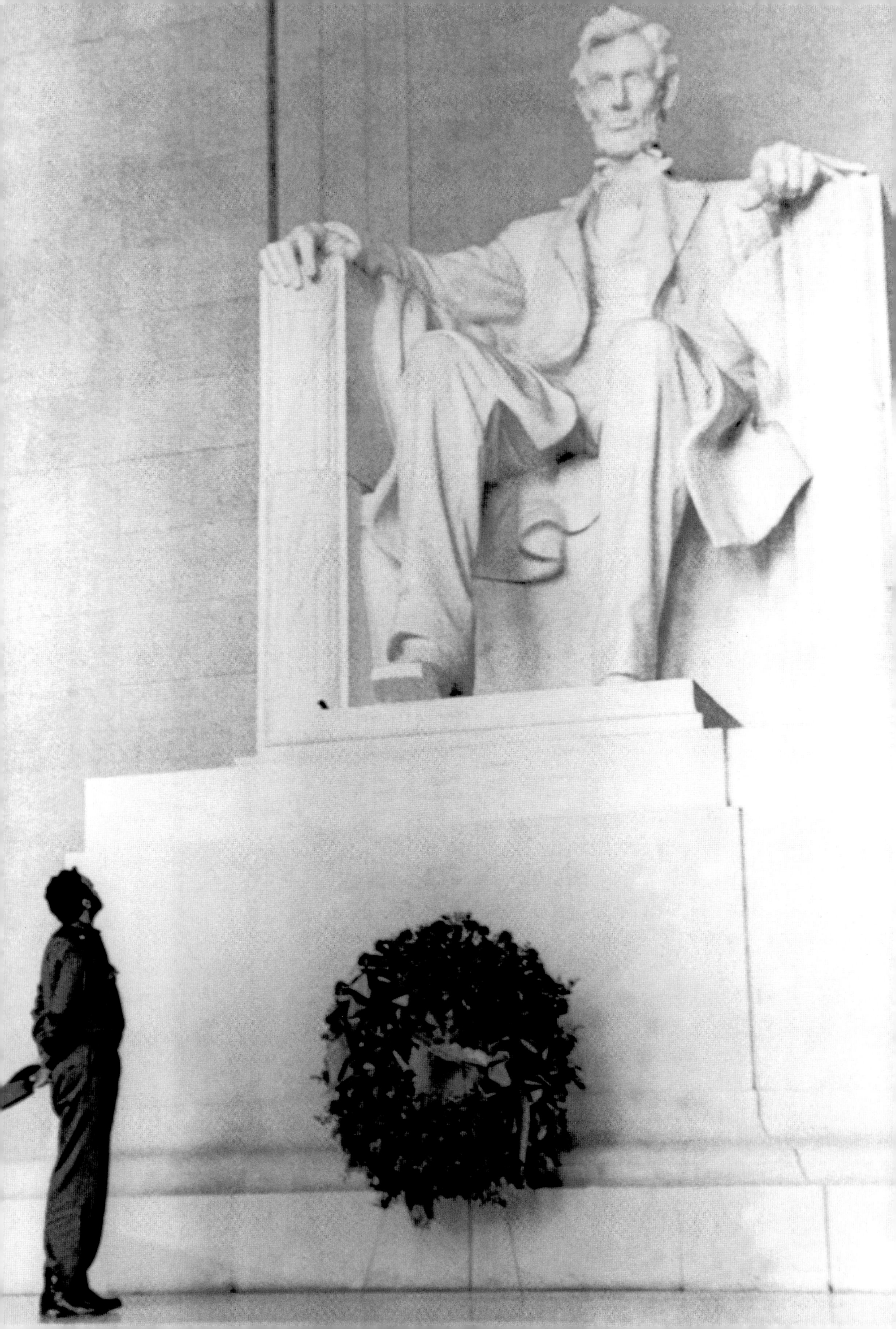

At the start of March 1960, more than a year after taking power, the French cargo vessel *La Coubre* from the General Transatlantic Company arrived in port at Havana. It was carrying a second load of munitions that the Cubans had succeeded in buying from Belgium, in spite of Washington's opposition. But on March 4, two enormous explosions shook the city. The attack killed 81 port workers and wounded another 200. Fidel blamed the CIA and this carnage ended any hope of

"At the foot of the podium draped in black crepe, my eye pressed to my old Leica, I was focusing on Fidel and the people around him. Suddenly, through the 90 mm lens, Che loomed above me. I was surprised by his look..."

reconciliation with the United States. Gilberto Ande, a photographer with the magazine *Verde Olivo*, found Che trying to help the wounded but Che forbade him from taking any photos. It seemed heartless to be the object of attention in such circumstances. The next day during the funeral service for the victims at Havana's cemetery, Korda was there for the newspaper *Revolución*. He took photos of Fidel Castro during his angry speech, some of Che Guevara, and others of Jean-Paul Sartre and Simone de Beauvoir, the French intellectuals who had just arrived in Cuba. They had come to study for themselves the revolutionary process that had enthralled the whole world. Returning home, Sartre wrote a long series of articles entitled "Whirlwind in the Sugarcane." He concluded: "Cuba wants to be Cuba, and nothing else."

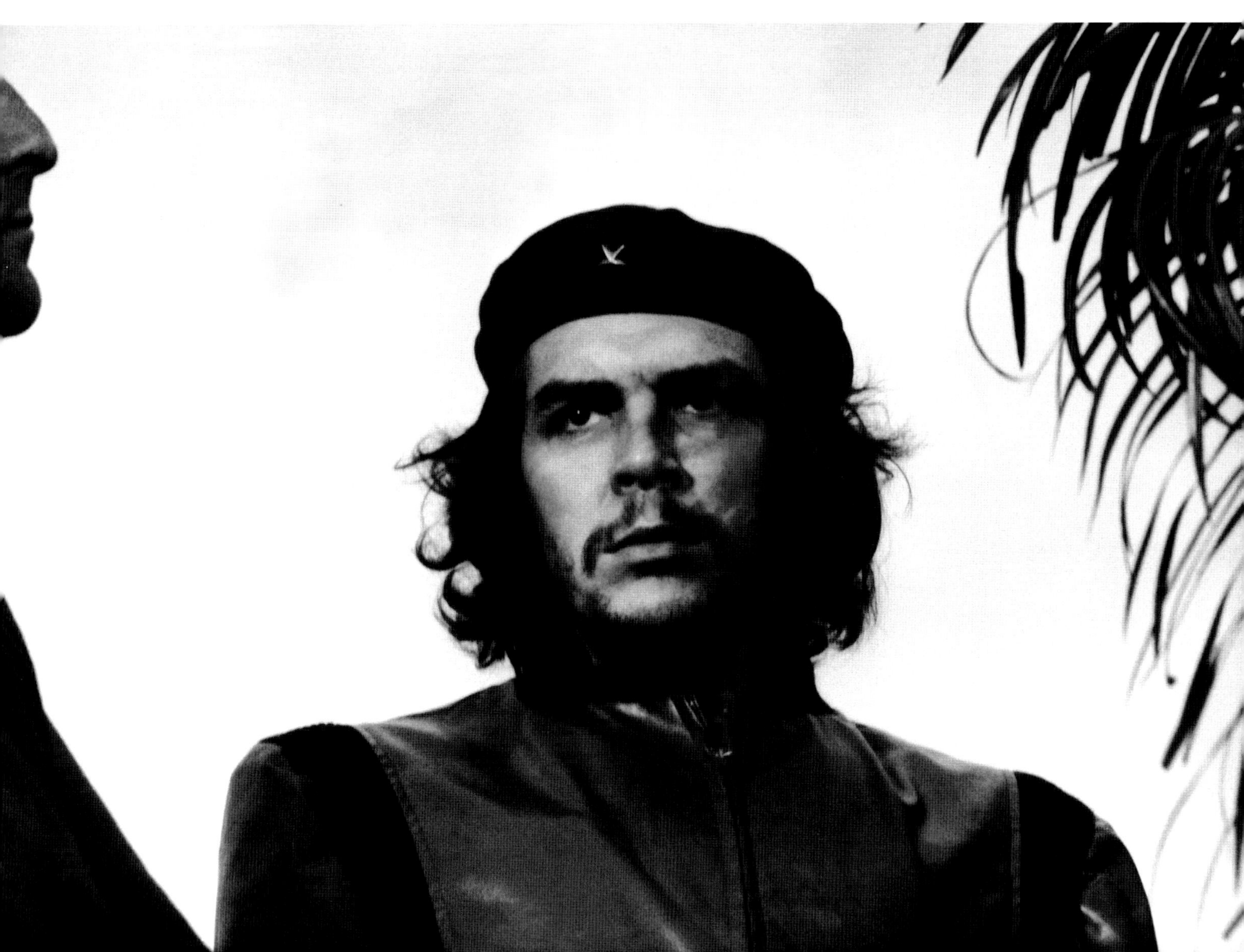

"By reflex, I snapped twice—one horizontal shot and one vertical. I didn't have enough time to take a third photo, as he stepped back discreetly into the second row. Back in my studio, I developed the film and made a few prints for *Revolución*. Because there was a head showing over his shoulder in the vertical shot, I cropped the horizontal photo. The editor-in-chief chose to publish a photo of Fidel on the front page instead, but I liked the Che portrait so much I later made a bigger print, 11 by 14 inches, and hung it in my studio..."

Korda didn't use this vertical shot, published here for the first time. He decided to crop the horizontal photo (previous page).

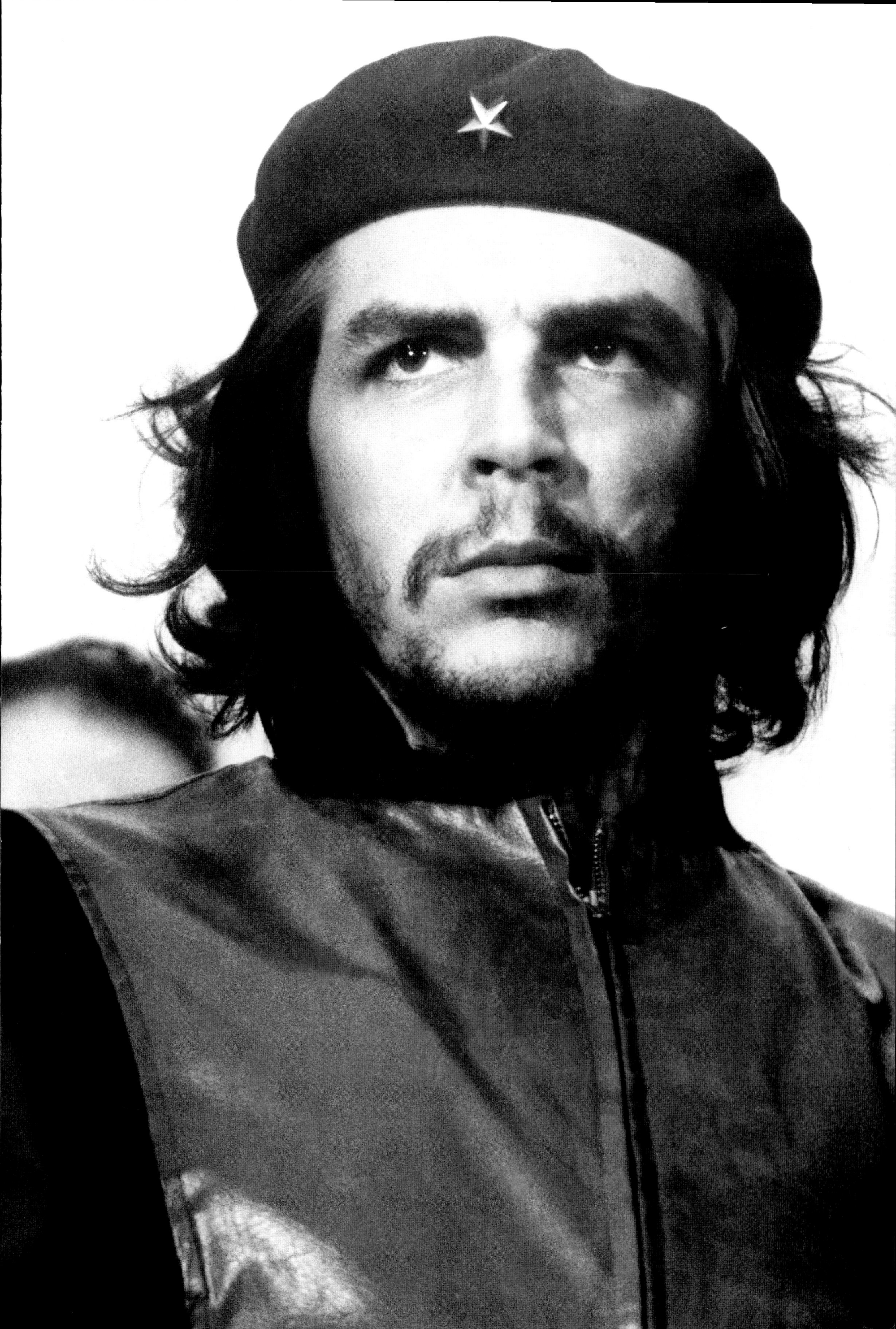

In June 1967, seven years after the explosion of *La Coubre*, the entire world was asking itself what had happened to Guevara. No one knew that he was trying to open up a new guerrilla front in Bolivia. In Havana, the Italian publisher Gianfranco Feltrinelli was looking for a good portrait of Che. He arrived at Korda's studio with a recommendation from Haydée Santamaría, one of the earliest revolutionaries. Based on this introduction, the photographer gave Feltrinelli a present of two prints of the photo. In October the same year, Che was taken prisoner and executed by the Bolivian army. A few months later, Fidel Castro sent Che's *Bolivian Diary* to Feltrinelli, who agreed to publish it and send the profits to the Latin American revolutionary movements. At the same time, the publisher printed the first thousands of posters featuring Korda's photo of Che. The poster became iconic around the world and millions of copies would be distributed without crediting the photographer. Korda never received a cent of royalties from the sale of the posters.

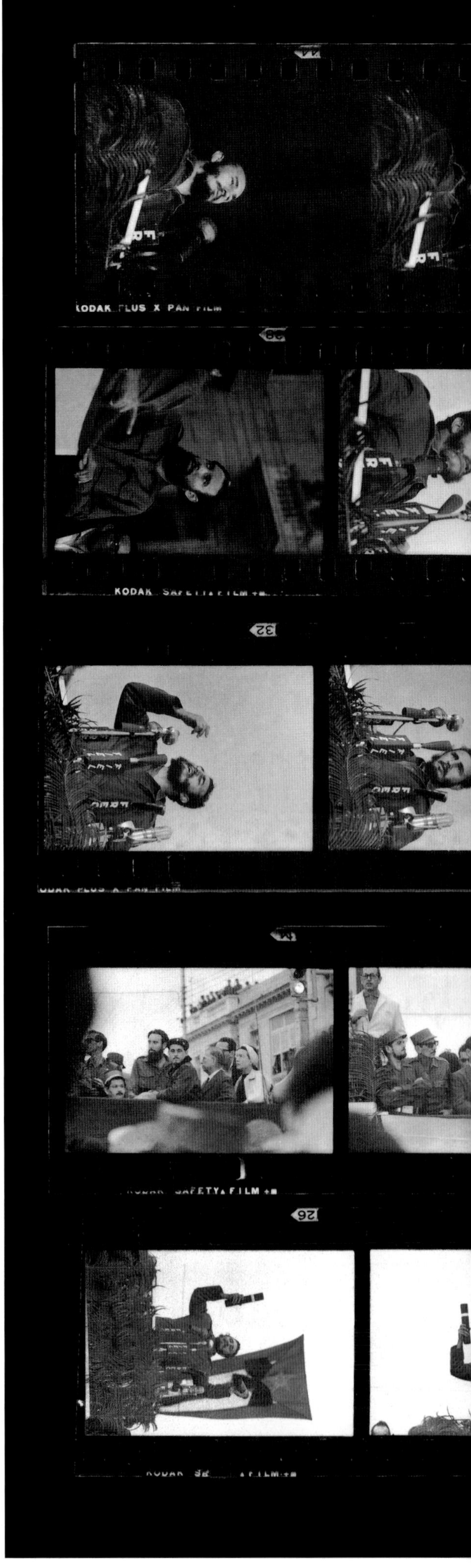

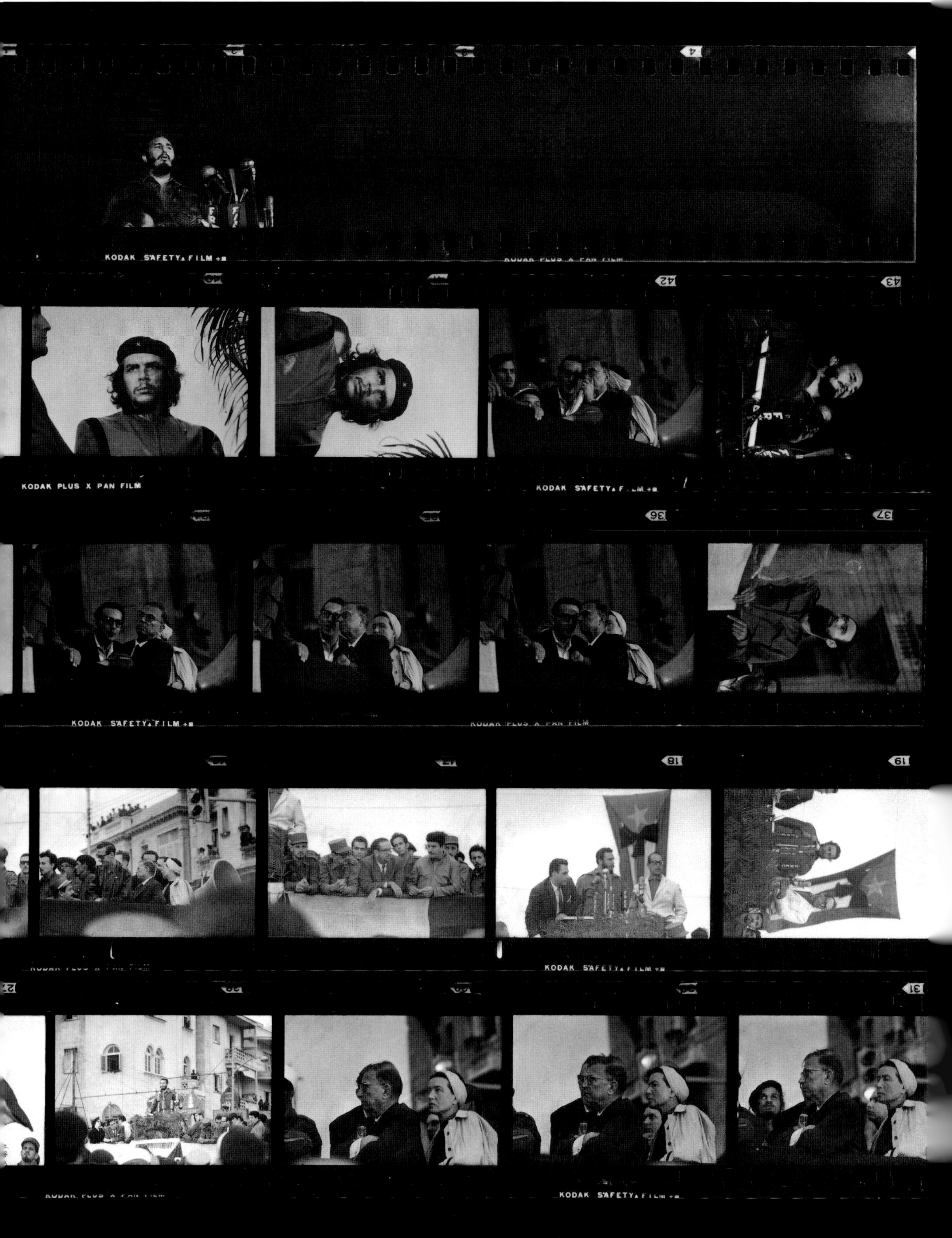
KODAK SAFETY FILM
KODAK PLUS X PAN FILM
KODAK SAFETY FILM
KODAK SAFETY FILM
KODAK SAFETY FILM
KODAK SAFETY FILM

"Here's one of the photos that was published the next day on the front page of *Revolución*: Fidel brandishing two explosives [like those used in the sabotage], during the speech in which he introduced the new catch-cry: *'¡Patria o Muerte, Venceremos!'* My photo of Che was not used on this occasion. It was only a year later in April 1961 that the newspaper used it to announce a TV interview with *comandante* Guevara..."

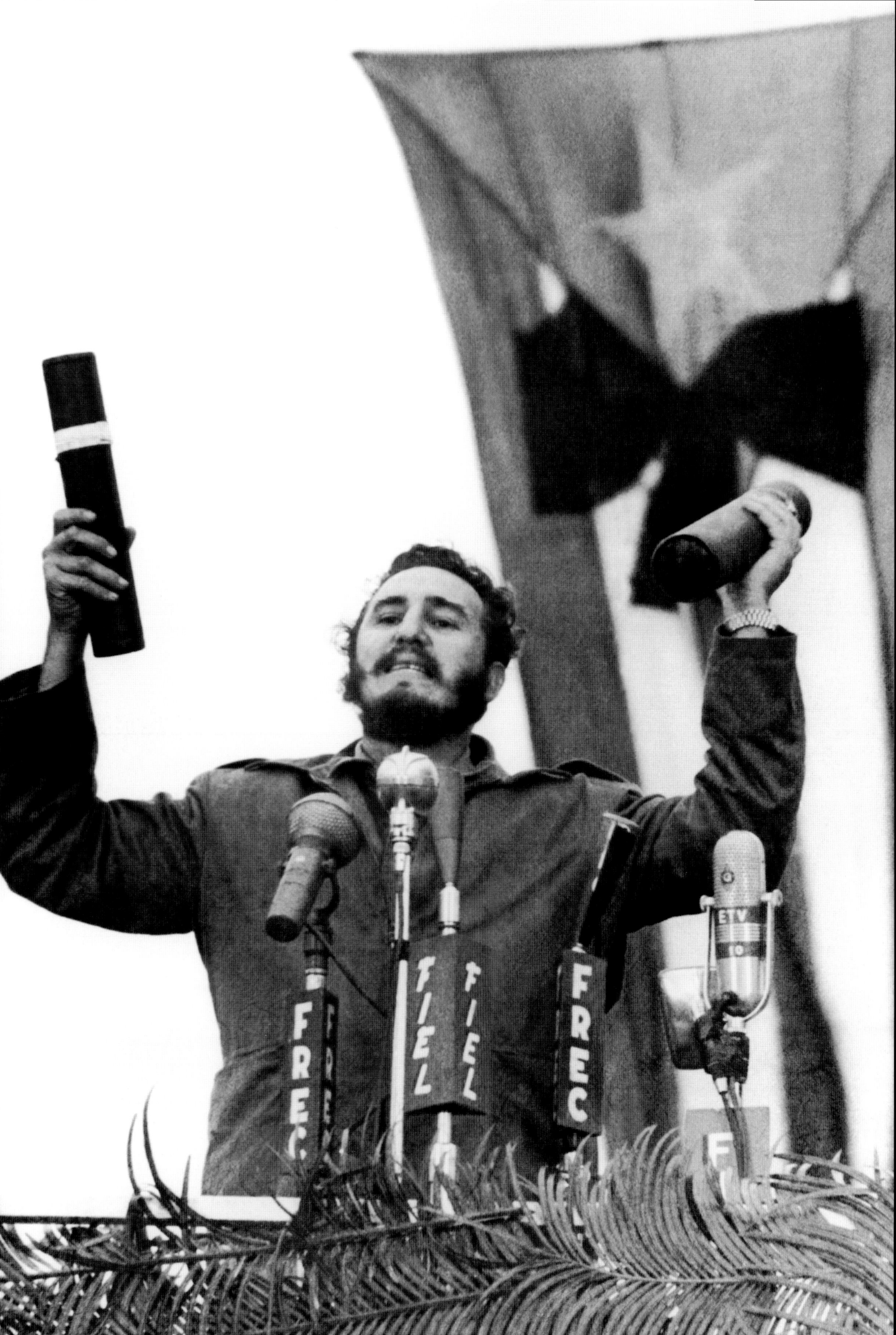
FREC
FIEL
FIEL
FREC
ETV
10

"While we were traveling by car, Sartre asked Fidel: 'Fidel, if the people asked you to do the impossible, what would you do?' Fidel replied: 'If they asked me, then I'd have to do it.' That night, near midnight, Che welcomed the two intellectuals to his office in the Ministry of Industry—he worked so much that he often received visitors as late as four in the morning. The interview was in French. When we left his office, the duty sentry was asleep, his cap over his face. Sartre commented to de Beauvoir that with the long hair tied back in a ponytail, you couldn't tell if it belonged to a man or a woman. . ."

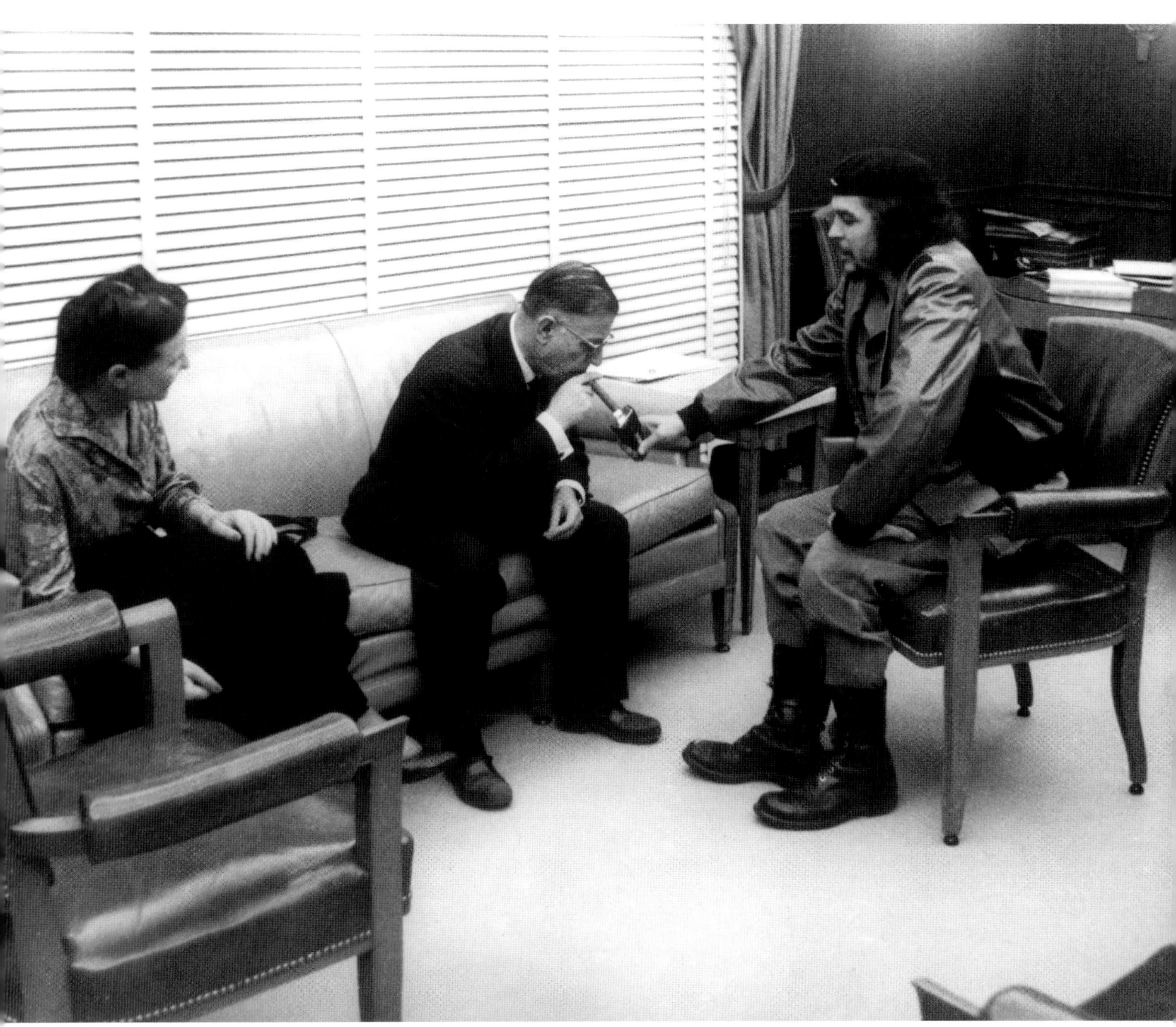

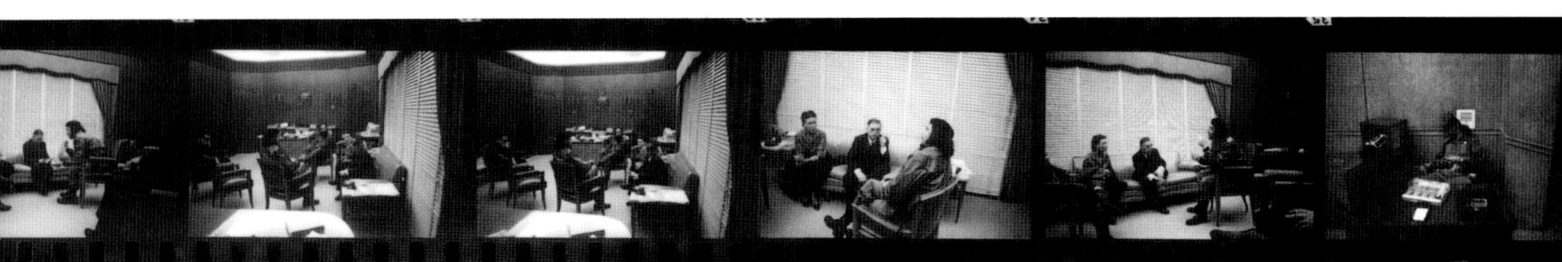

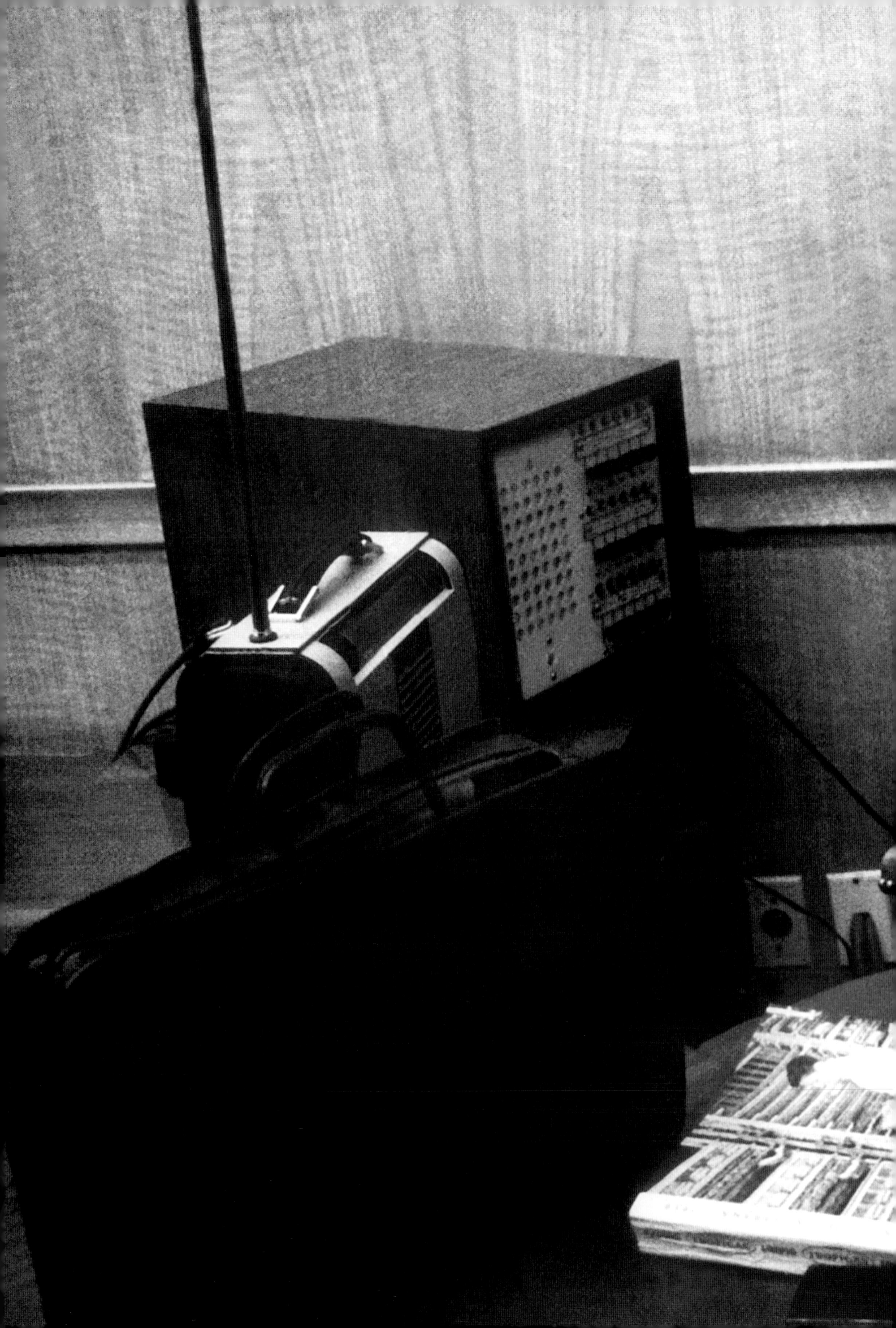

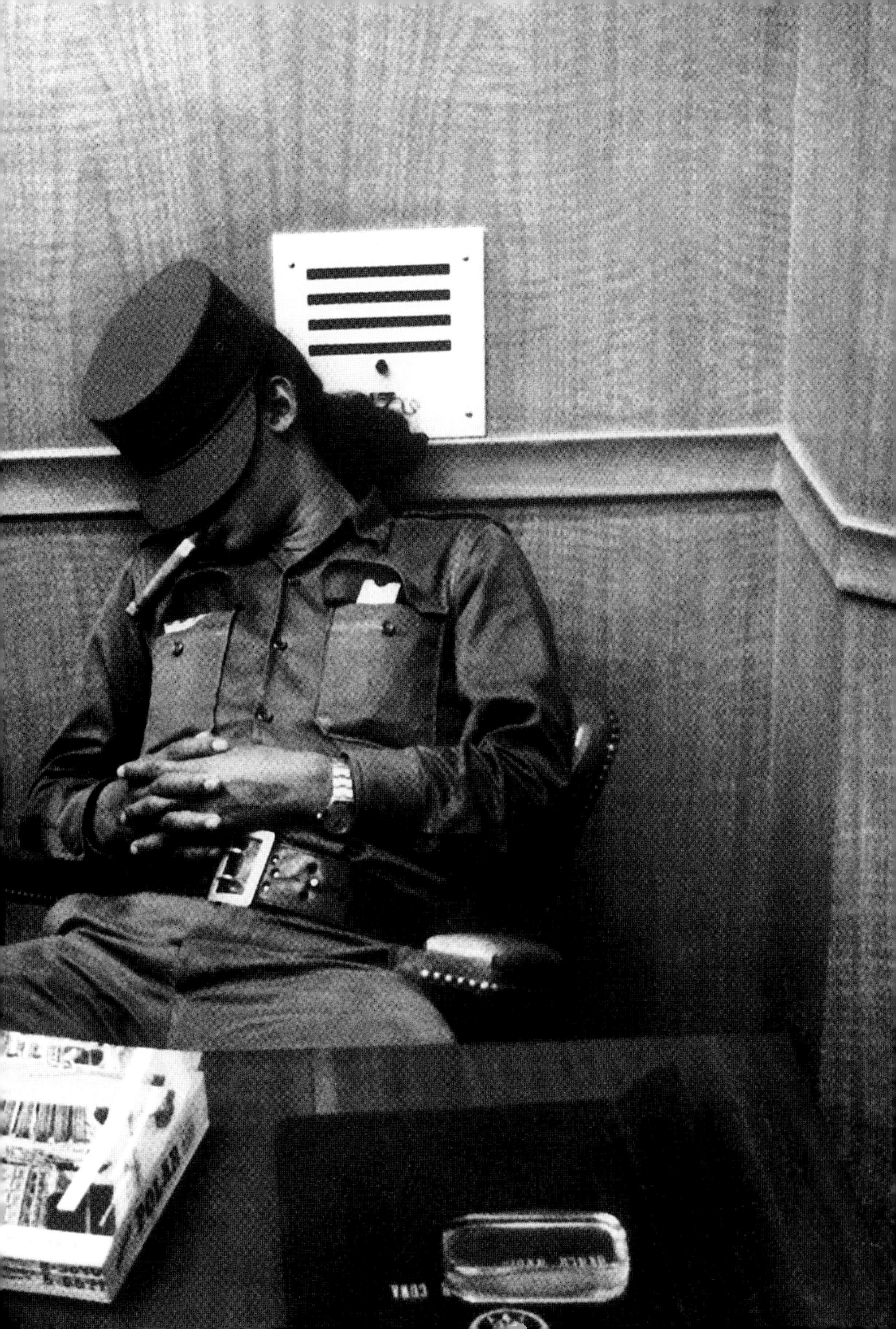

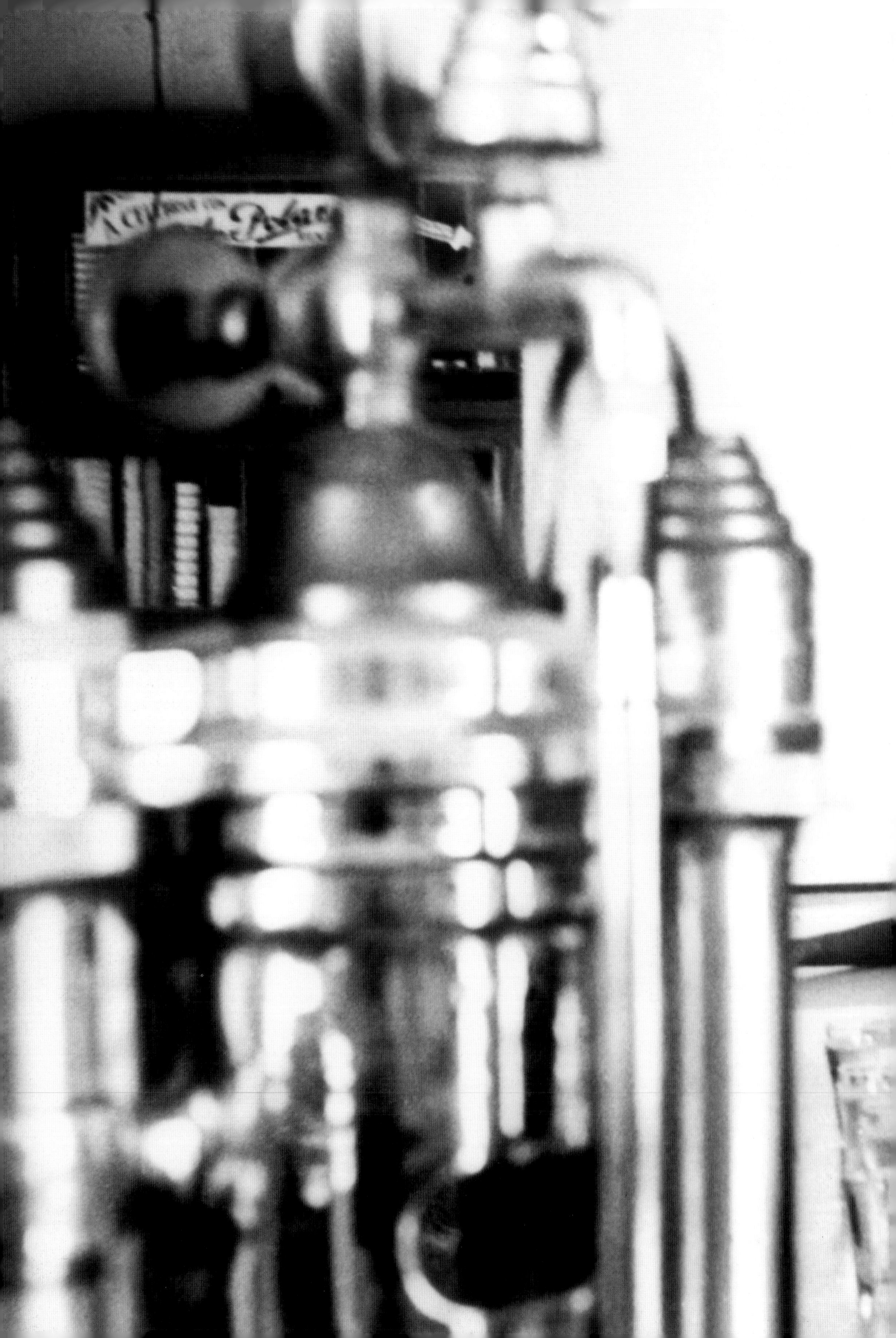

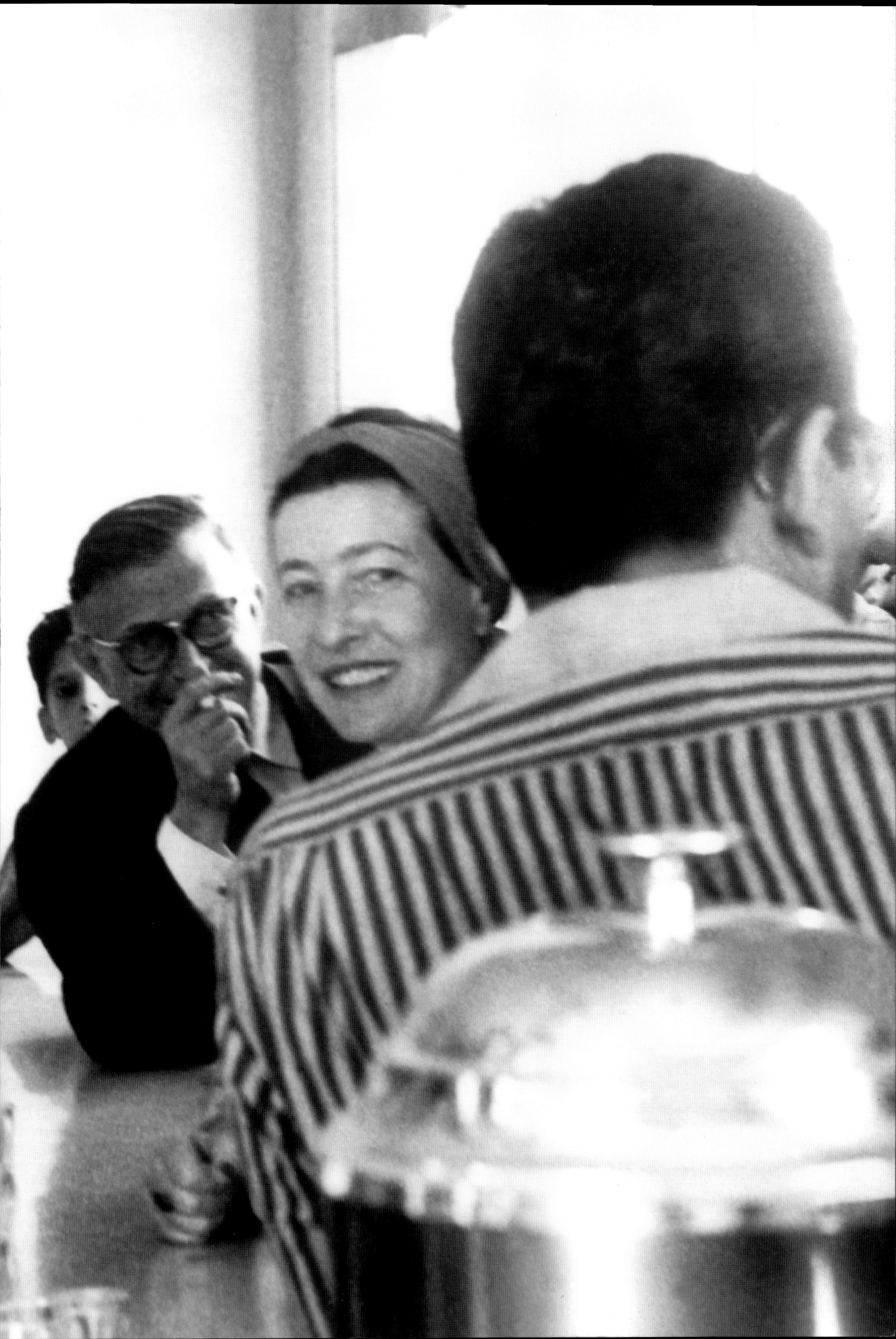

Until that time, the relationship between the big neighbor to the north and the little rebel island had always been one of dependency. After the end of Spanish domination in 1898, the United States acted as the new colonial power. In 1959, Americans in Cuba controlled 75 percent of commercial transactions and owned 90 percent of mines and telecommunications. "They owned a big part of the country's land," wrote Louis Pérez Jr., a professor at the University of North

"One day, President Eisenhower made the front page of the *New York Times* after scoring a hole-in-one during a golf match. In jest, Fidel asked Che to teach him how to play..."

Carolina. "They ran the best colleges, headed the most prestigious clubs. They lived a privileged life in Havana and on the sugar plantations. They became financiers and, as landowners, became a powerful force in government. They bought politicians and hired policemen just like they were doing with farms and factories." Cuba before the revolution, with six and a half million inhabitants just 200 kilometers from the Florida coast, was completely dependent on its neighbor. Annexation pure and simple would have been the natural step. This situation created an "anti-gringo" feeling, progressively isolating Batista and those who profited from this dependence while trading on the dignity of the Cuban people. And while the middle class of the major towns lived at a level almost comparable to their US neighbors, the peasantry lived in poverty.

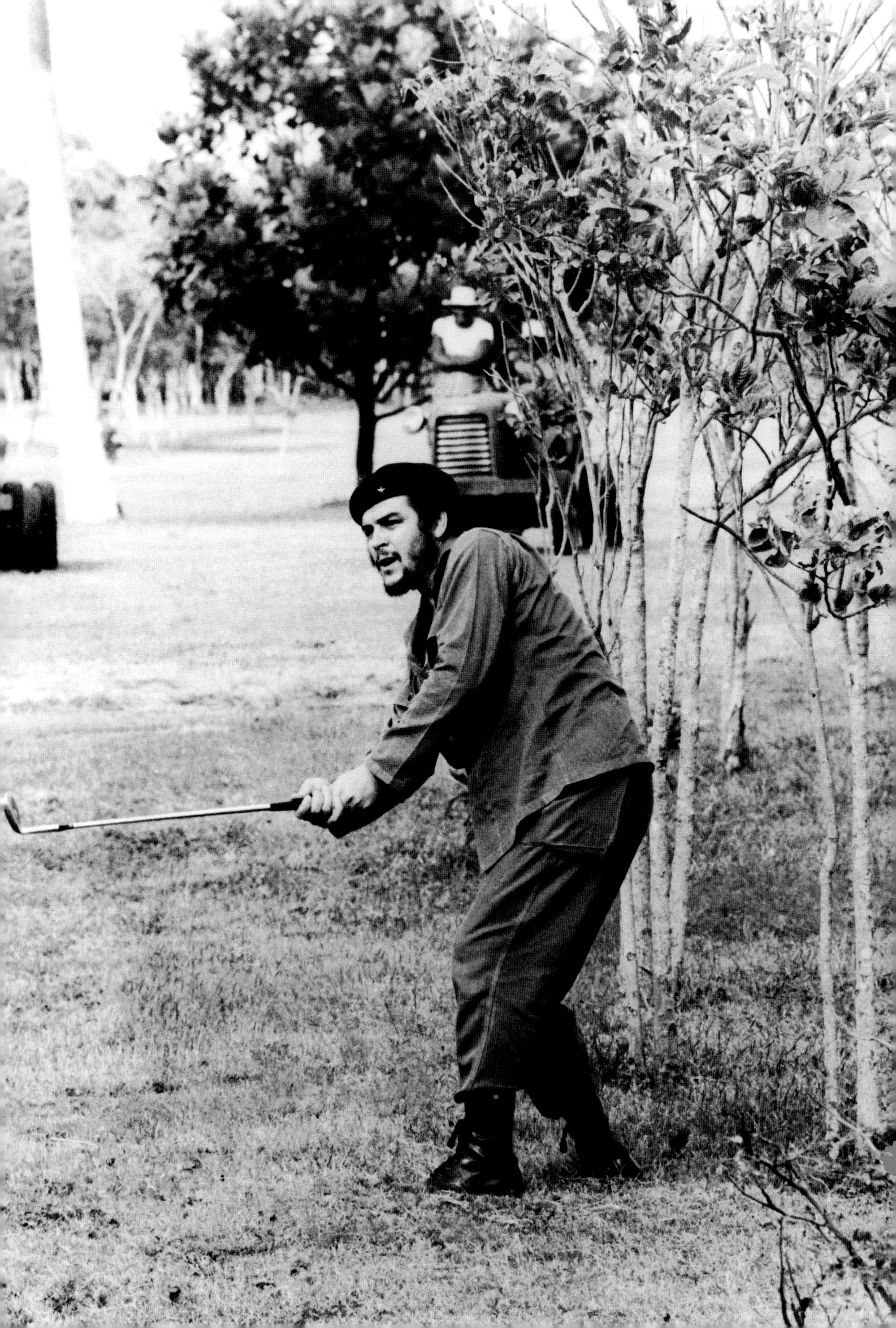

On March 17, 1960, just 12 days after the burial of the victims of *La Coubre*, President Eisenhower gave the CIA the green light to launch a series of clandestine anti-Castro actions. This included the training of a paramilitary force which could be used for guerrilla activity. Fidel Castro was warned by his new G-2 intelligence service and thought that the United States might try a repeat of the 1954 coup in Guatemala: an invasion of mercenaries to overthrow the progressive

"Che knew how to play golf from his childhood in Argentina. Fidel asked me along to take some photos..."

Árbenz government, an episode the young Che Guevara had witnessed directly. In fact, the United States was more and more convinced that "Cuba wanted to introduce the communist bloc into the Free World," as shown by the Cuban-Soviet rapprochement since the start of the year. During his visit to Cuba in February, the vice-president of the Soviet Council of Ministers Anastase Mikoyan signed a major trade agreement—the Soviet Union would buy 700,000 tons of sugar immediately and another million tons over the next four years. As minister of industry, Che was convinced that the famous "sugar quotas" bought by the United States at nearly double the market rate were an instrument to "enslave" Cuba. The island was completely dependent on the cultivation of sugar and the United States benefited from customs preferences for its products.

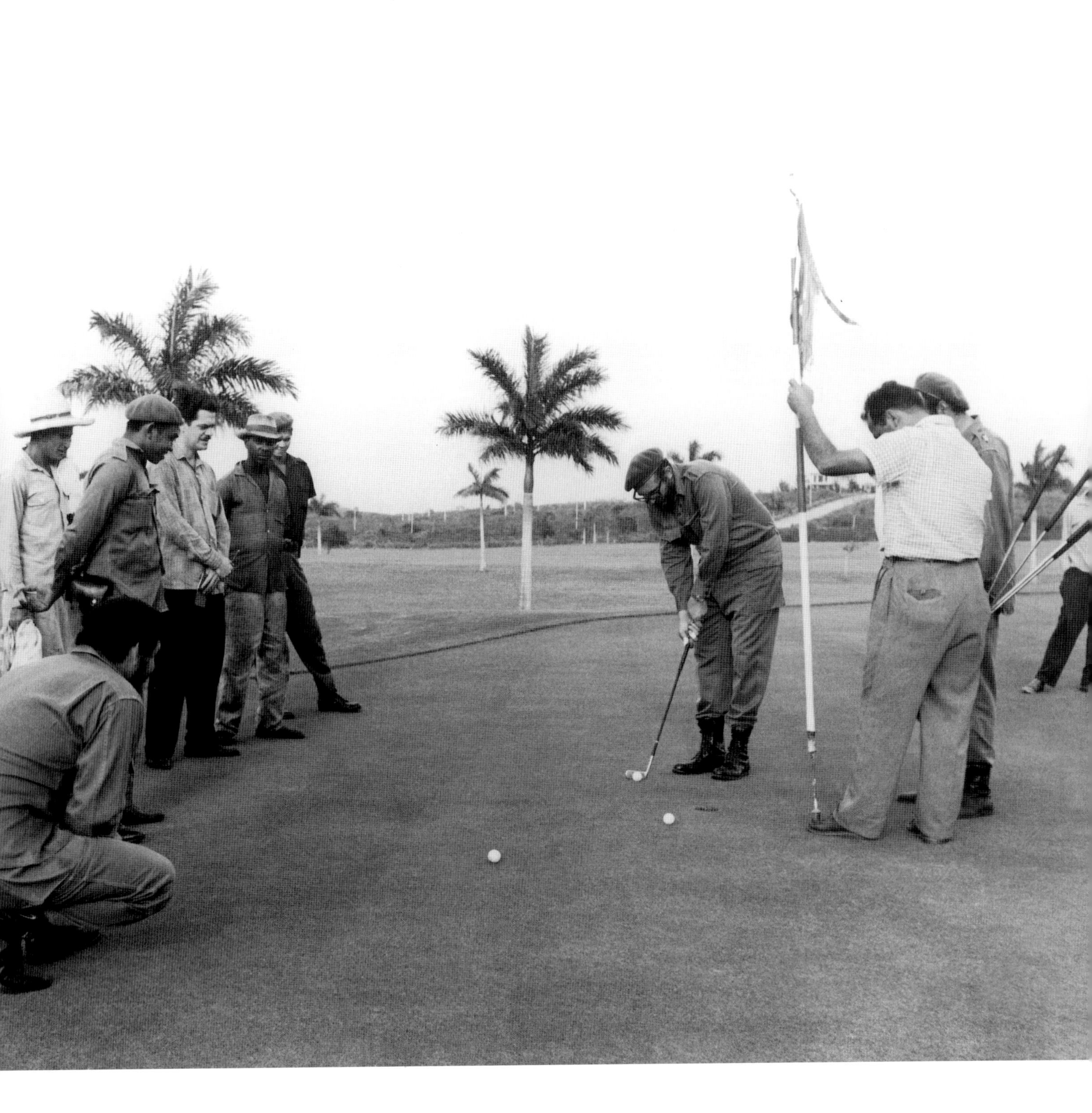

"'Chico, with your cameras around your neck, you look like a Yankee!' Che joked when I started to photograph him playing golf. 'Do you realize how much it costs the country for all the film spilling out of your pockets?' I didn't reply, but thought to myself: 'What's the problem? I paid for all the film myself!' It was only much later that I understood, when the blockade of Cuba began."

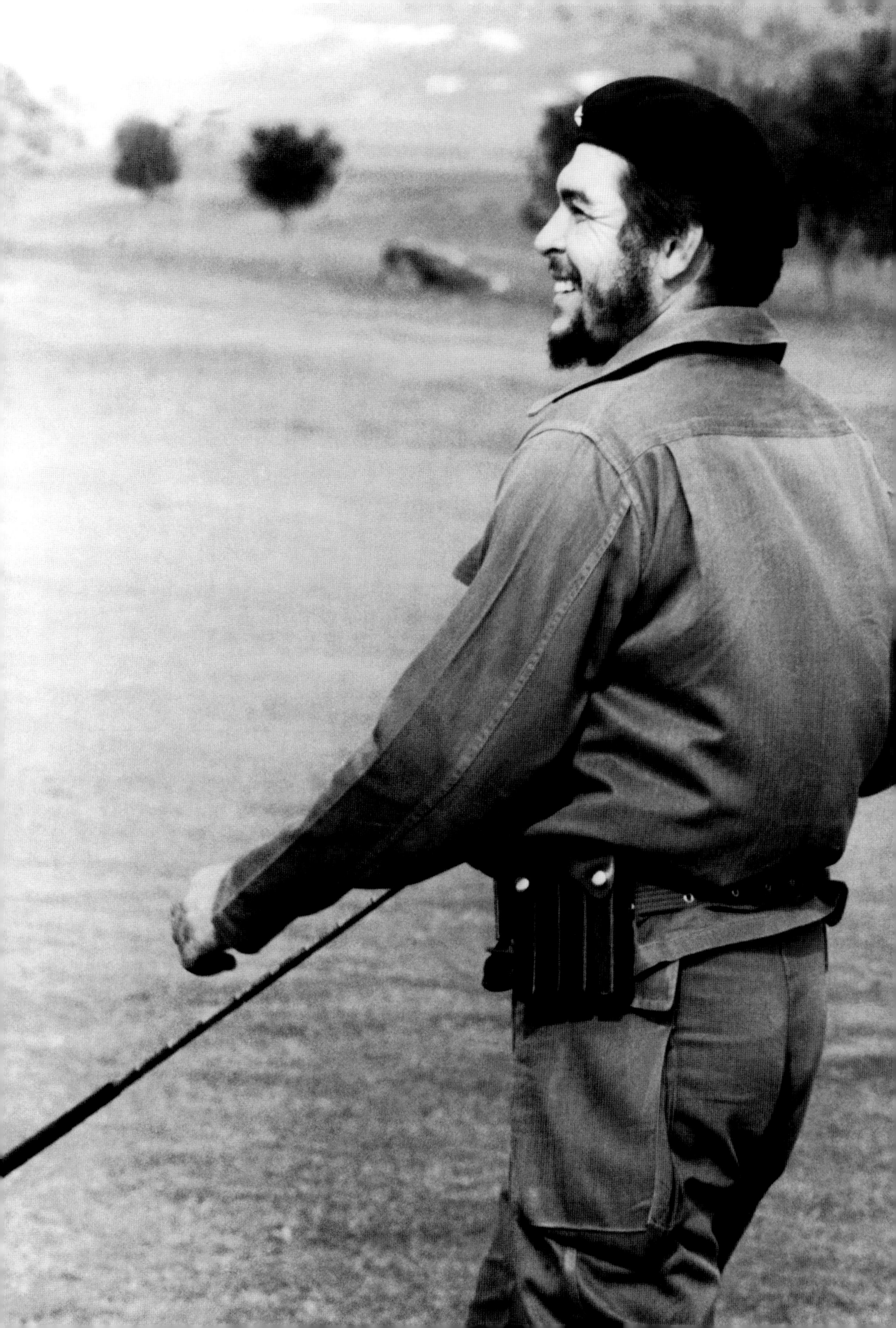

From the end of June 1960, the economic war between Washington and Havana escalated. On June 21, US Secretary of State Herter asked congress to pass a law authorizing the reduction of Cuba's sugar quota. On June 29, Fidel Castro seized the facilities of Texaco's Cuban subsidiary and then the assets of Shell and Esso on June 30, just as the US congress was voting on the Herter bill. On July 6, the Cuban government passed a law authorizing the expropriation

"The Russians agreed to pay for our sugar with petrol for a very low price. The first tanker arrived on July 4, Independence Day for the United States. For us, this day in fact marked a new independence for Cuba..."

of foreign assets "each time this measure conforms to the national interest." The same day, Eisenhower announced that he would not allow the importation of Cuba's remaining sugar quota for the year, which meant a loss of $80 million for Cuba. Three days later, Nikita Khrushchev delivered a shock: "The Soviet Union will lend a helping hand to the Cuban people, and if necessary, the flames of our missiles can support their military power." He did say, however, that he was speaking "metaphorically." More practically, the secretary of the Communist Party of the Soviet Union agreed to purchase the sugar that the United States had rejected. On August 7, before 50,000 people gathered in a stadium, Raúl Castro helped his exhausted brother read out a list of US companies that had been nationalized. On October 18, Washington imposed an embargo on all exports to the island. Cuba would suddenly discover that everything consumed on the island was manufactured in the United States.

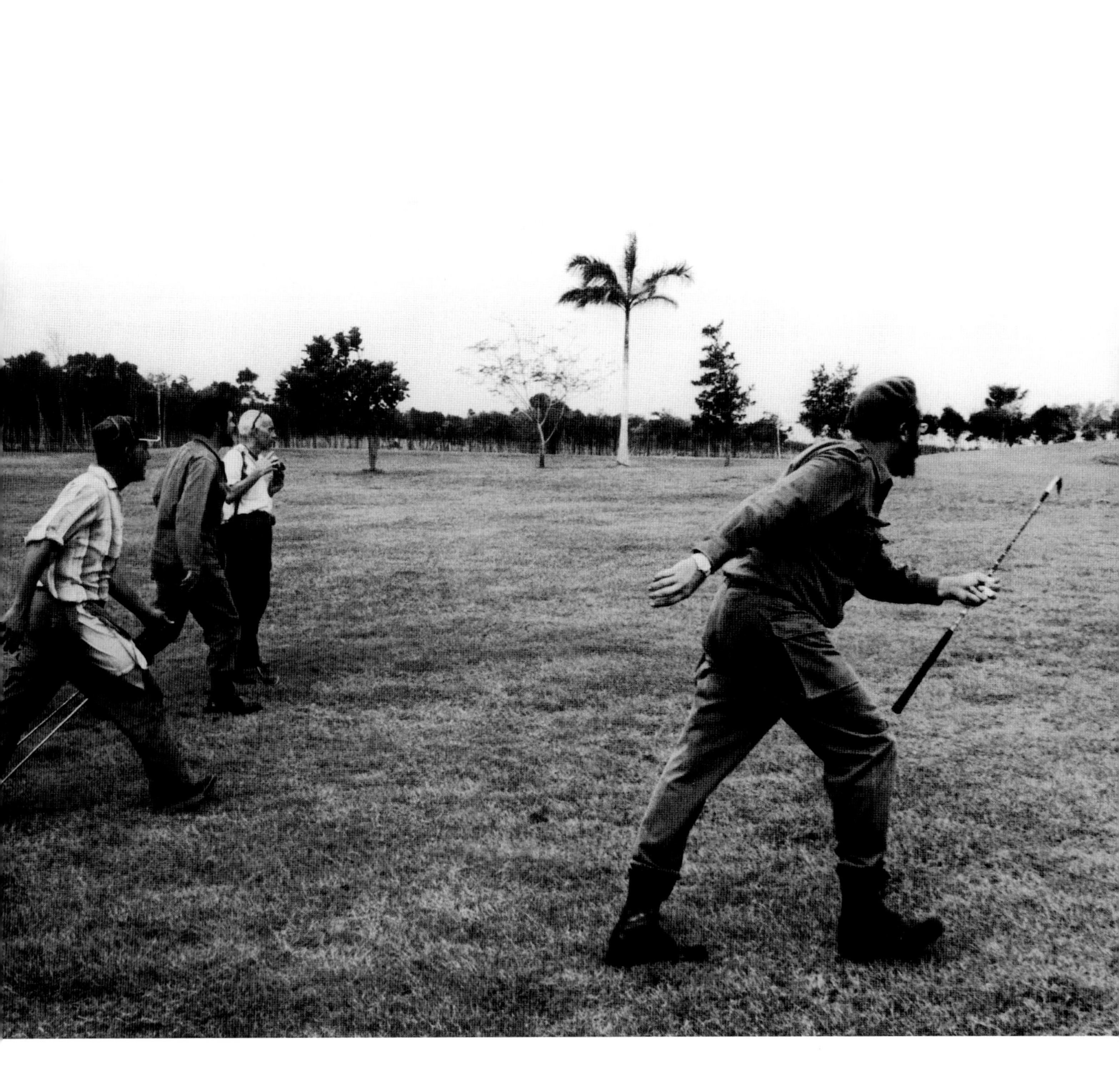

The first assassination attempt against Fidel Castro took place in the middle of Manhattan. On September 18, 1960, he arrived once again in New York, at the head of the Cuban delegation which was taking up its seat at the United Nations. Before his arrival, on the orders of Deputy Director Richard Bissell, the CIA used former FBI agent Robert Maheu to make contact with John Roselli, listed as "an important member of an organized crime syndicate." Roselli convened a

"In this period, Fidel often said that it was natural that his enemies should try to kill him. There were dozens of attempts. They even tried to poison the mouthpiece of his snorkel."

meeting with Mafia godfathers Sam "Momo" Giancana from Chicago and Santos Trafficante of Florida. During the 1950s, these men had transformed Cuba into a floating casino off the US coast. Thanks to their collaboration with the dictator Batista, they developed a hotel industry based on casinos, prostitution, drug trafficking, and abortion clinics. They had lost hundreds of millions of dollars during the revolution, so they accepted the contract on the Cuban head of state with a certain enthusiasm. The CIA had developed highly toxic but rapidly dissolving pills, which only took effect two or three hours after being swallowed. But in New York, all attempts to give the pills to Fidel Castro failed. Other attempts were then mounted in Cuba, notably through a barman of the Hotel Habana Libre, who tried but failed to dissolve a capsule in Castro's chocolate milk shake.

Fidel was a great fan of underwater spear fishing. He introduced Korda to the sport, and Korda later went on to create the photographic department of Cuba's Institute of Oceanography.

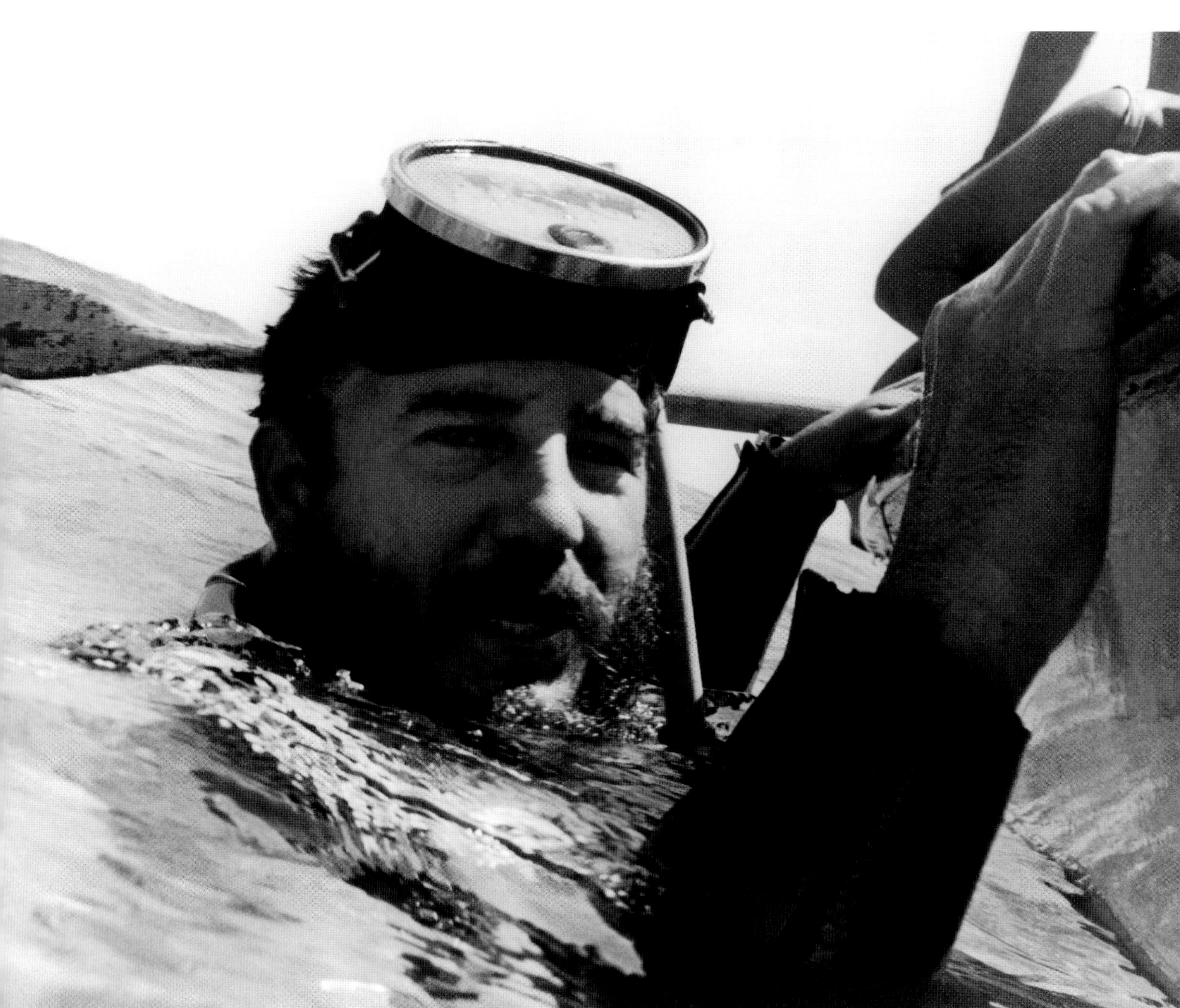

On January 3, 1961, the United States formally broke diplomatic relations with Cuba. In Washington, they believed that this year would see the final liquidation of Fidel Castro. In contrast, the year that marked the third anniversary of the revolution was proclaimed as the "Year of Education." With the cry of *"Cuba Libre,"* Fidel launched a massive campaign against illiteracy. One hundred thousand young instructors from the cities were sent to run literacy programs in the

"'Except when he is reading, Fidel can't last five minutes without talking to someone. He doesn't know how to do nothing, to remain by himself and rest.' It's not me who says this, it's his own brother Raúl."

countryside, in the mountains, and in the poorer suburbs. Freeing themselves from family bonds, a whole generation of young boys and girls went on a crusade. All they carried was a blanket, a teaching text in one hand, and a lamp in the other. Meeting with farmers, Afro-Cubans, and the poor, they wanted to build a collective feeling based on the idea of sharing reading and writing with those who hadn't been to school. Armando Hart, the minister of education and culture, announced the results: from 970,000 illiterates, 700,000 had benefited from the campaign. As well as the health sector, education was to become one of the two main pillars of the revolution.

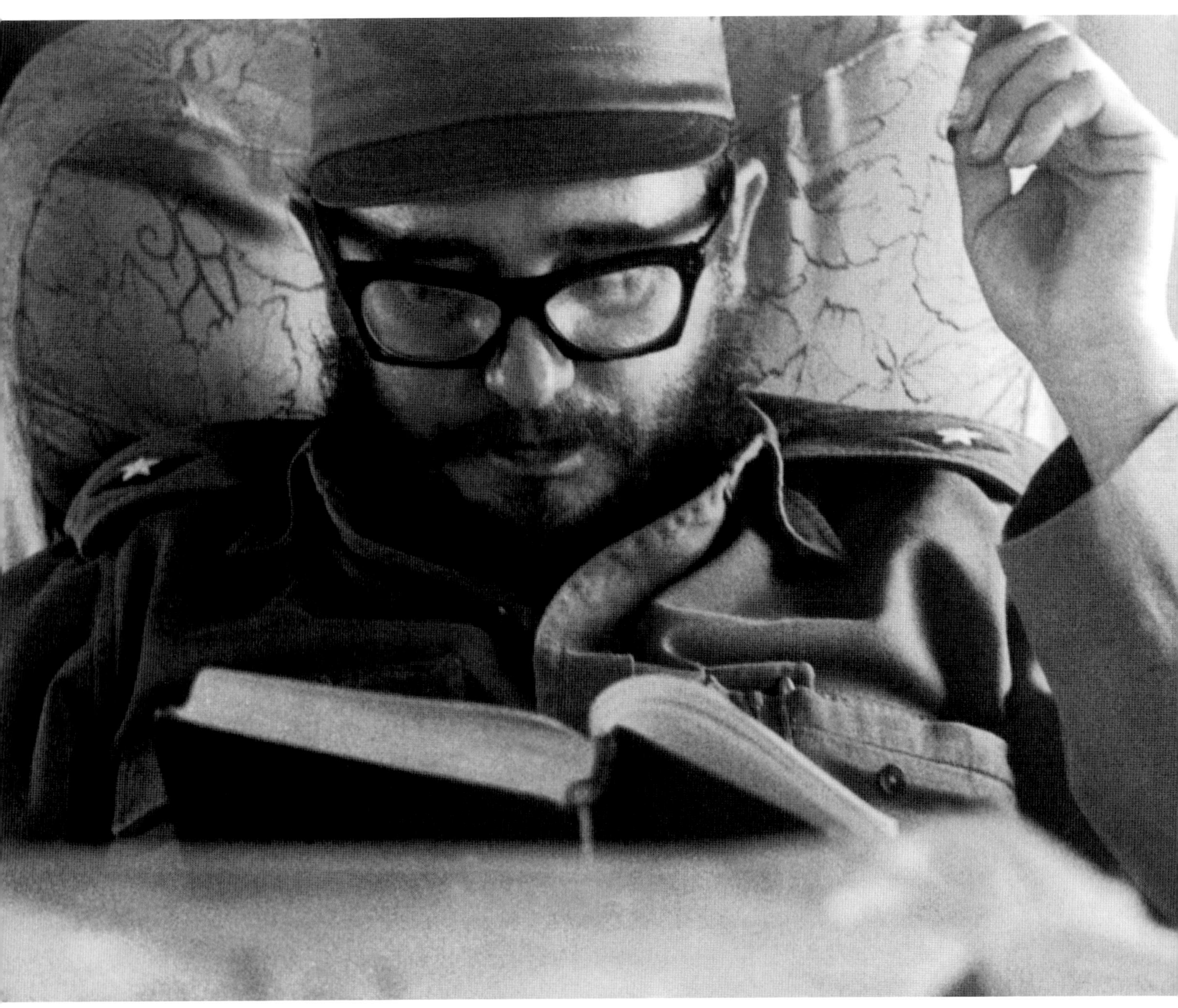

In the United States, the hardliners grouped around CIA Director Allen Dulles carried the day. As well as planning the assassination of Fidel Castro, they decided to mount an invasion of the island using Cuban exiles. John F. Kennedy inherited the plan following his victory over Richard Nixon, when he took the oath of office on January 20, 1961. Groups of Cuban émigrés were already training in secret CIA camps in Guatemala. The new president didn't feel comfortable

"The mercenaries disguised their planes with the colors of our air force, as they wanted us to believe that our own pilots were betraying us. But they had forgotten one detail: their B-26 bombers had a metal nose, while ours were made of Plexiglas..."

with the plan, and put the brakes on—but he didn't yet control all parts of his administration. On April 15, eight B-26 bombers crewed by former Batista pilots took off from airfields in Nicaragua to bomb Cuban airports. Only one plane was shot down by young militiamen above San Antonio. But the object of the attack—the destruction of Cuba's small air force on the ground—was only partially achieved. Castro was able to protect eight of the 13 planes, by leaving decoys on the airstrips. The next day, speaking at the funeral ceremony for victims of the attack, he drew comparisons with Pearl Harbor. For the first time, he referred to the revolution as socialist: "What the United States can't stand is that we have created a socialist revolution under their noses... This is a revolution of the humble, by the humble, for the humble, and we swear to protect it, to the last drop of our blood..."

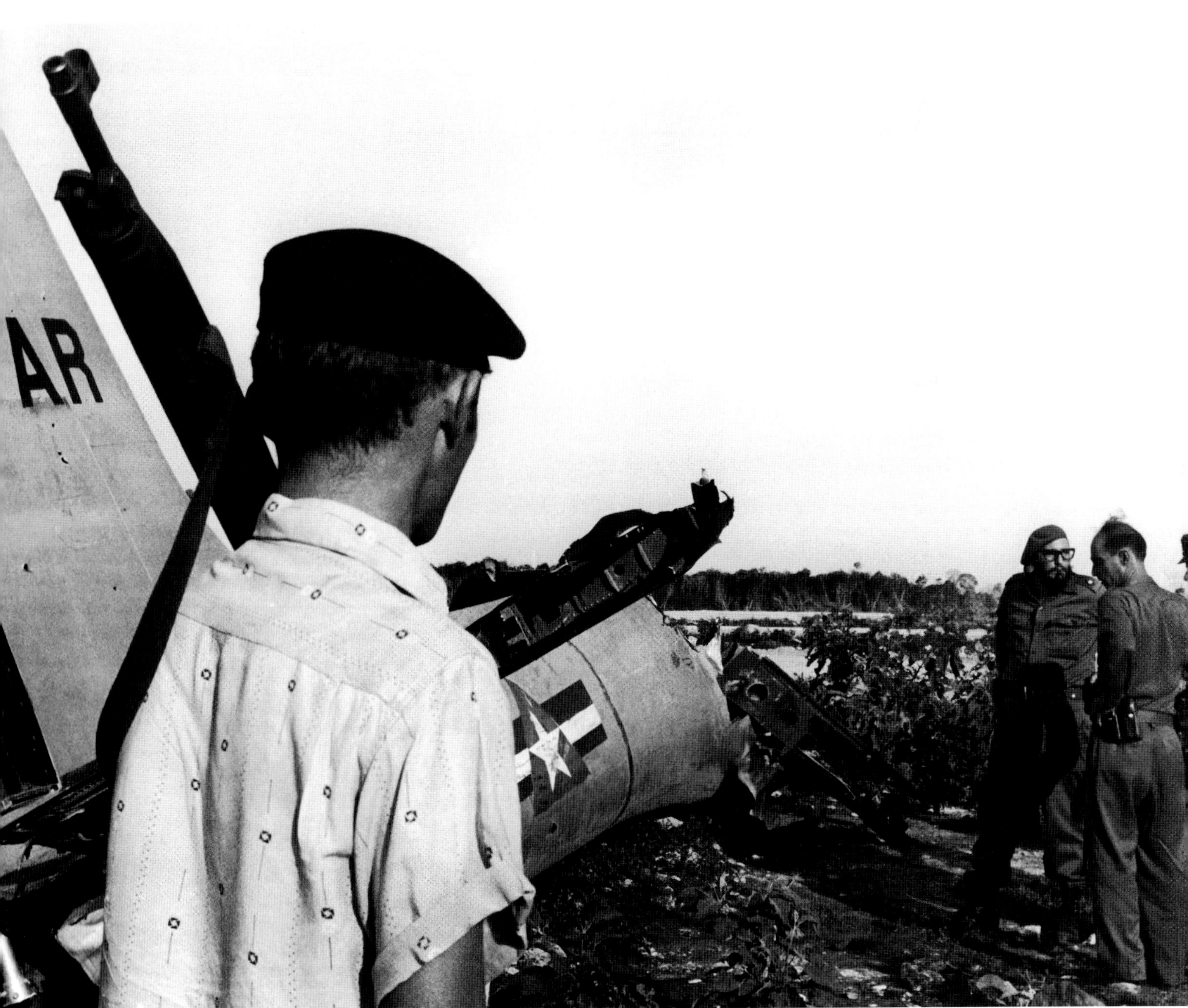
AR

During the air attacks, more than 200,000 men and women across the country mobilized along with the army. This mixed militia was the backbone of the Cuban defense. When 1,400 men landed on April 17 at the Bay of Pigs—an area of marshes to the southeast of Havana—they were spotted first by a militia patrol. Castro immediately ordered the seven (just seven!) air force pilots to attack the cargo ships which were transporting the exile brigades. Two ships were sunk

"The CIA brains-trust had hoped to land the mercenaries in a quiet corner. Their intelligence told them that there were only mosquitoes and alligators at the Bay of Pigs. But this region was one of Fidel's favorite holiday retreats and he knew every inch by heart..."

and the others retreated, depriving the invaders of food and ammunition. Their retreat was cut off. By mid-afternoon, the commander-in-chief was on the spot. He was concerned that the United States was trying to establish a beachhead on Cuban soil, where they could land some exiled Cuban politicians, recognize them as a new government, and then provide direct military support. However, after two days of intense fighting, 114 of the attackers were killed and many more captured. Kennedy didn't send the US air force and navy to the rescue. He chose humiliation rather than have his hand dealt by the Pentagon and the CIA. The CIA would never forgive him for this defeat.

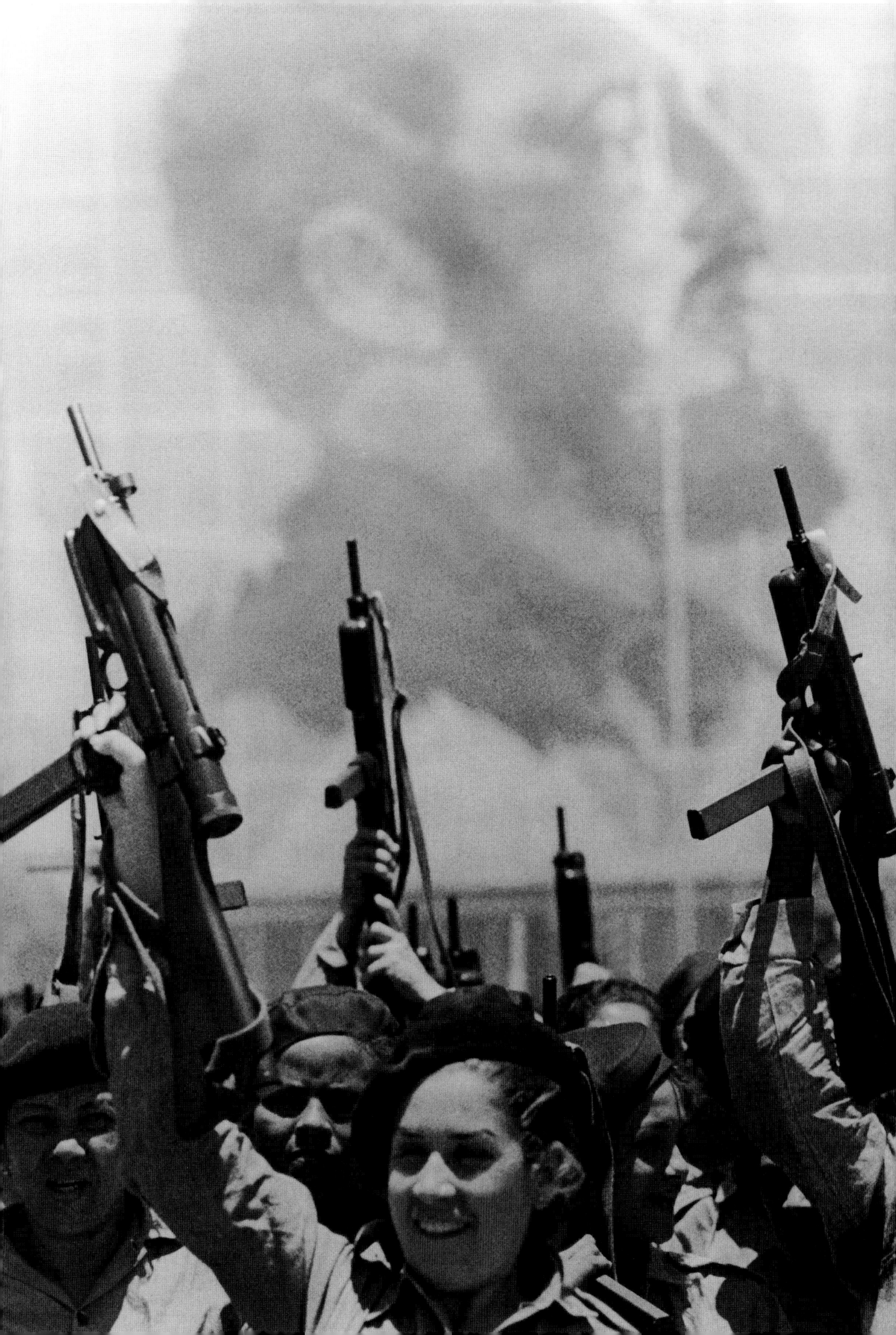

In January 1962, Nikita Khrushchev's son-in-law Alexei Adjoubei visited Havana, and told Fidel Castro that the Soviet intelligence services had discovered plans for an invasion of Cuba by US forces. Five months later, Marshall Biriouzov made a secret visit and suggested to the Cuban prime minister that they could deploy "defensive strategic weapons" in Cuba—in other words, nuclear missiles capable of striking US territory. Castro accepted the installation of the missiles in Cuba.

"During the Cuban Missile Crisis, Khrushchev and Kennedy were arm-wrestling without us having a say. But it was we Cubans who risked being wiped off the map..."

Although the first elements of the Red Army secretly arrived on the island in July, Khrushchev told the United States in September that there was no plan to install strategic weapons in Cuba. On October 14, however, an American U2 spy plane photographed a missile base being built in a field near San Cristobal. President Kennedy was informed on October 16. In a highly dramatic televised speech on October 22, Kennedy announced that he had decided to establish a quarantine zone around Cuba—in reality, a naval blockade designed to halt Soviet cargo vessels suspected of carrying troops and weapons. He threw out an ultimatum to the Soviet Union, calling on the Russians to dismantle the bases and withdraw any ships carrying military materiel. All humanity held its breath, on the brink of nuclear apocalypse. For the first time in a confrontation, the fate of the whole planet was under threat.

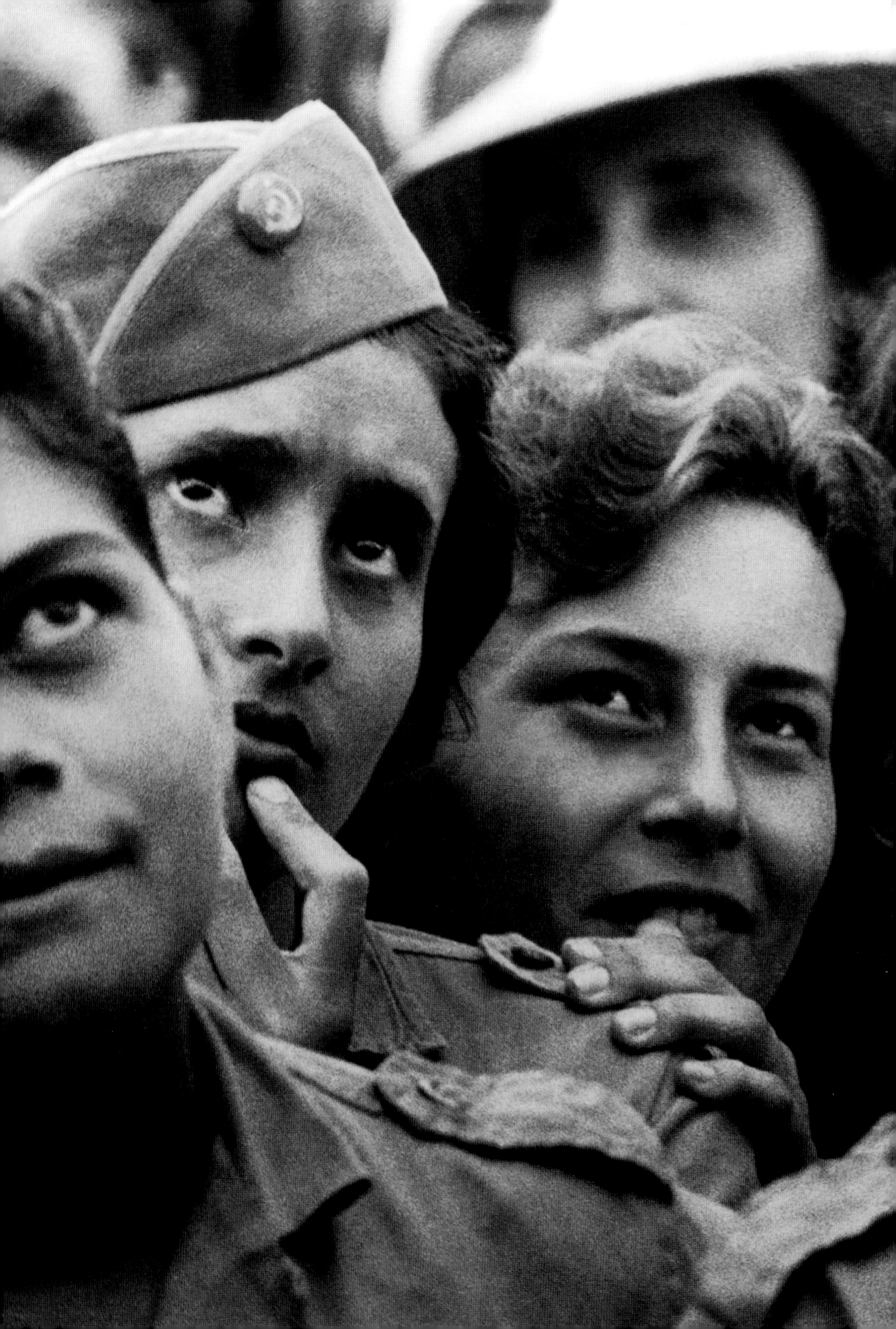

The alarm was real. For the first time, the US Strategic Air Command was placed on Defense Condition Two. All of its forces were placed on alert: 284 intercontinental missiles, 105 mid-range missiles in Europe, 1,450 bombers, amounting to 3,000 nuclear warheads with 6,000 megatons of destructive power. As well, the largest invasion force since World War II was assembled in Florida. The attack plans envisaged the deployment of 150,000 men, thousands of air

"Every morning, the gringo aircraft made low-flying passes over the city. Batteries of anti-aircraft guns were installed along the Malecón, the seafront avenue in Havana, near the hotels built by the North American Mafia..."

sorties, and the mobilization of three quarters of all cargo vessels on the east coast of the United States. The aim was to transport 42 million tons of materiel to the island in less than a week, including 300 tanks. The Soviet Union, for its part, placed all its conventional forces and intercontinental ballistic missiles on alert. Their nuclear submarines took up assigned positions and the 42,000 Soviet soldiers on the Caribbean island joined Cuban forces to prepare for the US invasion, which was seen to be imminent. On October 22, some nuclear warheads had already arrived, but they weren't located near the rockets. On October 24, Soviet navy vessels escorted by submarines came into contact with warships of the US navy. China had just attacked India in the Himalayas. Was this the start of World War III?

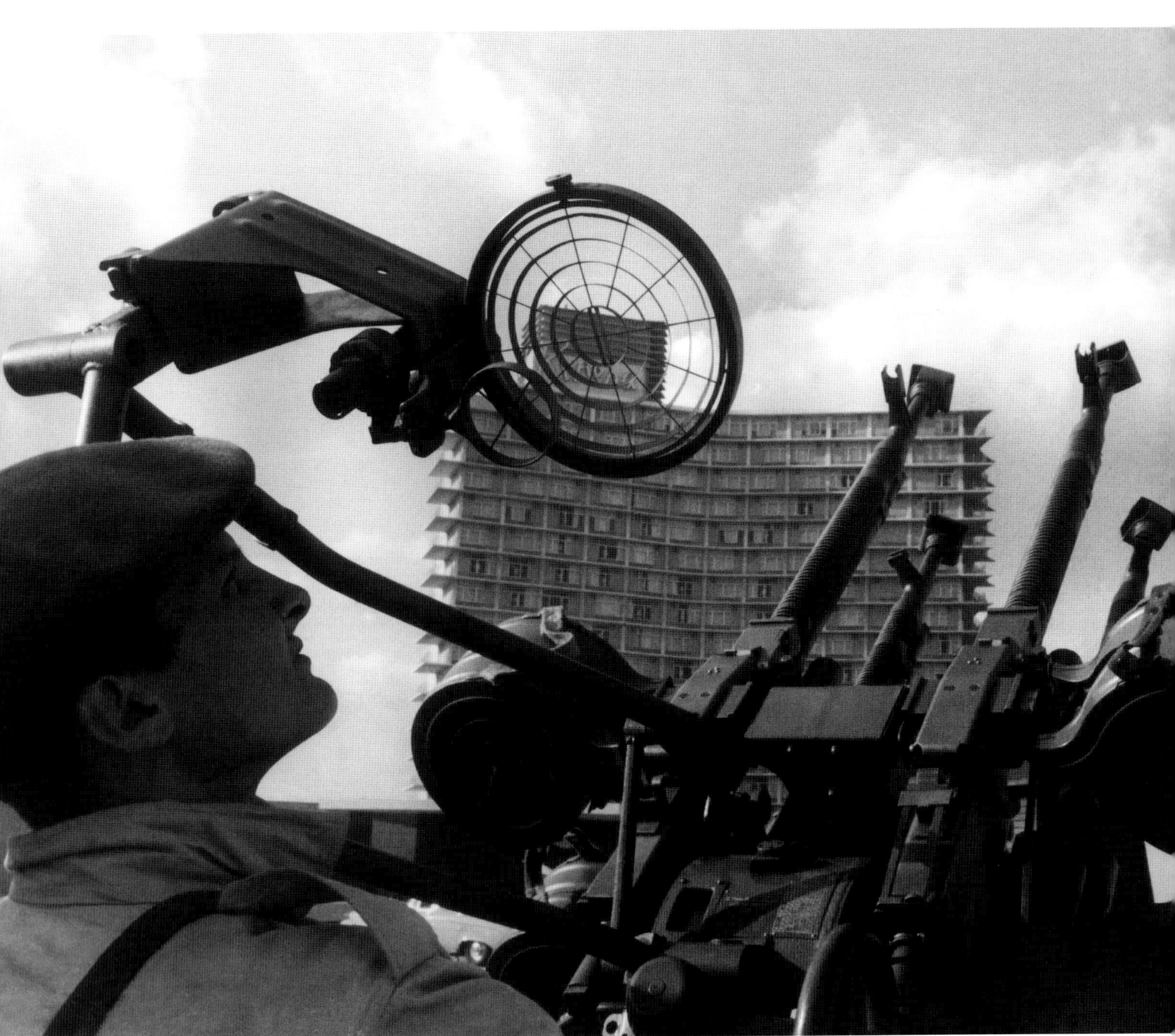

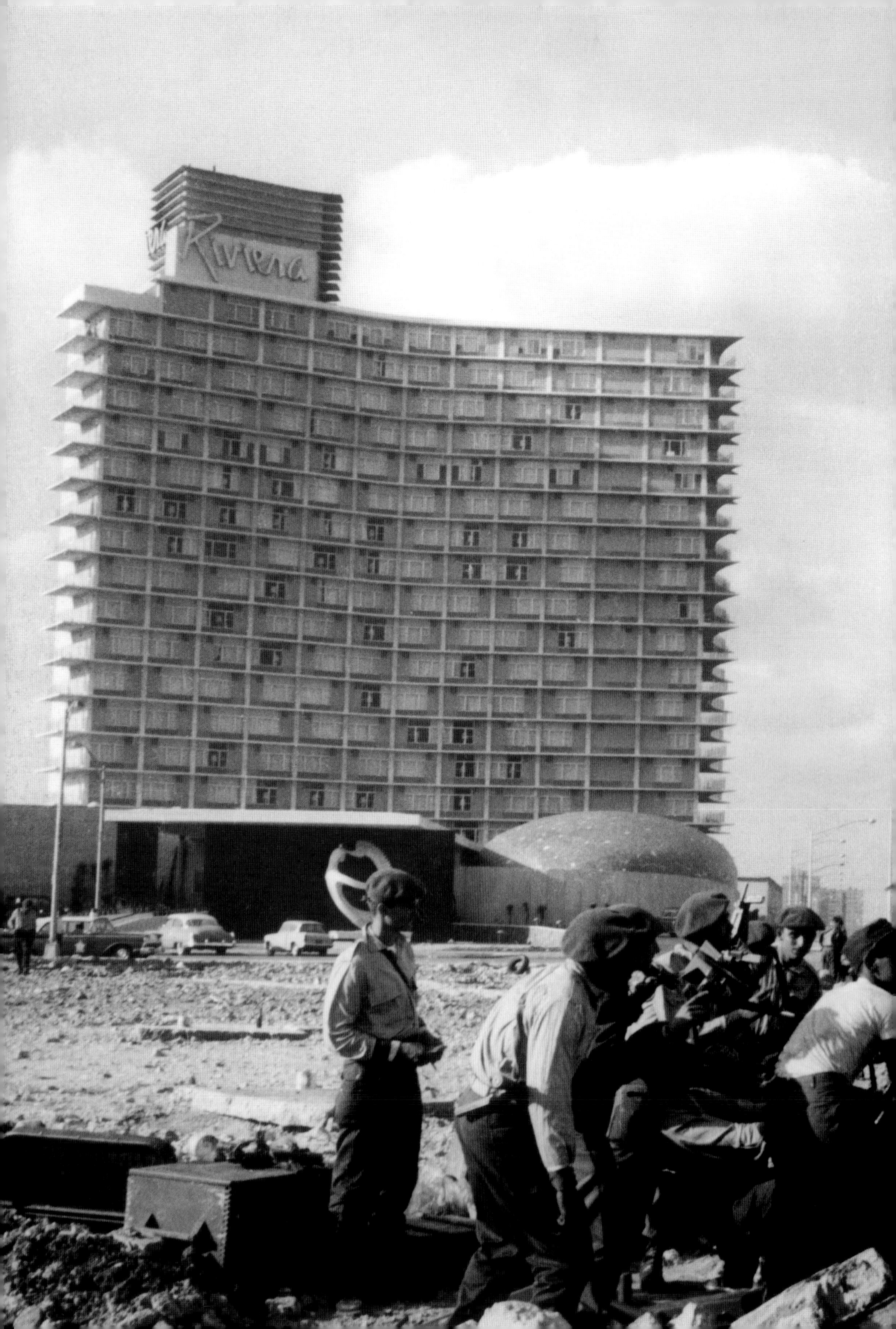
Riviera

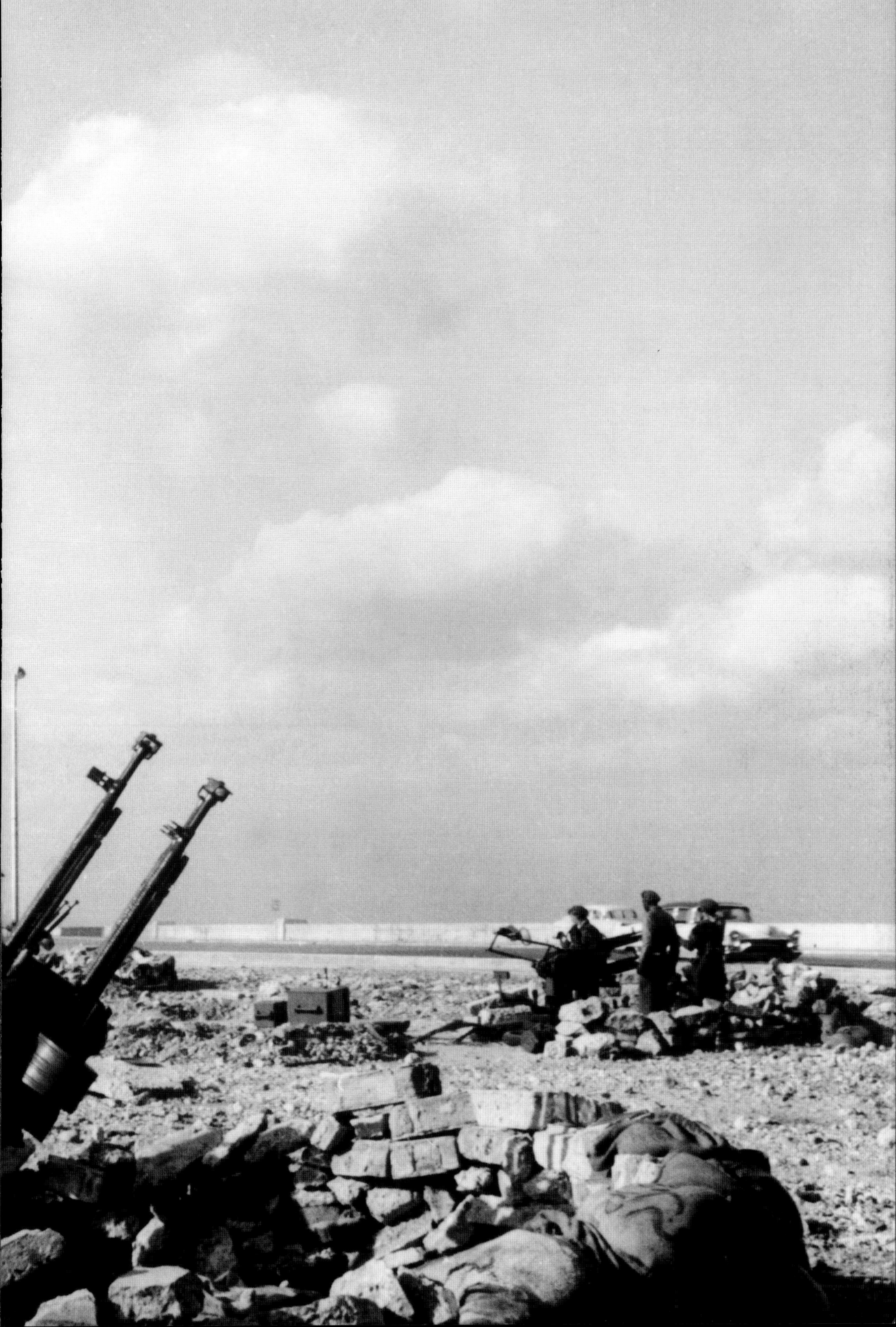

Why did Khrushchev want to install nuclear weapons in Cuba? The leader of the Soviet Union had all the reasons in the world to believe that the socialist regime in Cuba was threatened. The fact that NATO had installed missiles in Turkey, on Russia's doorstep, also encouraged him to take a decision that was audacious, but which he considered legitimate. The introduction of short-range ground missiles to Cuba, under the greatest secrecy, was supposed to be a *fait accompli*

"On October 23, Fidel received a message from Nikita announcing that the Red Army units in Cuba had received the order to prepare for combat..."

to encourage the United States to resume negotiations in Berlin on a new basis of equality, while protecting the Cuban Revolution by deterrence. Until then, maintaining a stockpile of nuclear weapons had allowed Moscow to negotiate with Washington on equal footing, but new advances by the United States in strategic missiles had challenged this status quo. Above all, the strategic balance was political and psychological as much as military and strategic. Prestige was at the heart of the competition with the United States, and Khrushchev viewed the installation of missiles in Turkey as an affront. On the other hand, the failed Bay of Pigs invasion reinforced his impression of US imperialism. On that occasion and at the time of his meeting with Kennedy in Vienna, he judged the new US president as "indecisive, badly informed, and unimpressive." Cuba, and everything that the victory of the socialist regime represented, was the opportunity for a stunning revenge.

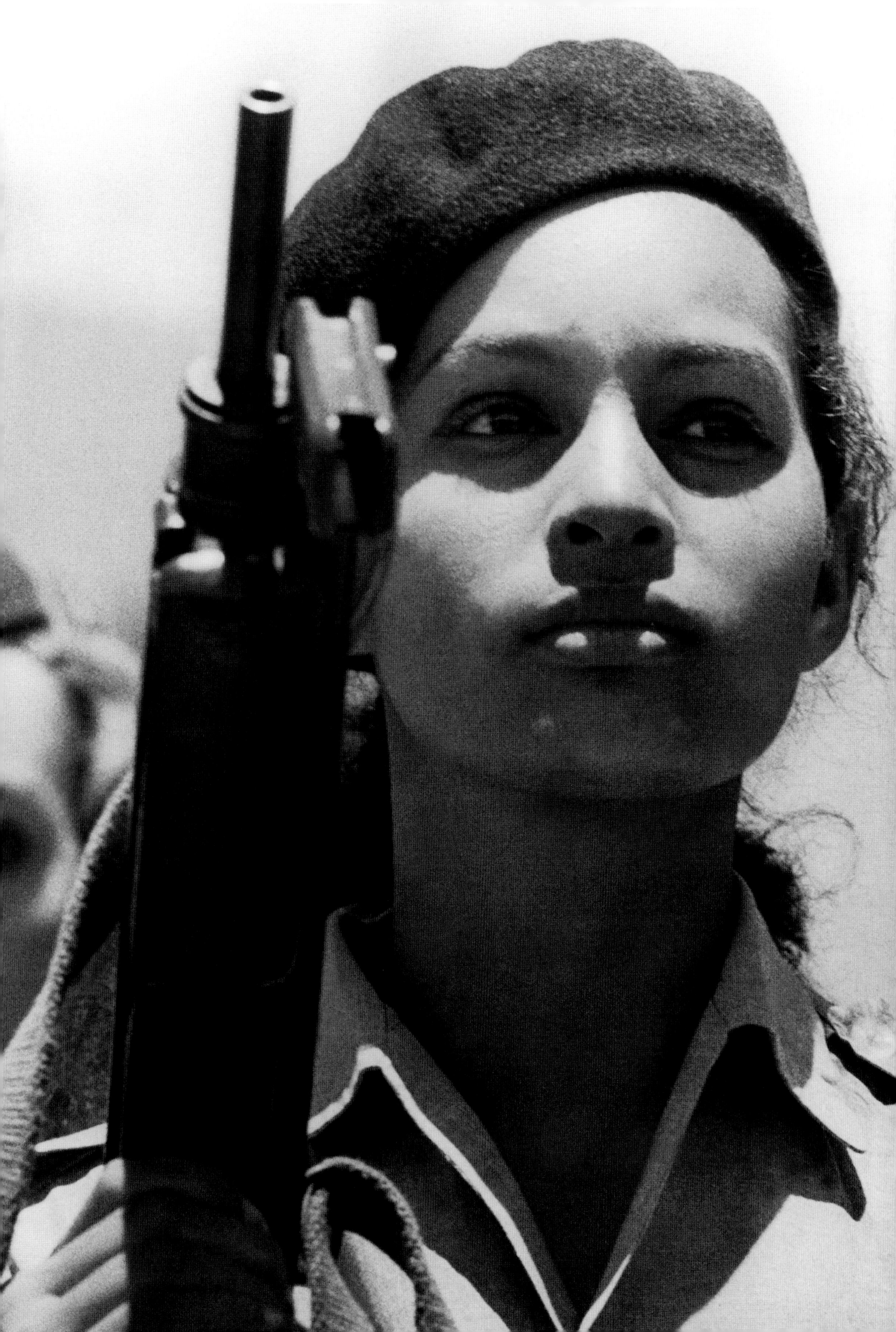

Why did the US president call for the removal of Soviet missiles from Cuba? Kennedy was angry. In his eyes, it was a deliberate provocation and Khrushchev had been caught deliberately lying. For weeks, Khrushchev had assured him personally on several occasions that he didn't intend to introduce weapons of mass destruction to the Caribbean. In two official statements, Kennedy had publicly committed himself to opposing their presence. In fact, each of the leaders

"The most remarkable thing during this period of tension was that the population, galvanized by Fidel, showed an unbelievable calm..."

saw their own weapons as strictly defensive, while the opponent's were undoubtedly offensive. The US president however did not attach much strategic significance to the weapons. Unlike his generals, he thought that a missile was a missile and their location was hardly relevant—whether they were fired from Moscow or Havana made little difference. Above all, the crisis went to the heart of a system based on the balance of terror. If the United States gave in over Cuba, it was probable that they'd give in over Berlin. During the first meeting of the Executive Committee, the White House's crisis team, the majority—including President Kennedy himself—were in favor of air attacks. But every military action ran the risk of a riposte in Berlin, which would leave the president no choice but to unleash a nuclear inferno...

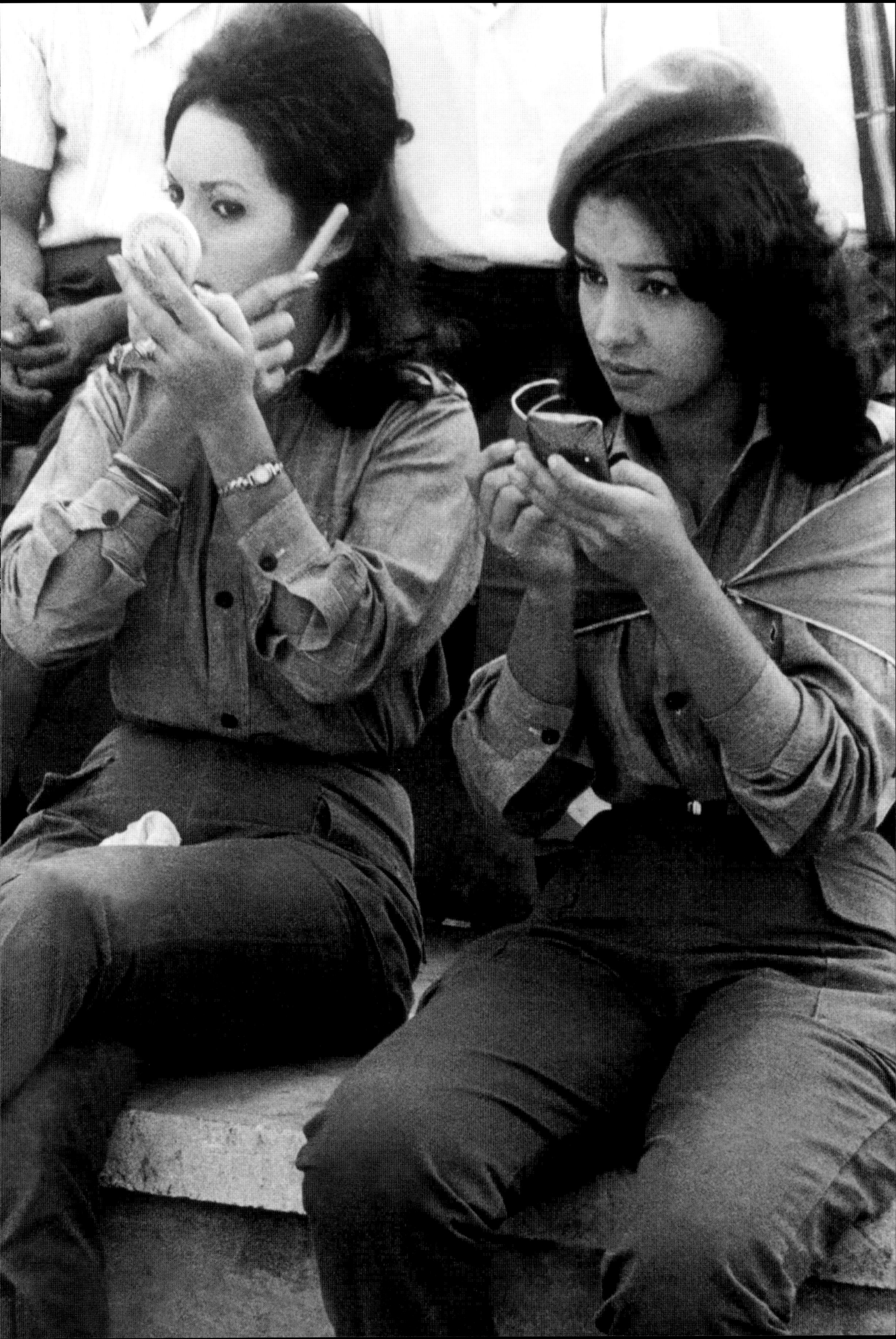

Once his anger had subsided, Kennedy abandoned the idea of aerial strikes, rejecting the advice of his generals. The fear of being held responsible for humanity's greatest cataclysm influenced his decision on October 22 to introduce a naval blockade, the least risky option. The analogy with the uncontrolled escalation that led to World War I frightened the US president. In his eyes, the main risk was the potential loss of control in an explosive situation, which could

"I believe that in spite of everything, Fidel had a certain intellectual respect for Kennedy..."

inadvertently lead to a nuclear conflict. On October 24, however, when Soviet cargo vessels and submarines came into contact with the US navy, they stopped trying to force a passage and turned tail. At the United Nations, Secretary General U Thant of Burma was trying to find a negotiated solution. Finally, several overlapping factors pushed Khrushchev to propose a compromise on October 26. The Soviet Union had heard the message placing US forces on alert, and had intercepted instructions for US hospitals to prepare to receive the inevitable casualties. This showed that Washington was really preparing for war and Khrushchev himself realized that the situation could get out of control. He wrote to Kennedy proposing the withdrawal of the missiles in exchange for a commitment not to invade Cuba. On Sunday, October 28, he opened the Presidium meeting with an unambiguous report: "To save the world, we had to retreat."

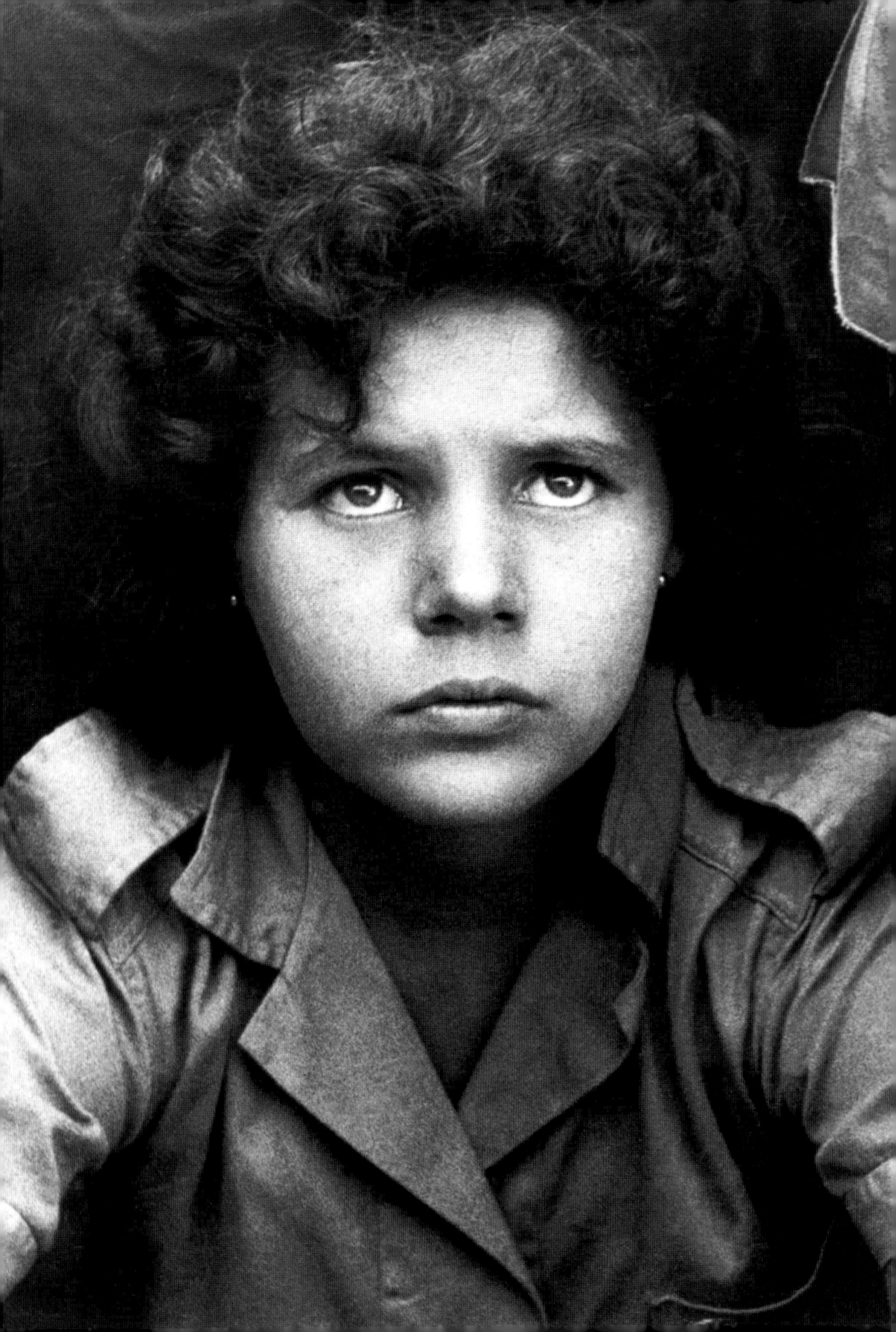

Fidel Castro was appalled by Khrushchev's decision, negotiated directly with Kennedy without consulting the Cuban leader. According to Che, he was furious. He punched the wall and broke a pair of glasses. He also issued several sharp messages to his "big brother"—confirmed then later denied—by giving interviews to European journalists. He reproached his ally for failing to publicly and clearly state that the weapons had been deployed in the legal framework of a Soviet-Cuban

"I was the first to leave the plane. The Russians saw my beard, and maybe they thought I was Fidel because they started applauding me..."

military treaty. To appease Fidel's anger, Khrushchev invited the youngest leader of the communist bloc on an official visit, which has gone down in the history books as one of the longest ever held. Castro and his entourage, including Korda, would spent more than 40 days visiting the Soviet empire. From Europe to the Pacific, from Central Asia to secret naval bases on the Baltic, the welcome was extraordinary. The trip, however, nearly began with tragedy. On April 27, 1963, the giant Tupolev aircraft made the non-stop flight from Havana to Murmansk in 14 hours. But arriving in Russia, the airfield was closed by thick fog. The fuel tanks of the jet were running low and so the pilot decided to land the plane through the fog without visibility—a style of landing worthy of the former guerrilla! After landing, unperturbed, Fidel put a cigar to his lips to avoid being kissed on the mouth...

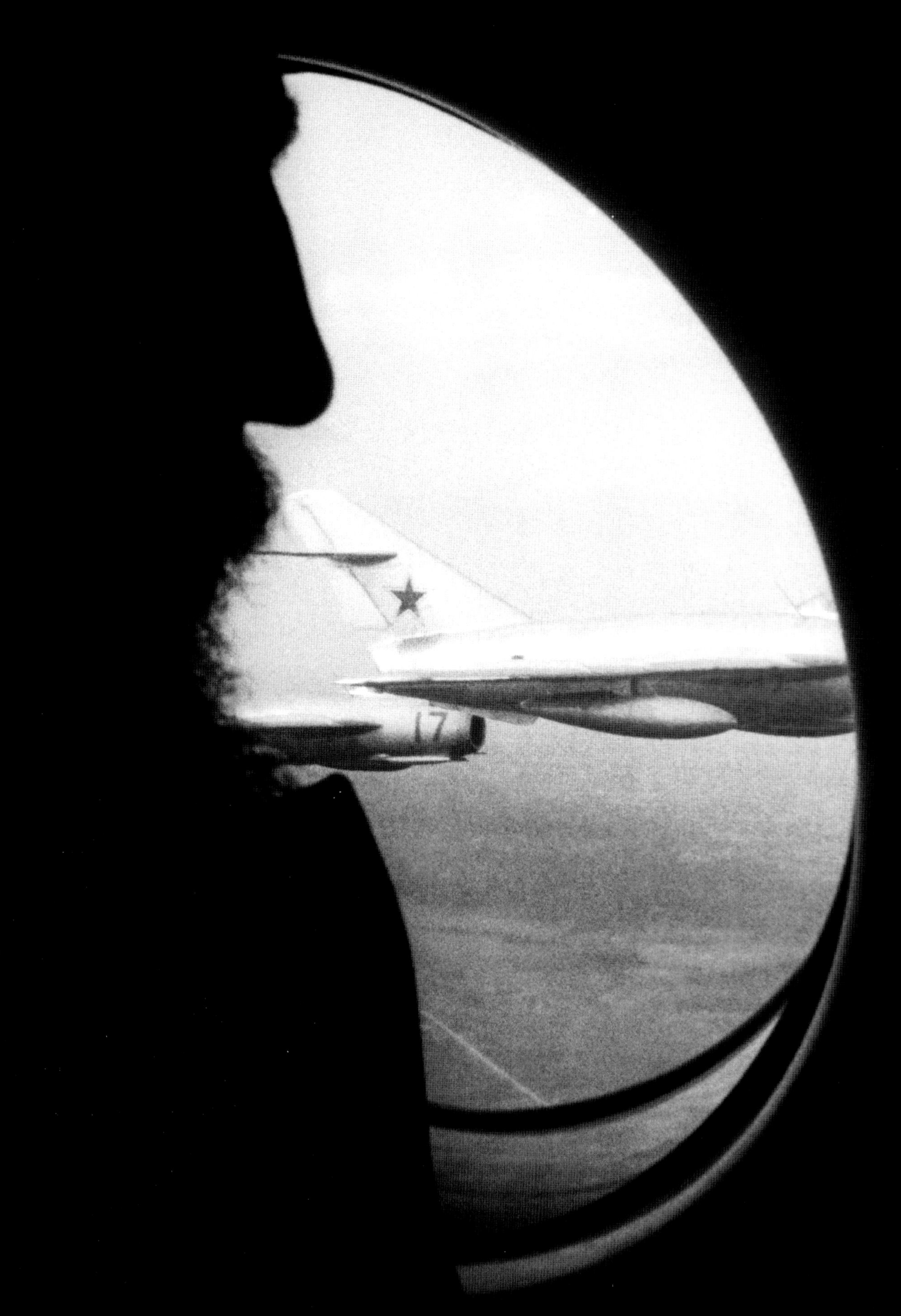
17

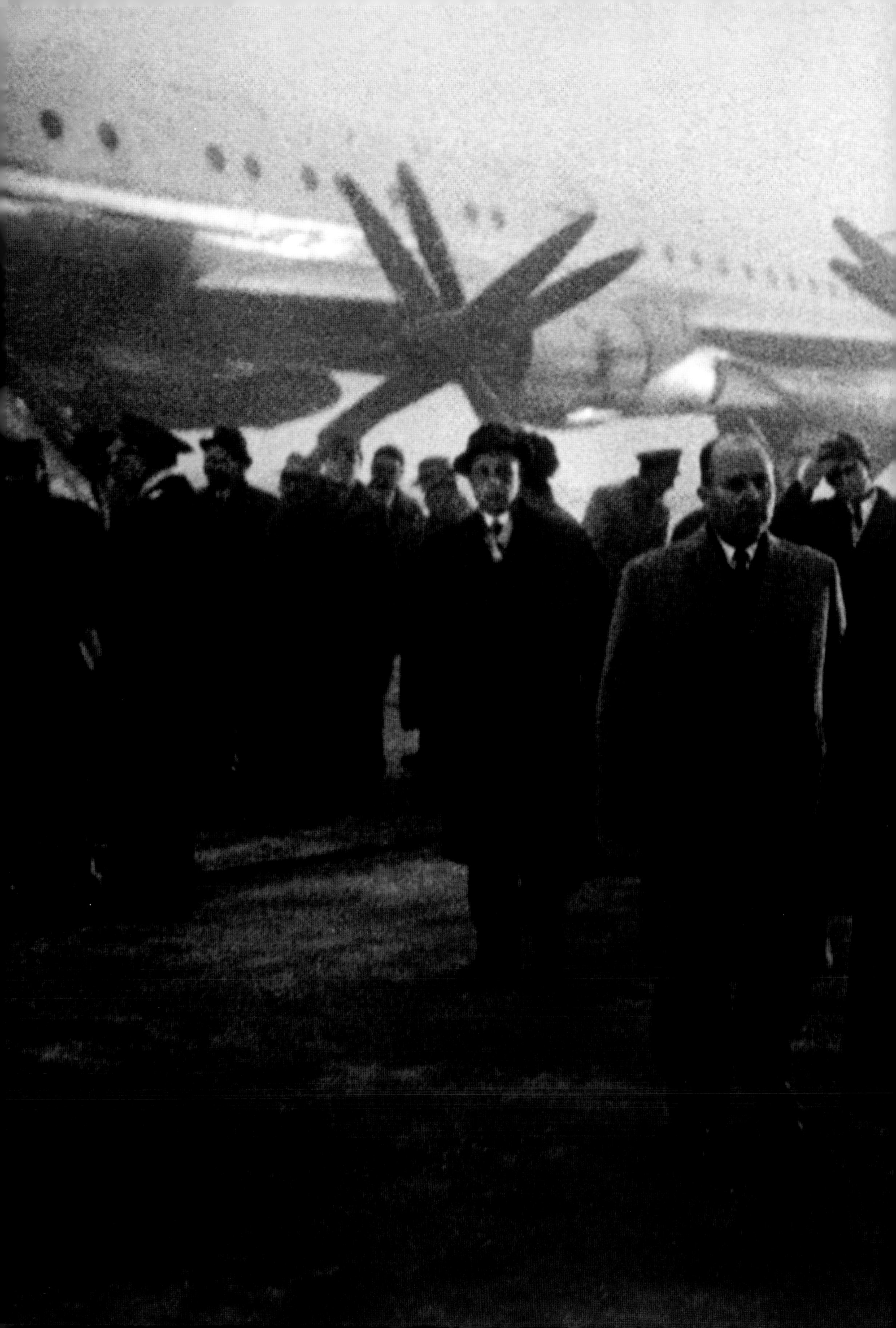

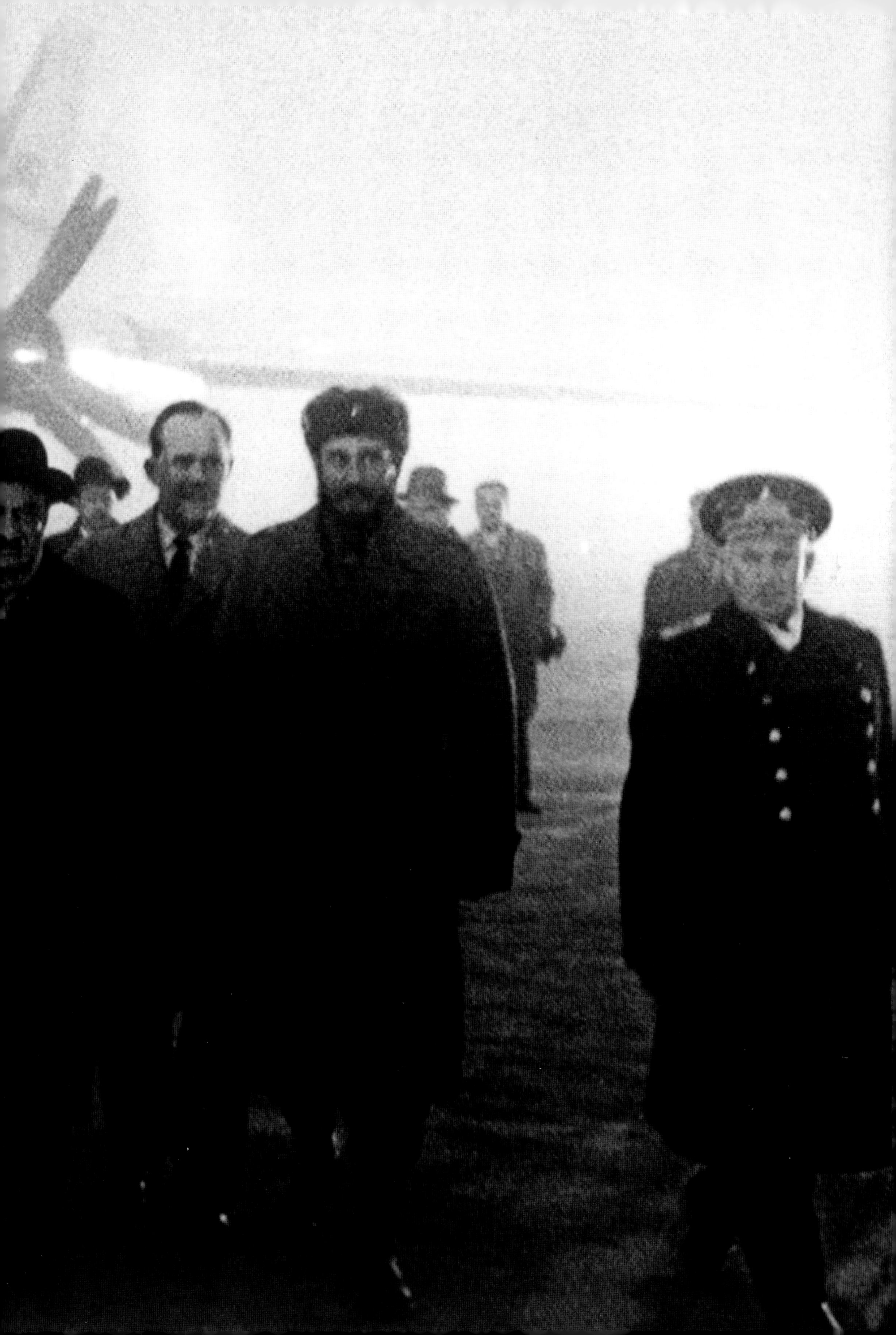

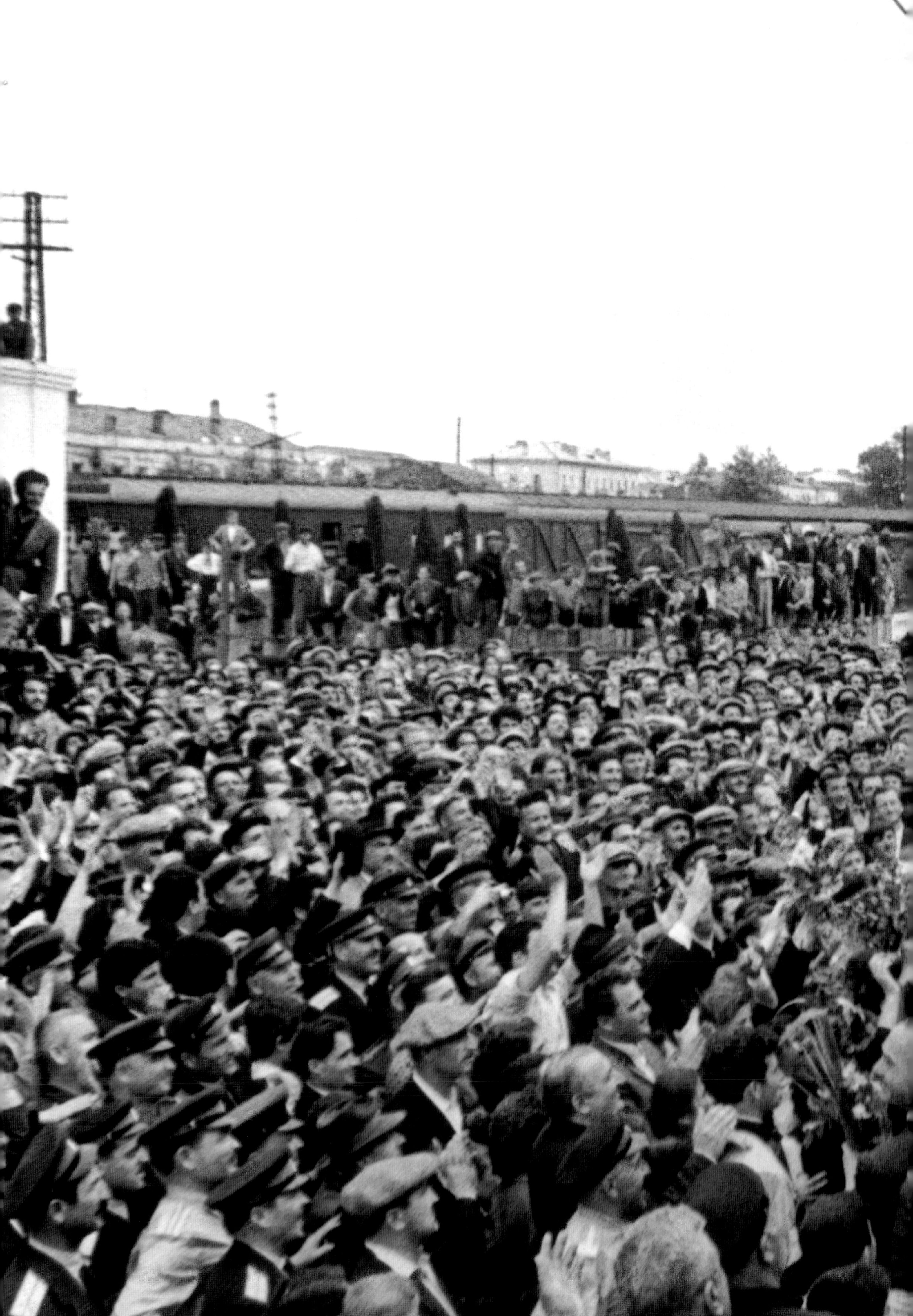

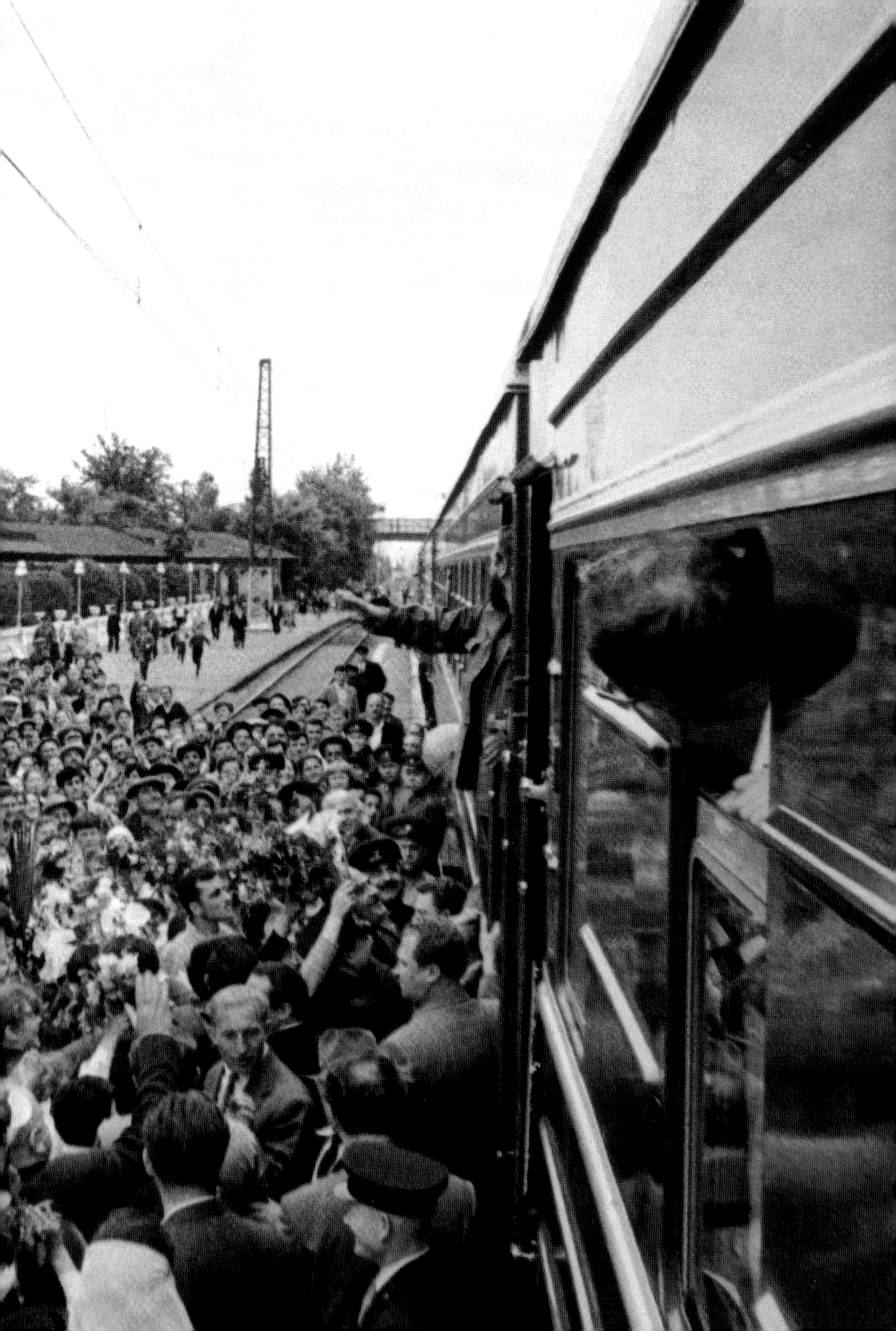

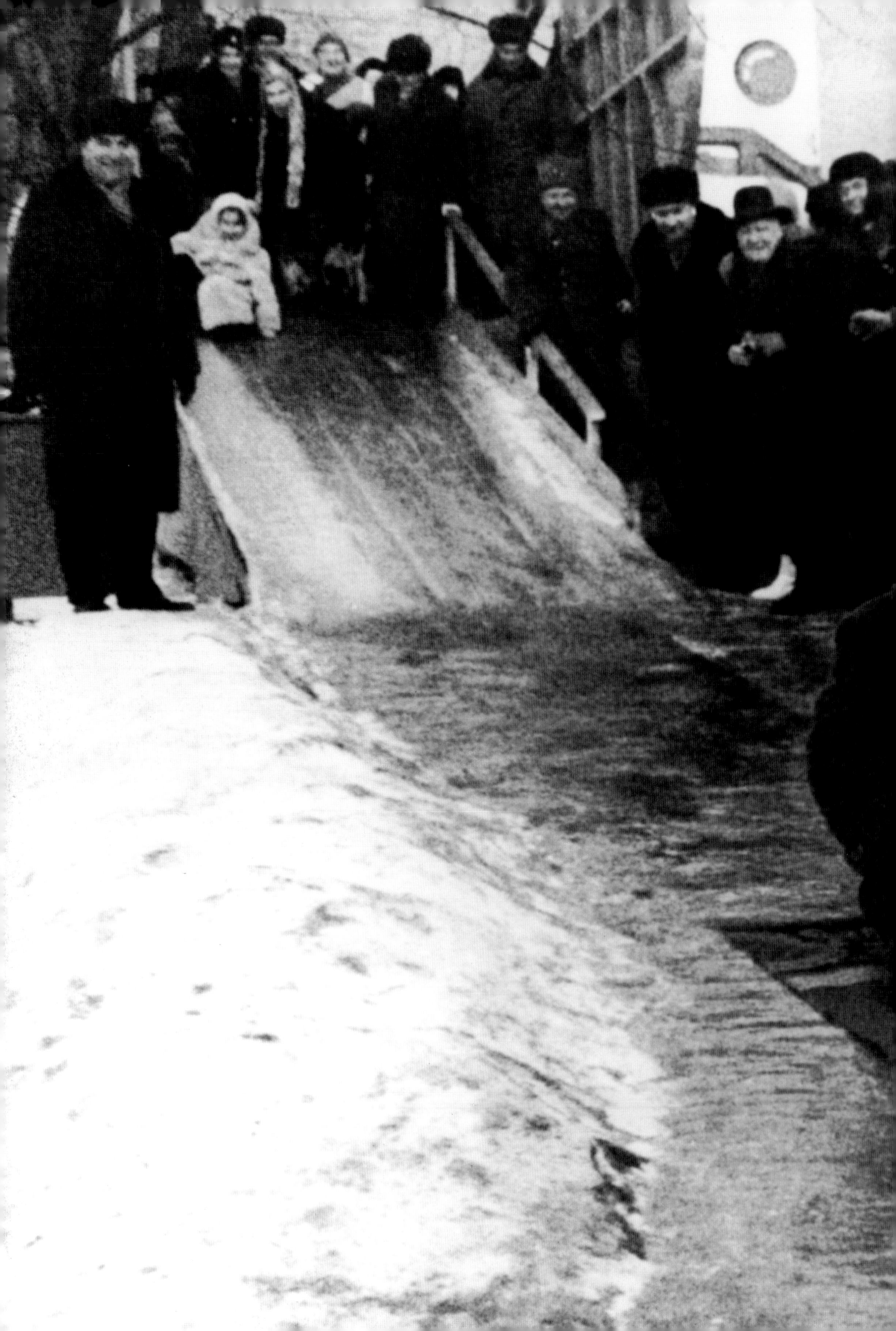

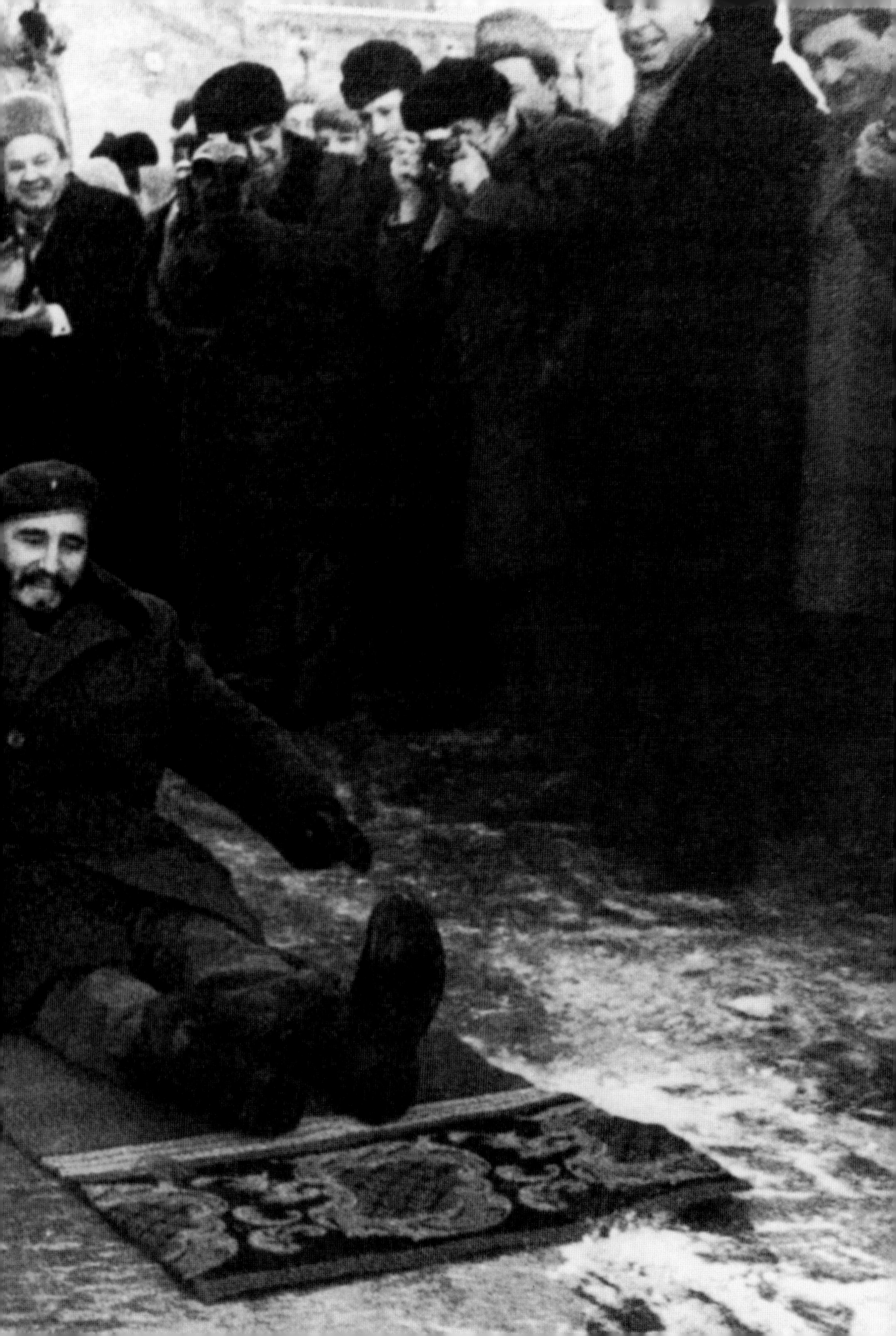

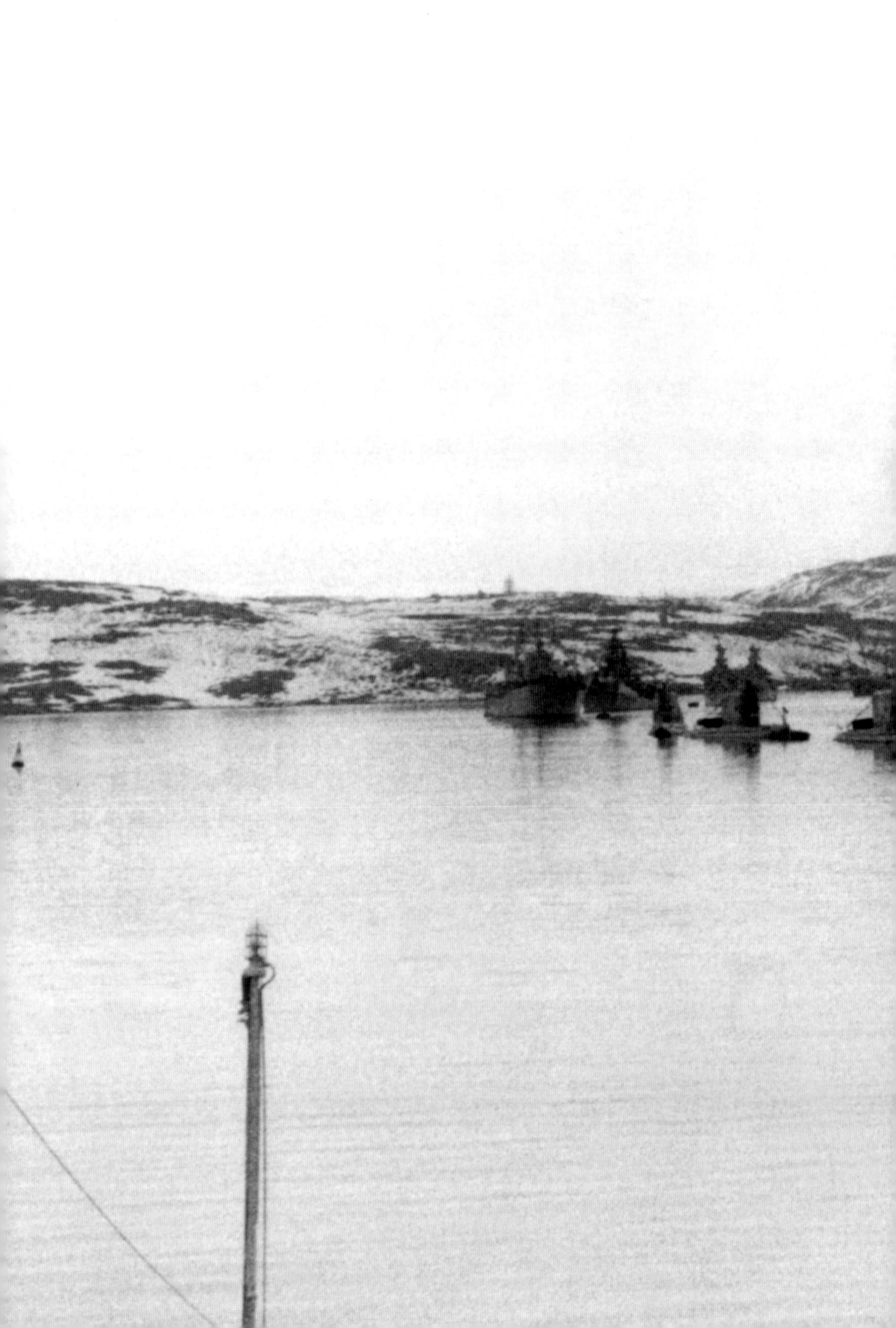

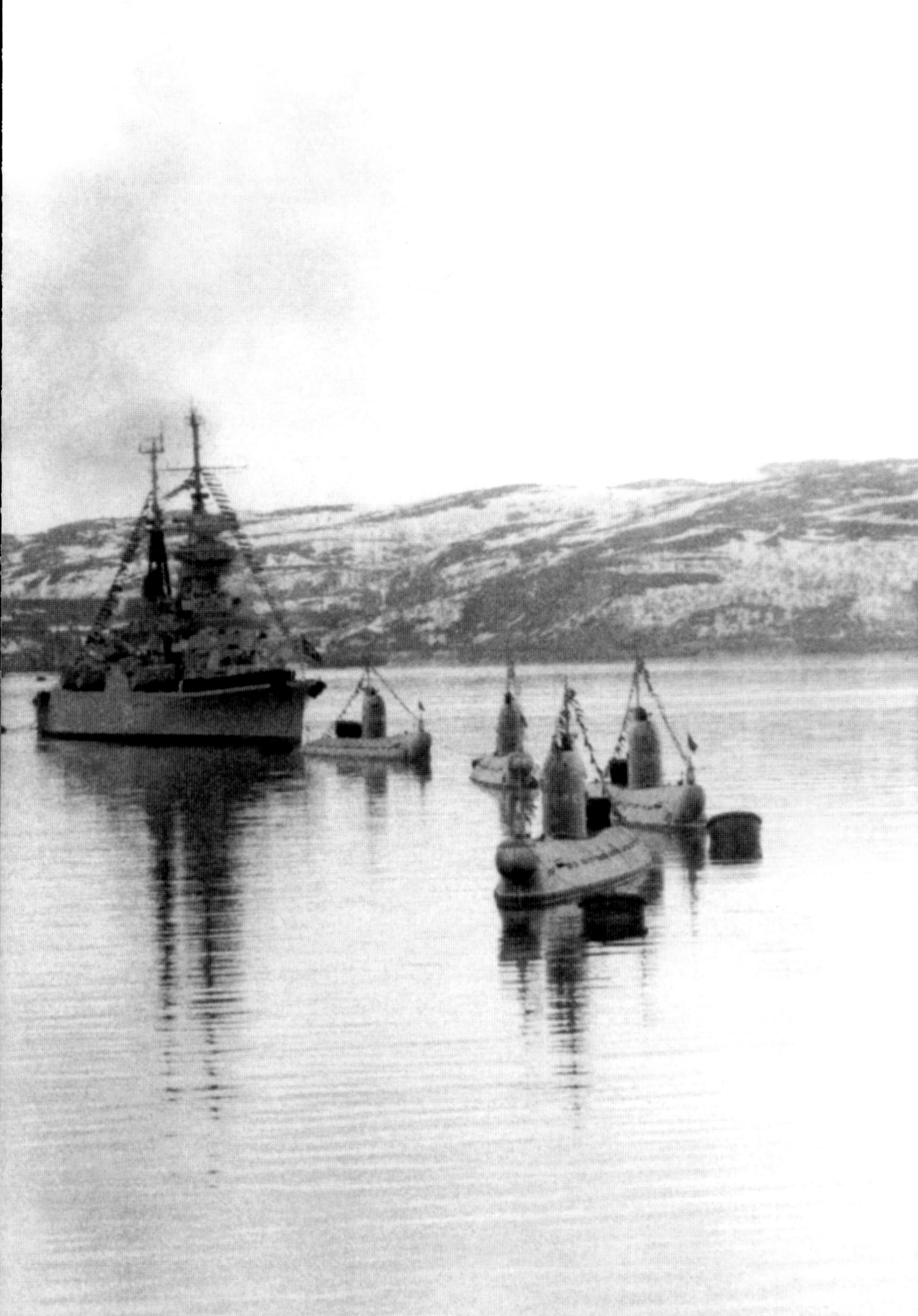

In the spring of 1963, Fidel Castro was 36 years old. His international popularity had reached its zenith in the countries of the communist bloc and in left-wing circles around the world. The French actor Gérard Philippe died in 1959 after a voyage to Havana, and after his widow Anne visited the country three years later, she wrote in *Le Monde*: "In no other country have I seen such a close relationship between a leader and a people. Everyone knows that Fidel might appear at any

"The Russians hadn't thrown such a party for anyone since the first cosmonaut Yuri Gagarin returned to earth..."

time, in a restaurant or in an isolated village where his helicopter could land. Most inaccessible leaders are just liked, but Fidel is adored with an overwhelming affection. When he appears in public, people look at his face and listen to his voice. And they often give him advice: 'You should rest more' or 'Look after yourself.' Everyone talks to him about their particular situation, explaining their daily woes or complaining about some injustice... And every time, as if by miracle, Fidel replies as if he personally knows the person he's talking to." Fidel was also an idol in Latin America, where Cuba was considered the "first liberated territory on the continent." In the Soviet Union, they lauded him as the hero from "the Island of Freedom," as the Russians had dubbed Cuba. After having acknowledged their generosity, Fidel Castro ended his first speech in Red Square by saying: "I thank you Lenin. Long live the Soviet Union!" In return, he received the large red medal of Hero of the Soviet Union.

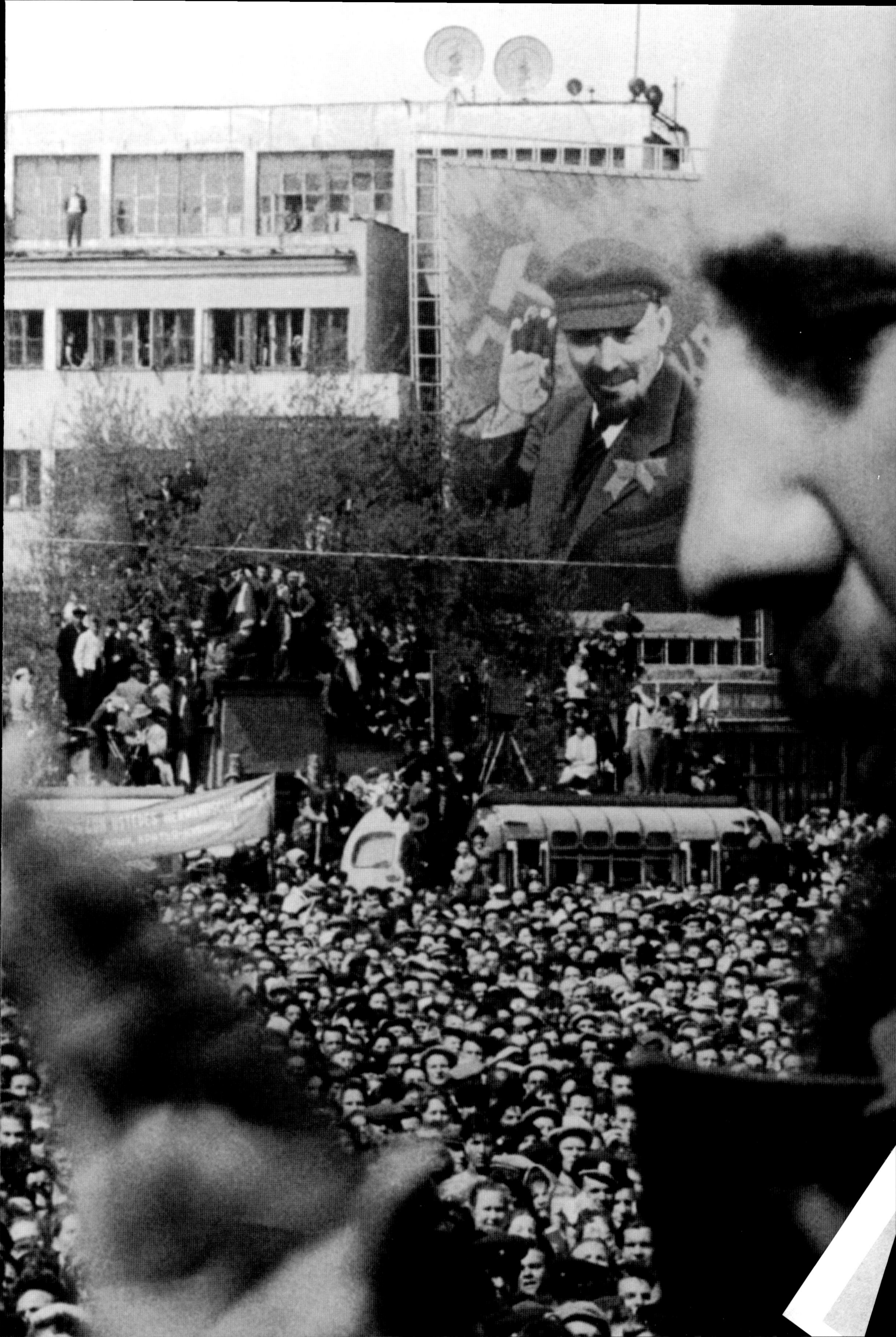

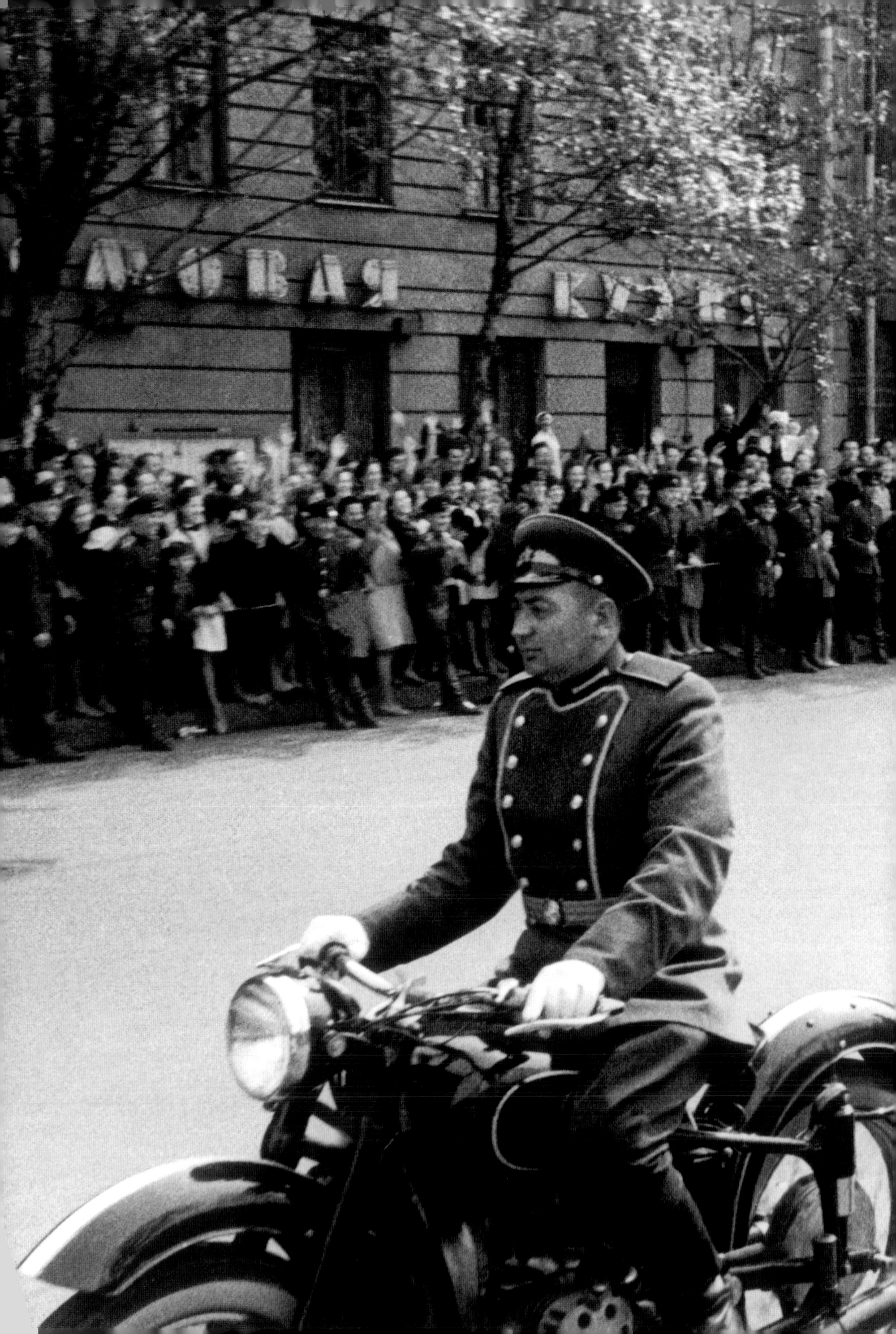

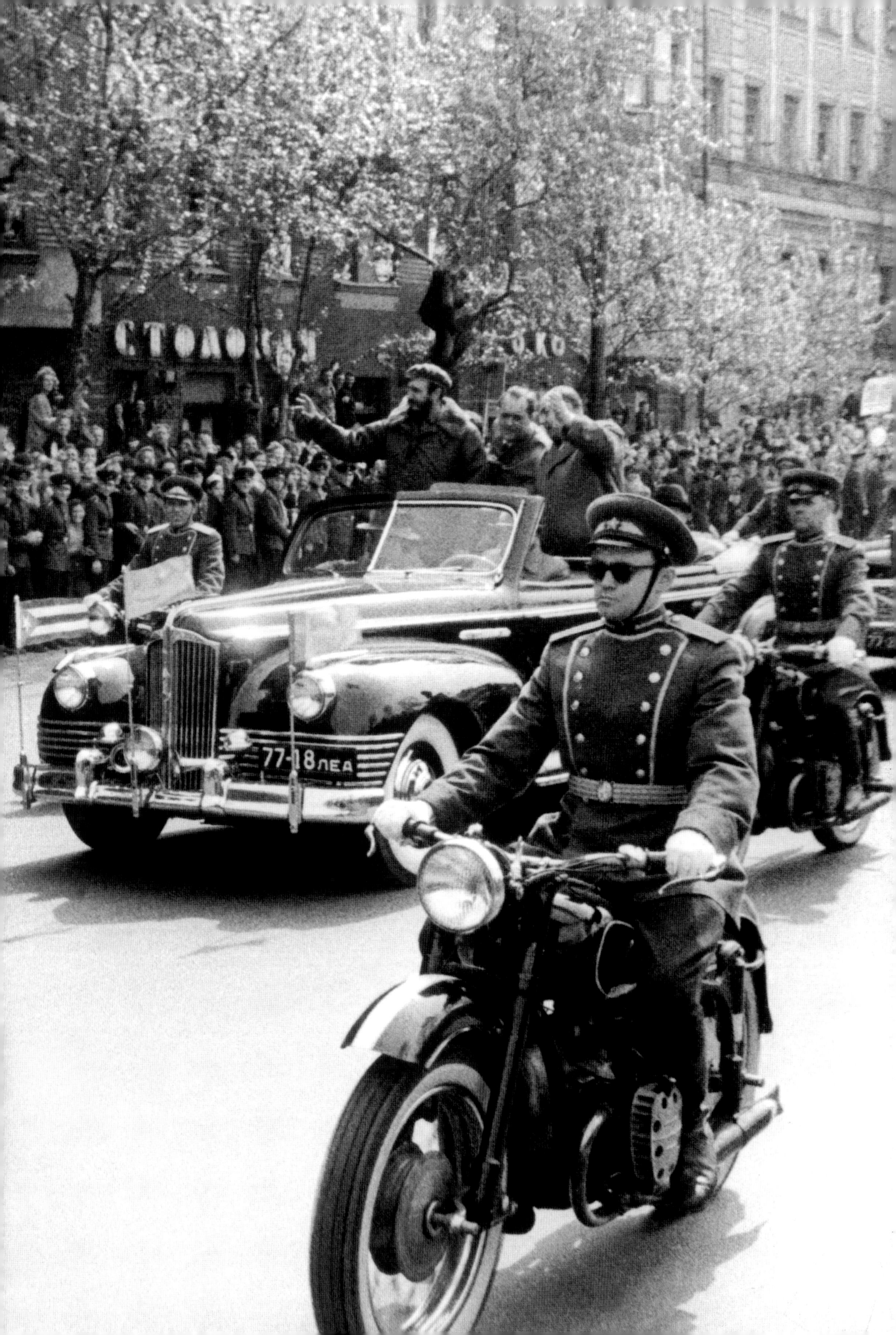
77-18 ЛЕД

Nikita Khrushchev and Fidel Castro met for the first time in September 1960 in New York, at the UN General Assembly. The leader of the second superpower had traveled to Harlem to embrace the young Cuban leader at his hotel. He praised Castro to waiting journalists, calling him a hero and declaring: "I don't know if Fidel is a communist but I am a *fidelista*!" In private however, he confided: "Castro is like a young horse that hasn't been broken in. He needs some more

"One weekend at Nikita's *datcha*, Fidel took some photos with a Polaroid camera. Nikita asked where this magical device had come from. With a beaming smile, Fidel replied: 'Boston, Massachusetts.'"

experience but he is full of spirit. We need to be very careful." In April 1963, Khrushchev received Castro at his *datcha* in Sabidowa. He read Castro letters from John F. Kennedy, one of which said: "We have fulfilled all our commitments and have withdrawn all our missiles from Italy and Turkey." The Cuban leader recognized the ulterior motives behind the Soviet offer to base missiles in Cuba. Much later, during a 1992 international conference in Havana which brought together a number of the key protagonists of the Cuban Missile Crisis, Fidel Castro concluded: "In light of what we now know about the balance of forces at that time [between the United States and the Soviet Union], we would have advised caution. Nikita was a cunning rogue, but I don't think he wanted to provoke a war, even less a nuclear war. He lived with the obsession of maintaining nuclear parity."

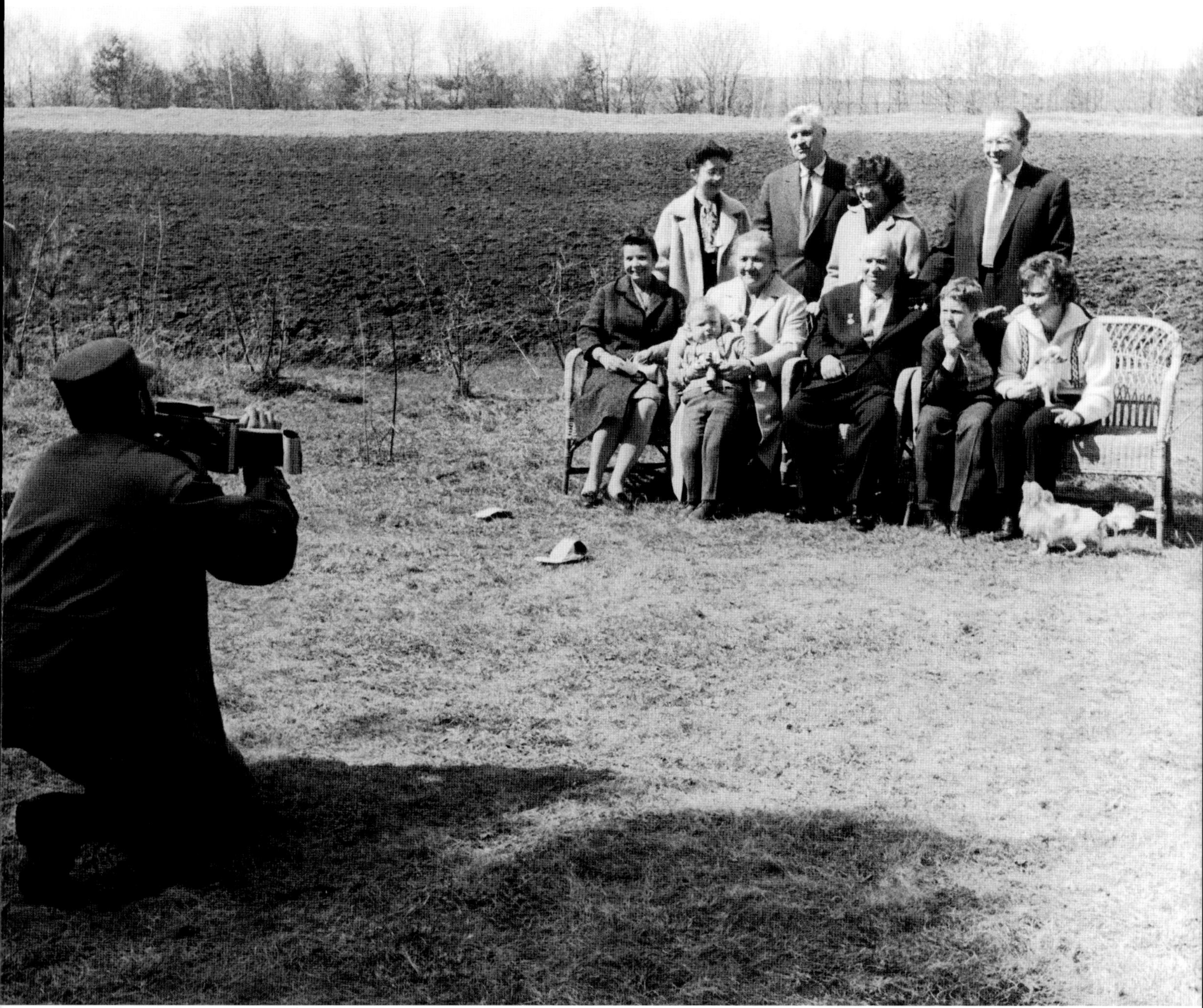

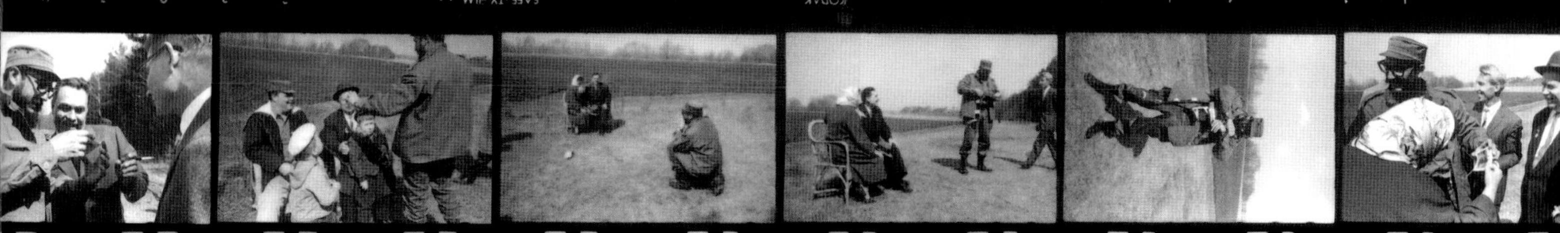

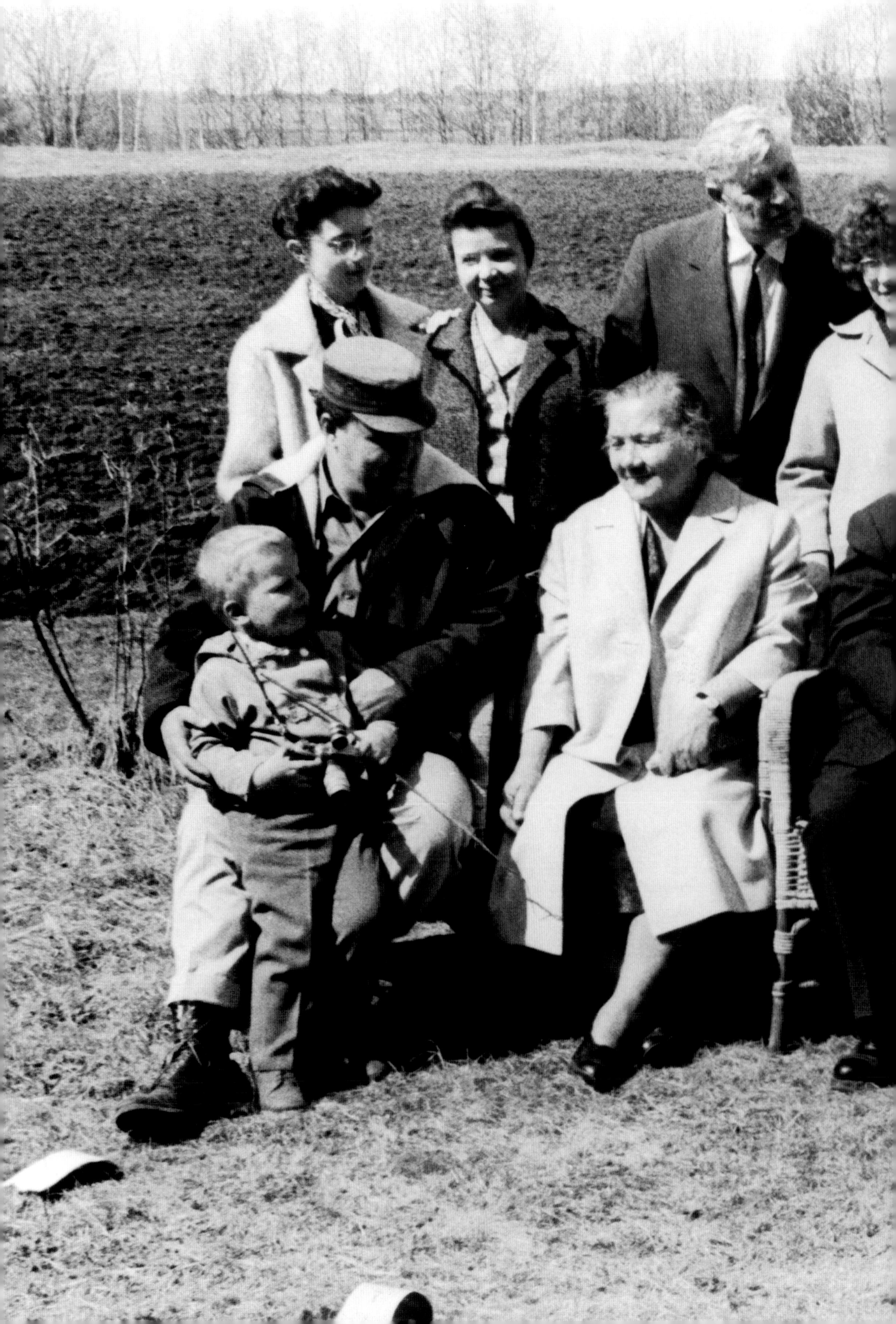

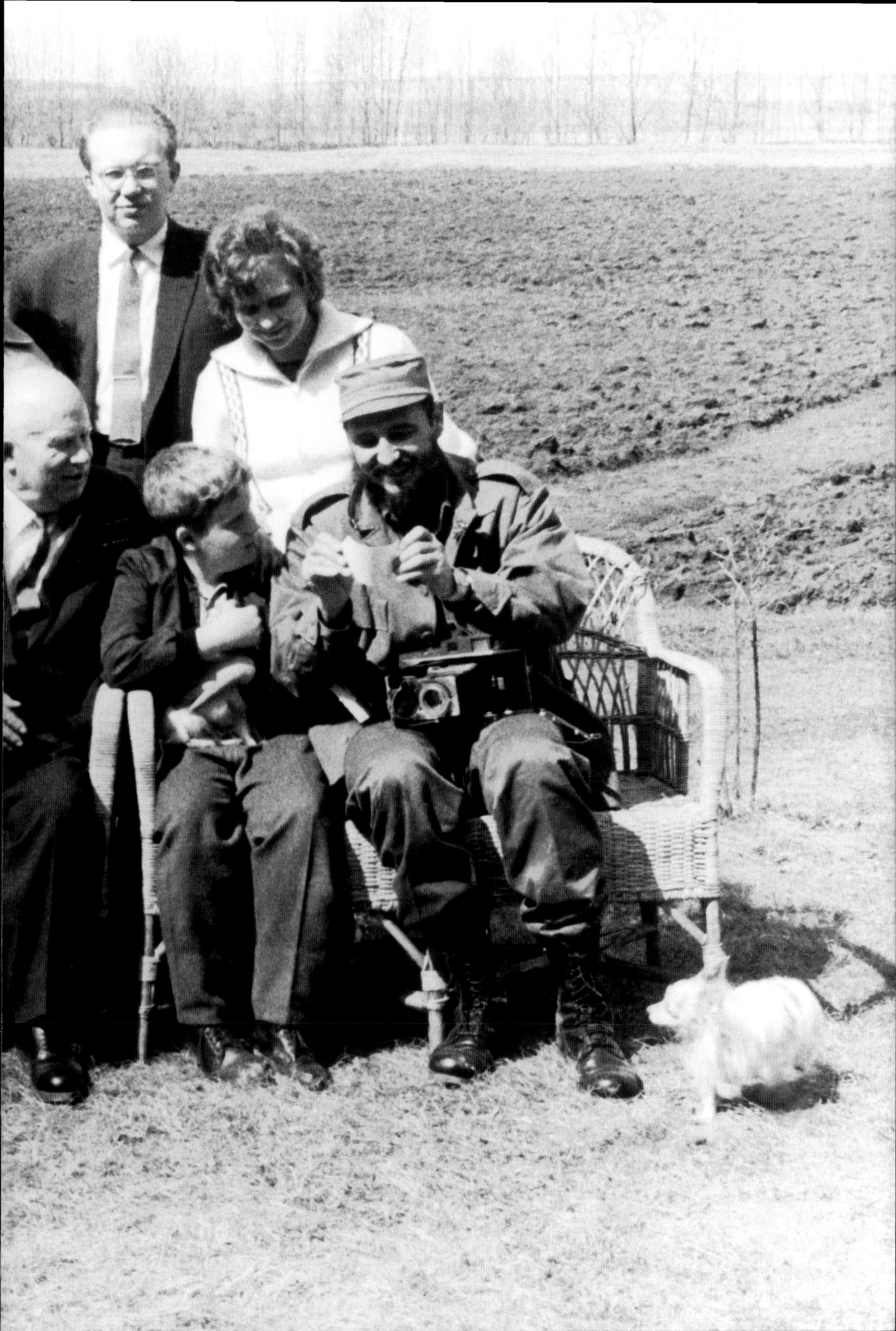

Born in 1894 to a poor family, Fidel's Russian host had been a shepherd, an ironworker, and a miner. Nikita Khrushchev participated in the Bolshevik Revolution, then forged his career in the party apparatus. In 1939, Joseph Stalin nominated him as a member of the Politburo, in charge of the annexation of eastern Poland after the Nazi-Soviet nonaggression pact. Then he led the defense of Ukraine and participated in the defense of Stalingrad during World War II. Finally, after

"At the United Nations in 1960, Nikita hit the podium with his shoe during an anti-Soviet speech by the Philippines delegate. Then he threw the shoe at the Francoist ambassador from Spain, just missing his head..."

organizing the funeral ceremony in March 1953 for "the little father of the peoples," he took over Stalin's position as first secretary of the Communist Party. Stalin's name disappeared immediately from the newspapers, while an amnesty decree allowed thousands of political prisoners to return to their homes. The 20th Congress of the Communist Party of the Soviet Union took place in the Kremlin in February 1956. In front of thoroughly traumatized delegates, Khrushchev read Lenin's testament and last letter in which the Bolshevik leader threatened to break off relations with Stalin. Then he accused Stalin of creating the concept of "the enemy of the people" and of massacring thousands of innocents. He condemned Stalin as largely responsible for the military disaster of 1941, by massacring the best officers of the Red Army and ignoring the Nazis' preparations for war. By charging the dictator and his soul mate Beria with all these sins, the new master of the Kremlin redirected the Russian people's anger on to the two dead leaders in order to save the Soviet regime—and himself.

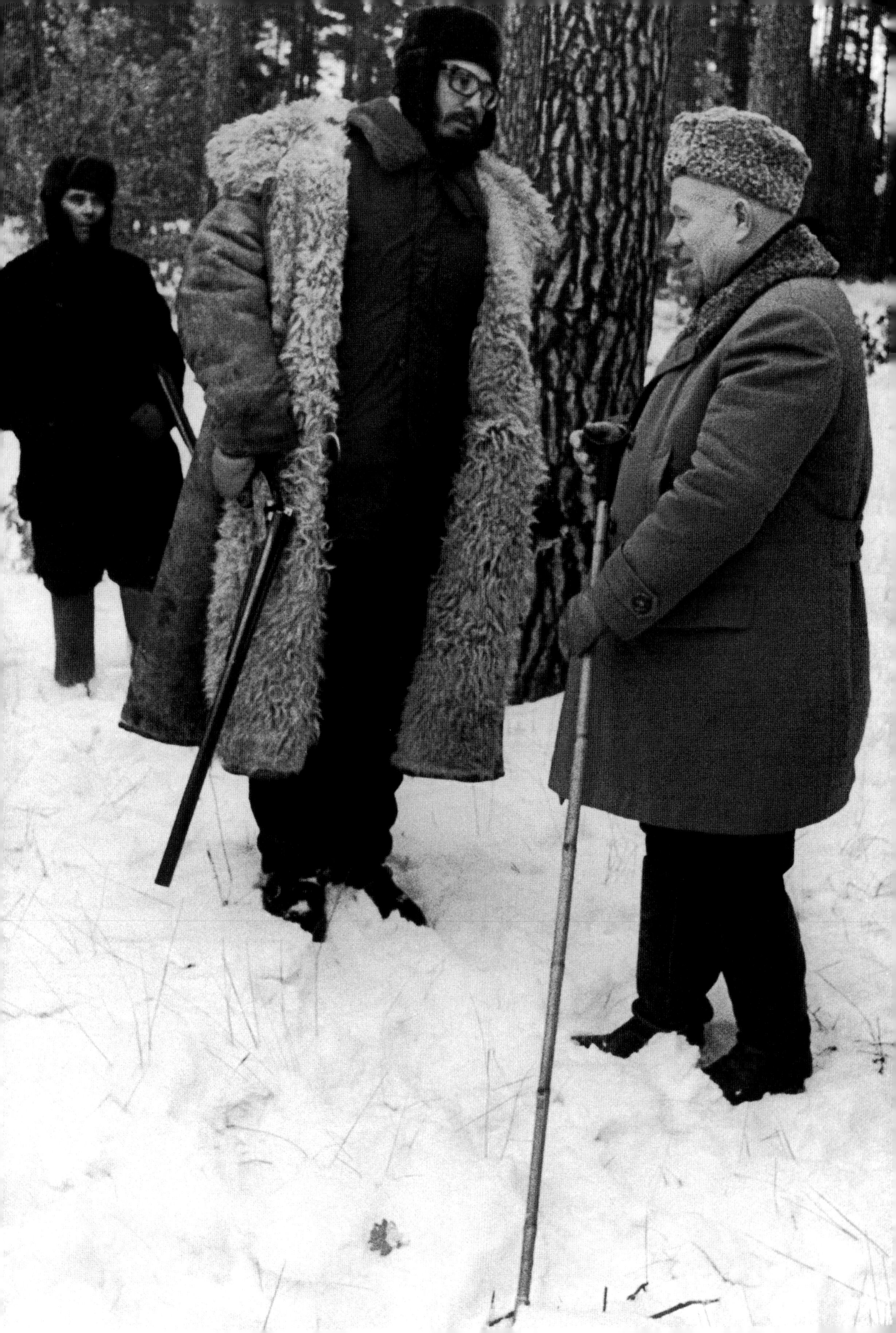

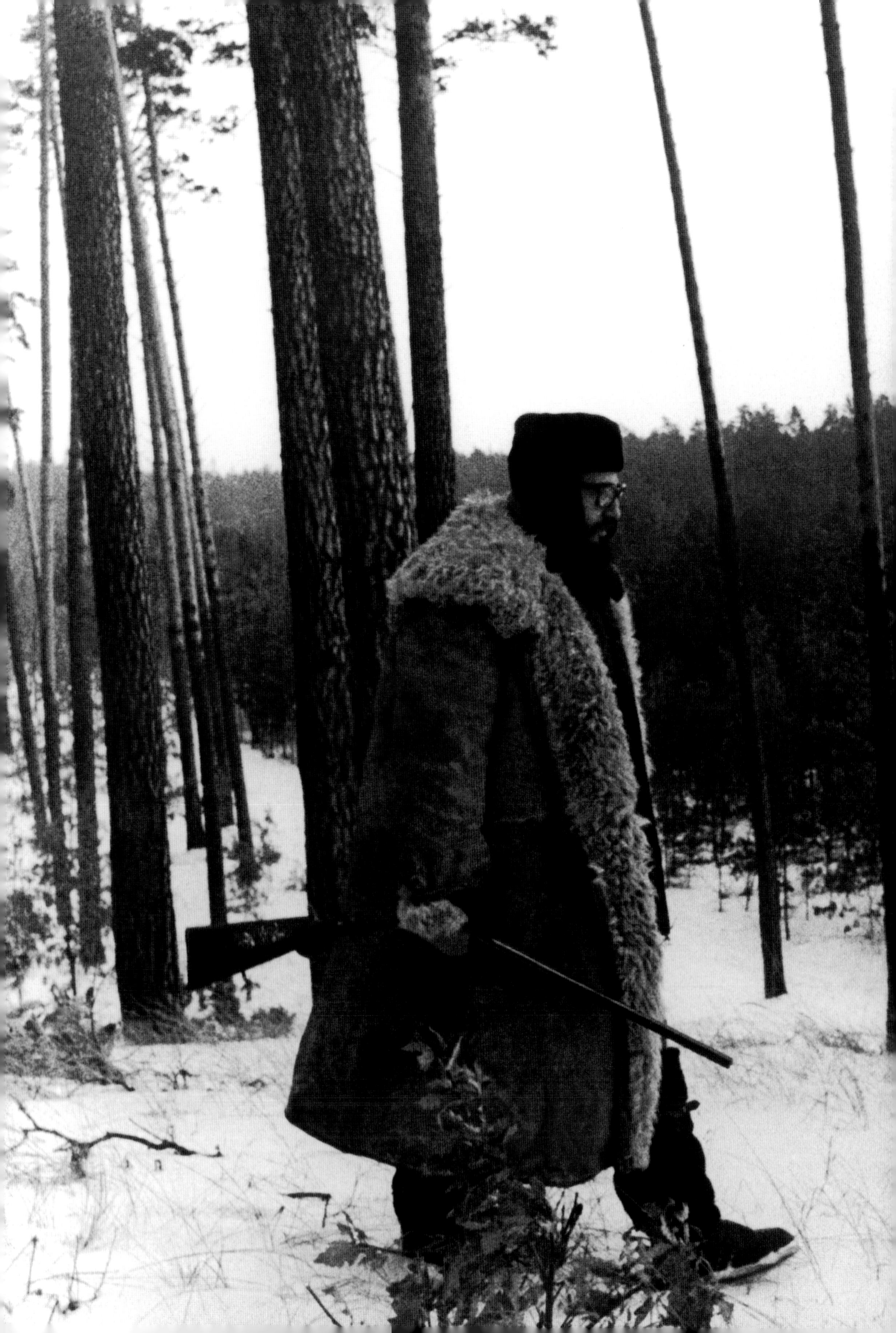

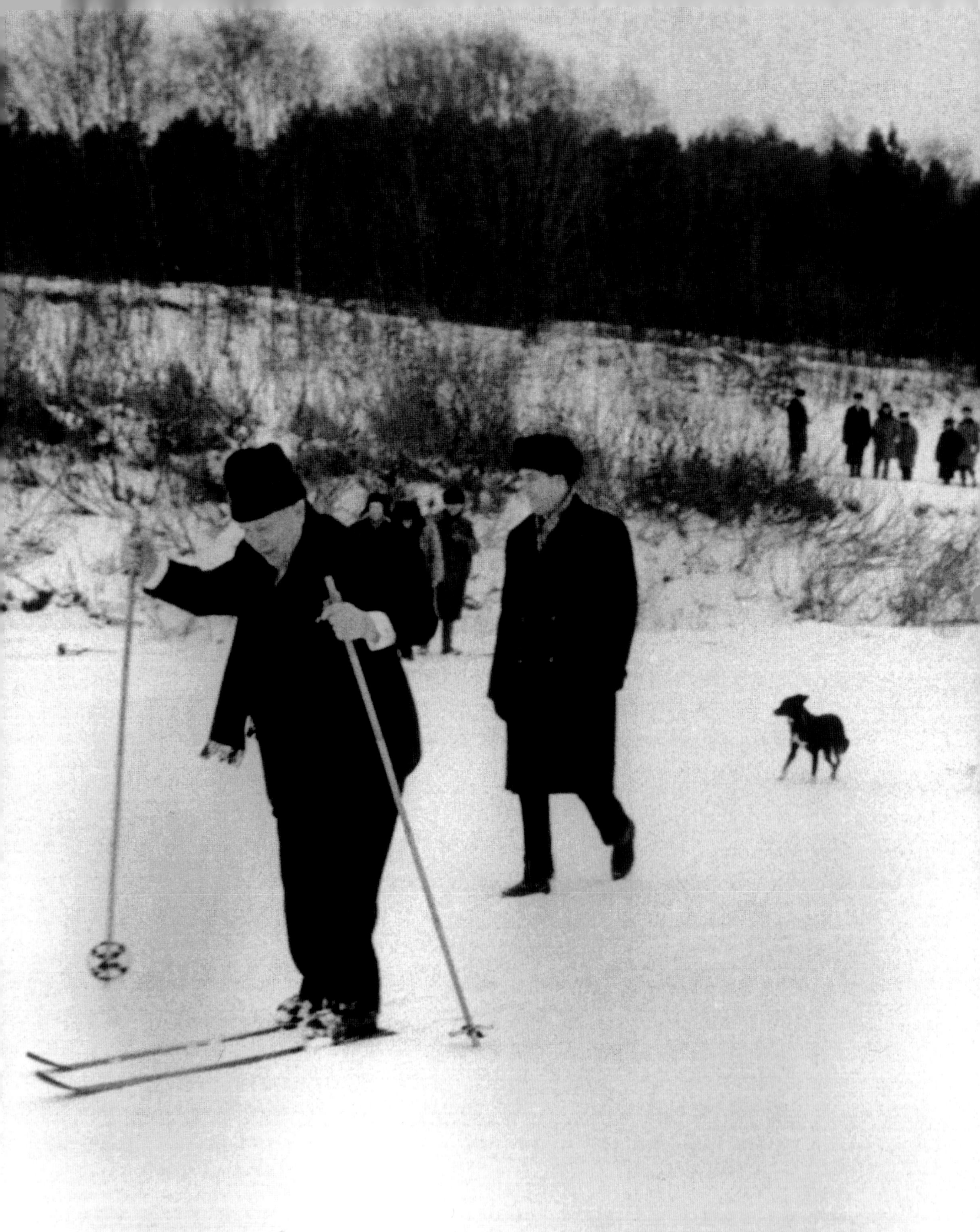

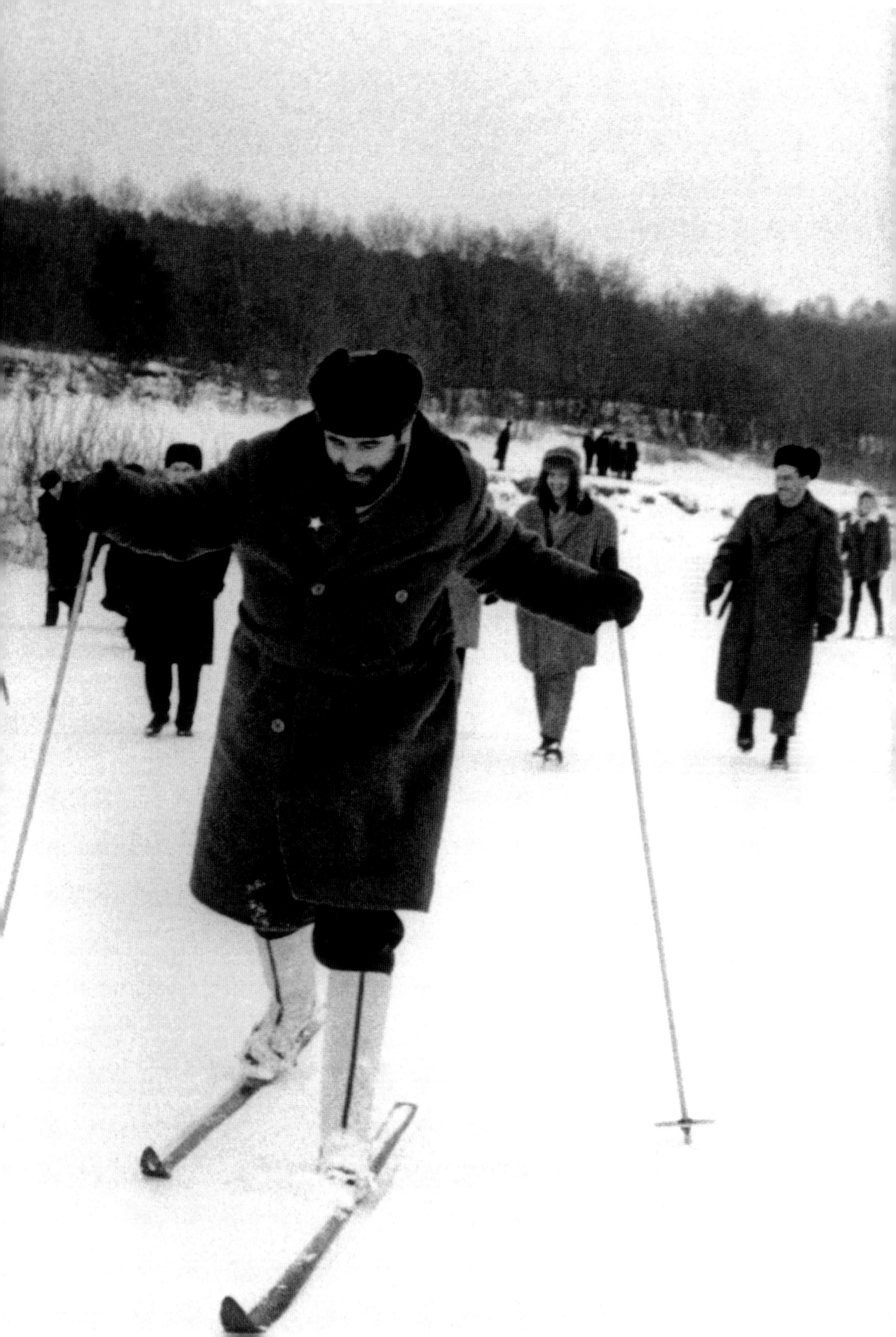

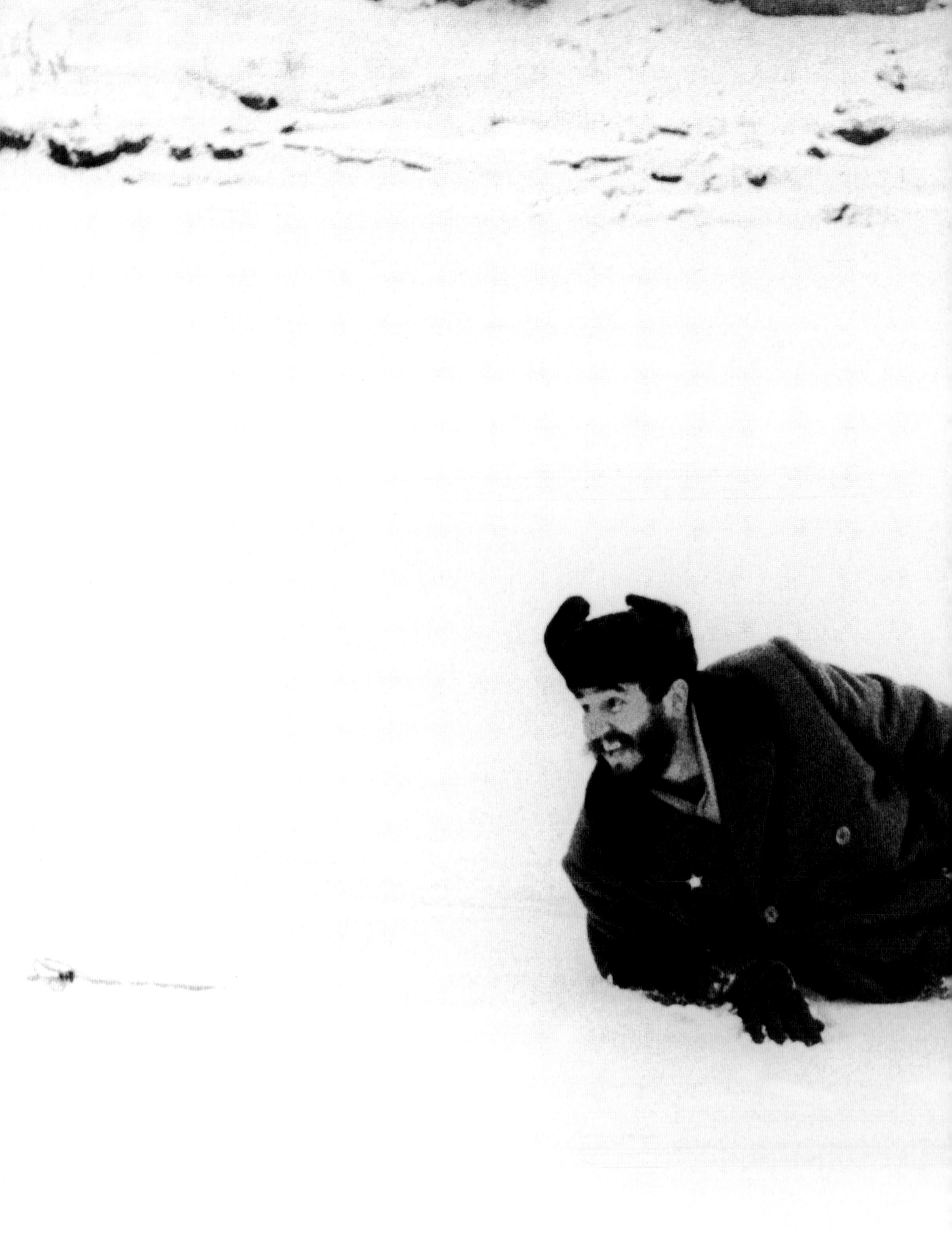

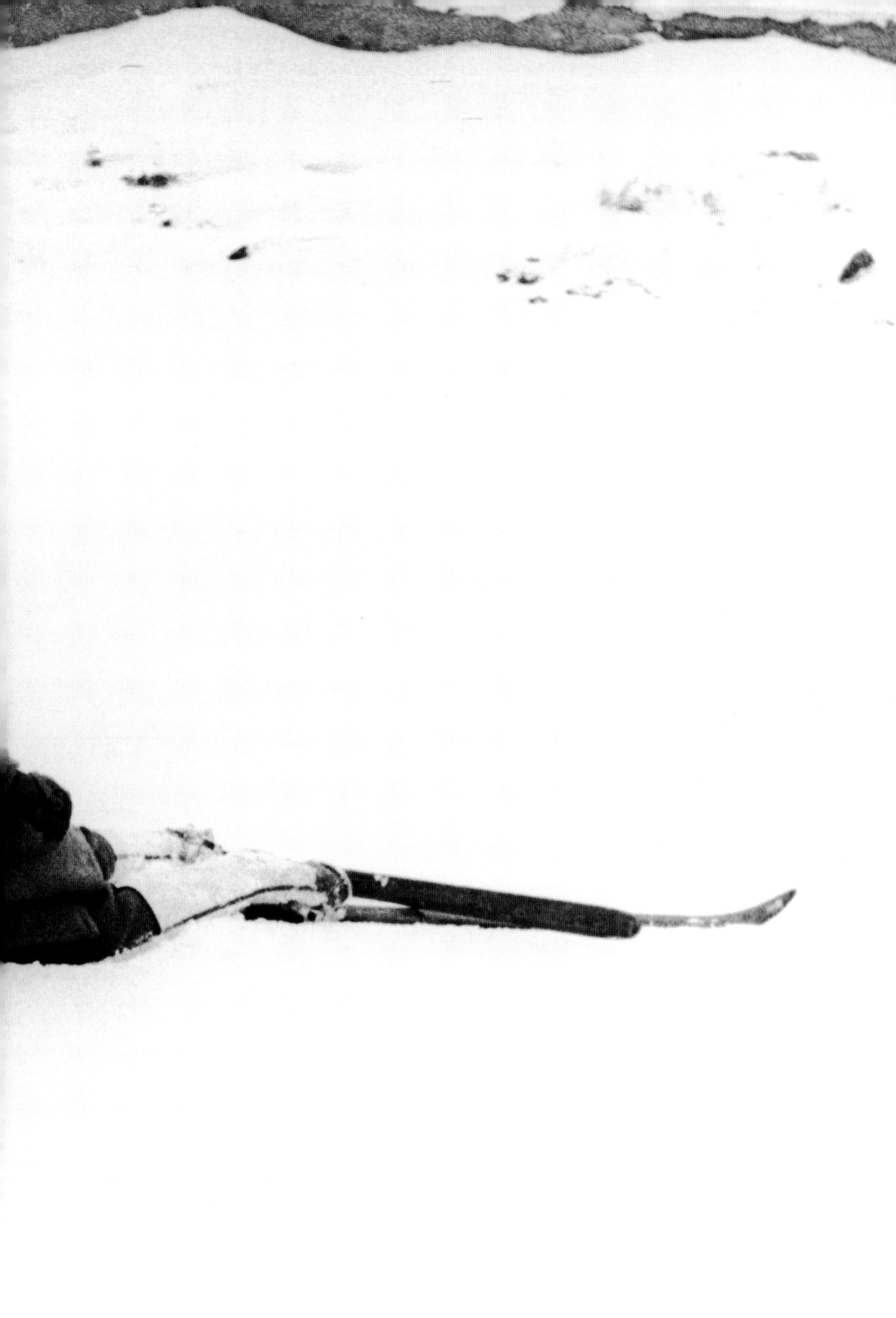

"Fidel went skiing for the first time with Nikita, when he returned to the Soviet Union a year later. He got the hang of it immediately. Another day, he saw some skiers on a frozen river. He called out to them and asked if he could try. It started well, but then crash! He was transformed into a snowball, and almost died laughing. But he never asked me not to publish that photo—so tell that to anyone who accuses him of not having a sense of humor!"

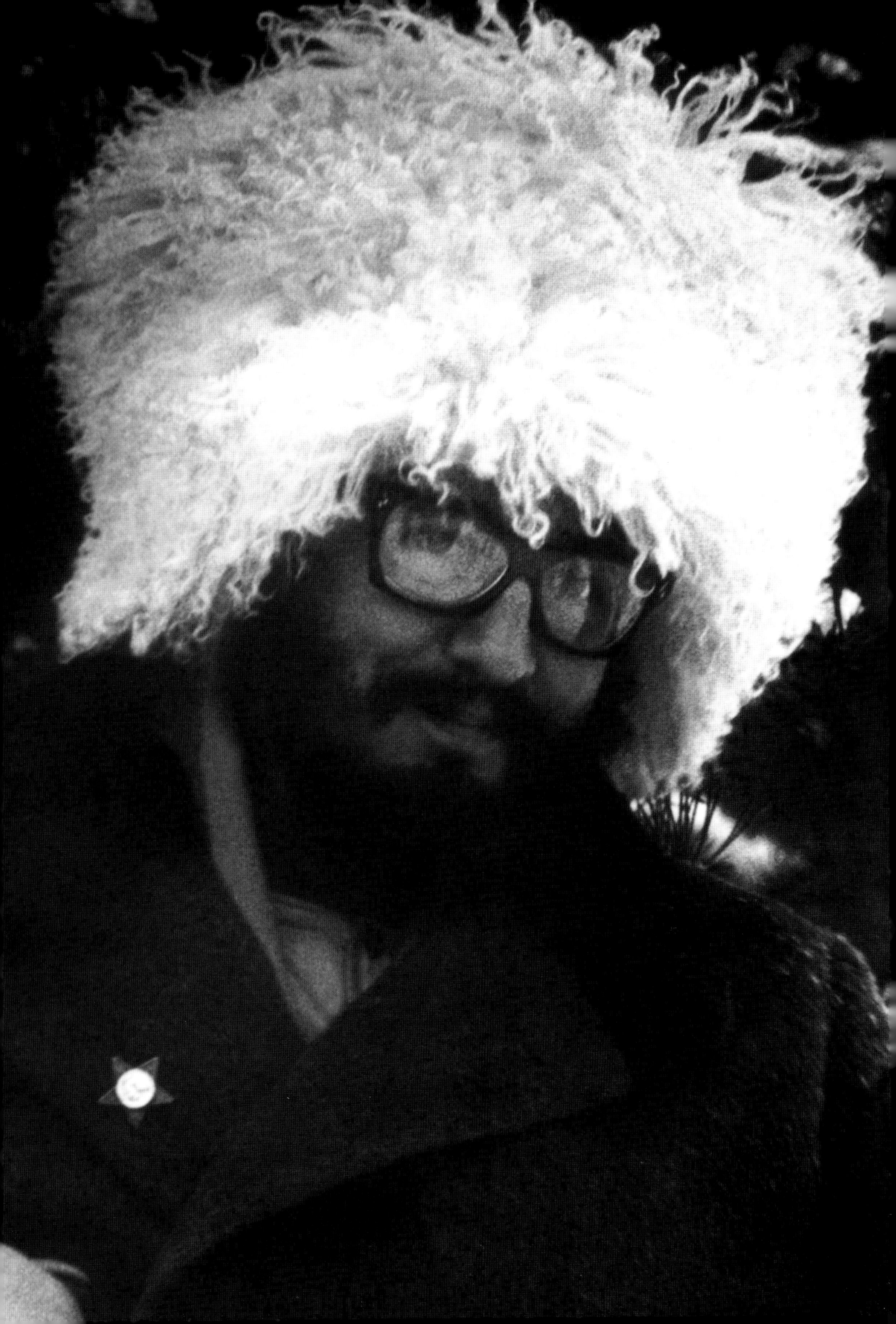

For over 11 years, Khrushchev ruled with a mixture of contradictory policies: destalinization, a cultural thawing, and the publication of Solzhenitsyn's books, but also the crushing of the 1956 Budapest revolt and construction of the Berlin Wall in 1961; "peaceful coexistence" with the capitalist world but also the placement of Soviet missiles in Cuba. He was popular around the world—to the point where Western newspapers had the habit of describing him by the

"The capacity of the Russians to drink alcohol and act like children was astounding. While they were out hunting, Nikita and Leonid's favorite pastime was to try to stuff snow down each other's pants..."

letter "K." This rotund smiling fellow was a pioneer of political theater, alternating between spectacular torrents of abuse and seductive moves. But setbacks to his economic reform program and his apparent capitulation during the Cuban Missile Crisis had earned Khrushchev some criticism from party leaders. The Presidium of the Central Committee invited him to resign on October 16, 1964, "because of his advanced age and failing health," even though the party's leading body was not short of aged and ailing men. Under his successor Leonid Brezhnev, Khrushchev's thaw froze over again, but without the bloody murders of the Stalin era. The proof of the new era was shown with Mr. K, calmly living out his remaining seven years in a prison-like *datcha* in the suburbs of Moscow, dictating his memoirs. It could not have happened under Stalin.

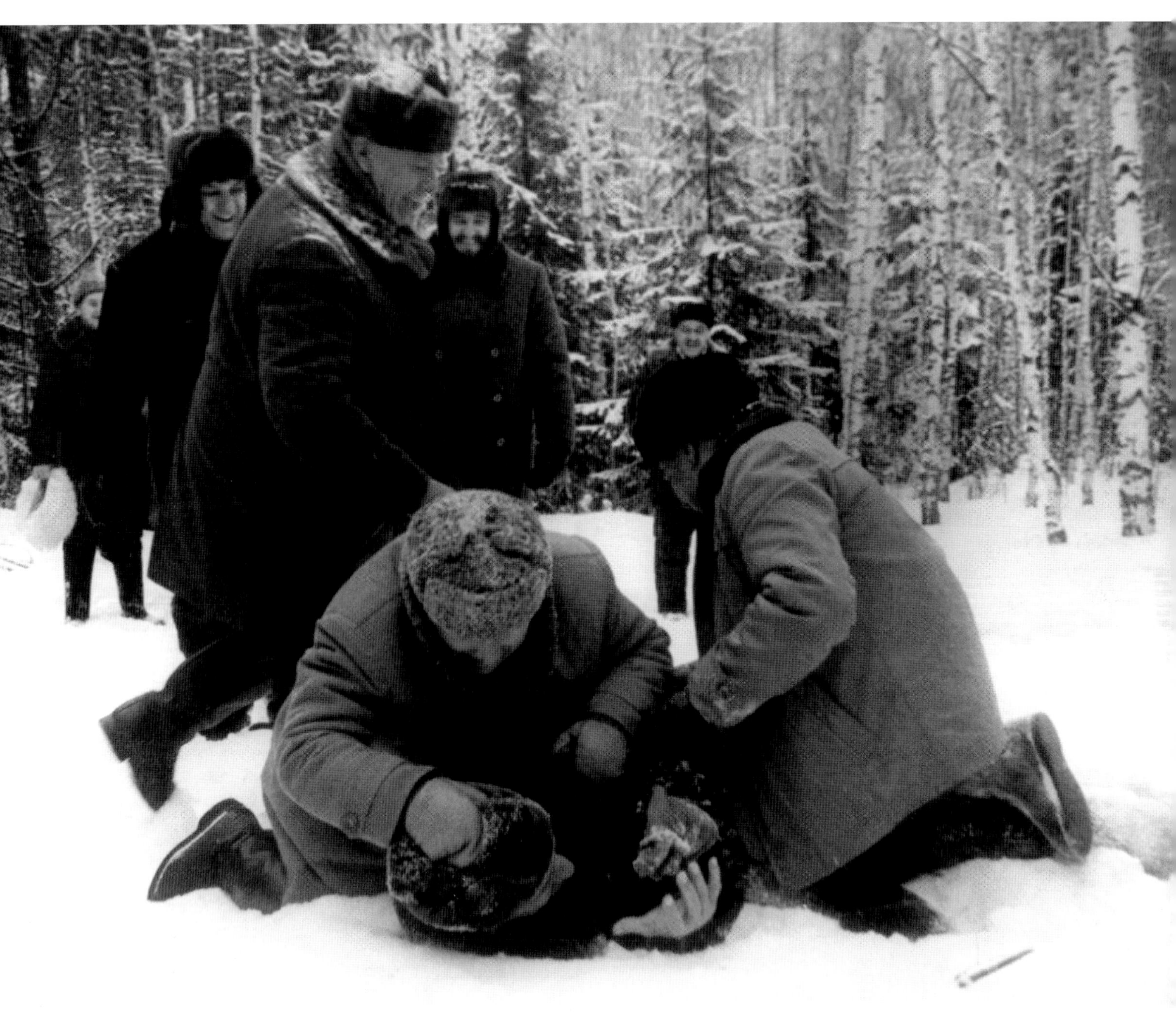

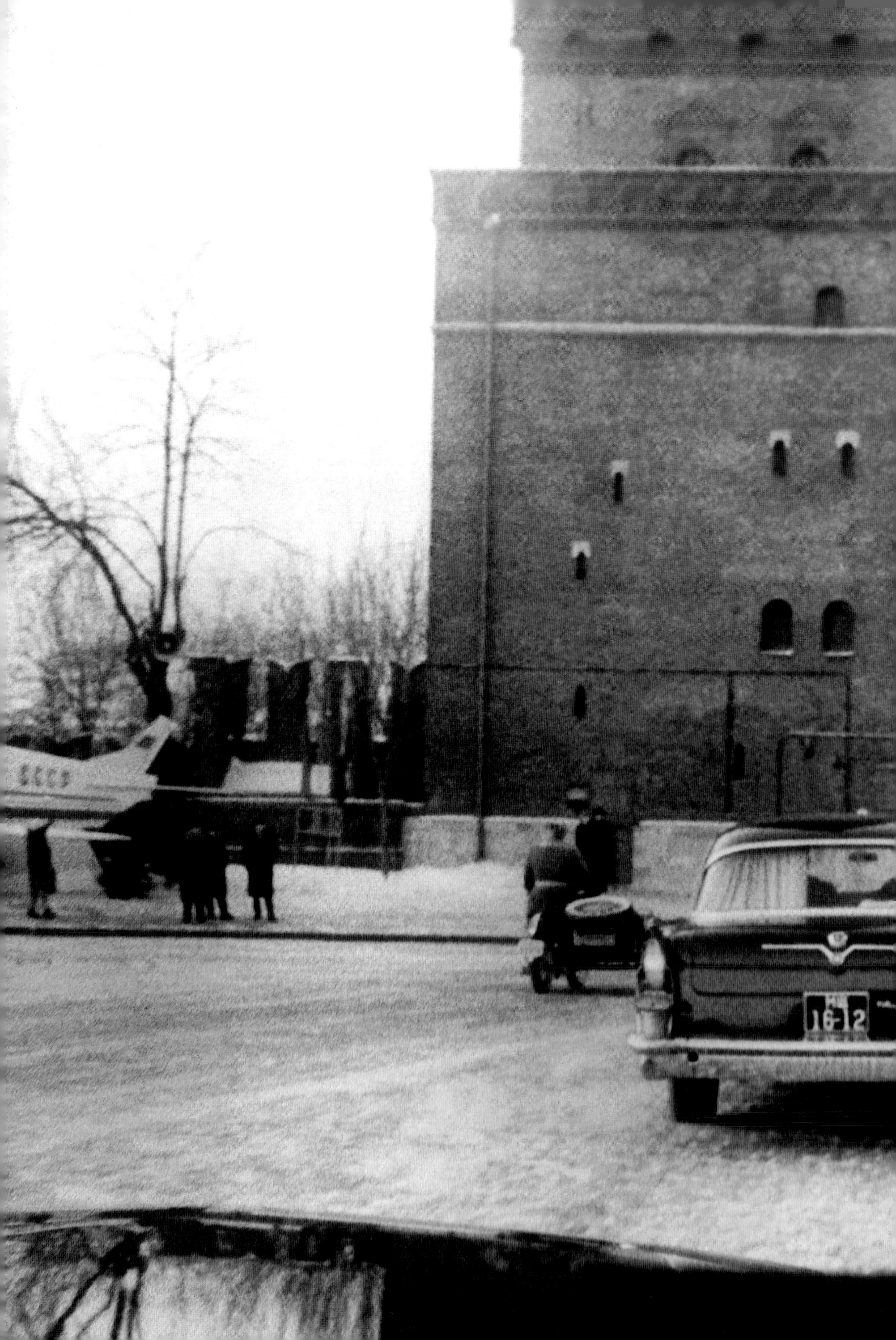
16-12

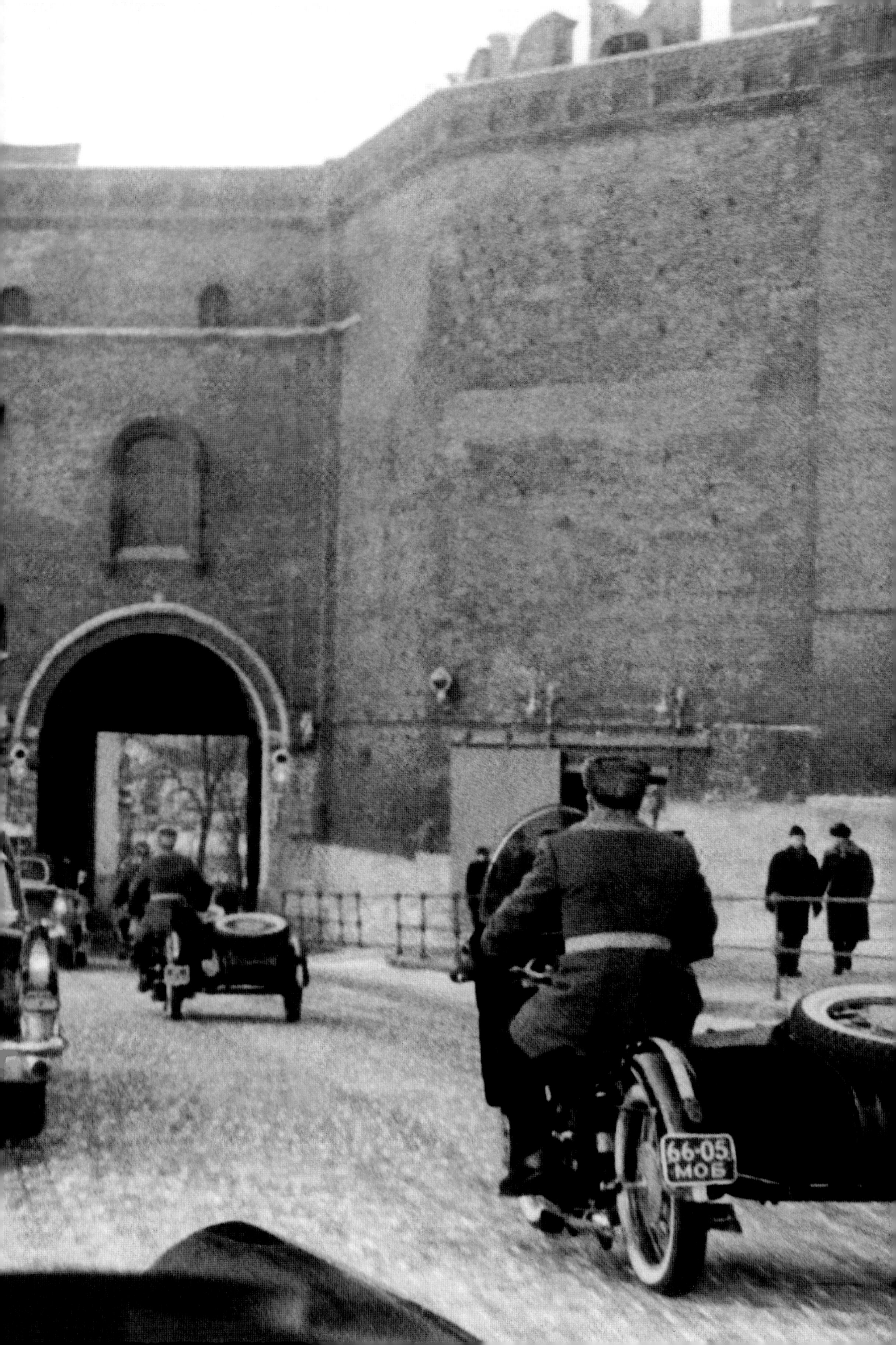
66-05
МОБ

In Moscow, Fidel visited the famous Spanish rebel La Pasionaria, whom Federico García Lorca described as "a woman of sadness and pain." Dolores Ibárruri was born in 1895 in the Basque province of Bizkaia (Biscay), to a poor, Catholic, and monarchist family. Like all young girls from her world, her education was interrupted so she could become a maid, then a serving girl. At 20, she married a socialist militant. Even though her husband spent more time in jail than at

"Fidel often cited a saying from the Spanish La Pasionaria, Dolores Ibárruri: 'It's better to die on your feet than live on your knees.' She welcomed him into her home in Moscow..."

home, she bore six children, four of whom died at an early age due to the family's difficult living conditions. At 25, she joined the communist party and became one of its leaders. She signed her first article "La Pasionaria" because it was written during a holy week. Dressed in widow's black, Dolores and her fine voice were found on the frontline of the strikes that shook Spain during this era. She was elected as a member of parliament for the Asturias region and set free all the political prisoners in the provincial capital Oviedo. She entered legend with the call she issued on July 19, 1936, the day after the uprising of Spain's fascist military forces in North Africa: "*¡No pasarán!*" (They shall not pass!). From 1939, the tragedy of the Spanish Civil War led her to play a decisive role in the leadership of the Spanish Communist Party, but from exile in Moscow. It was only in 1977, aged 92, that she returned to Spain to take up her position as deputy for Asturias. She died in 1989.

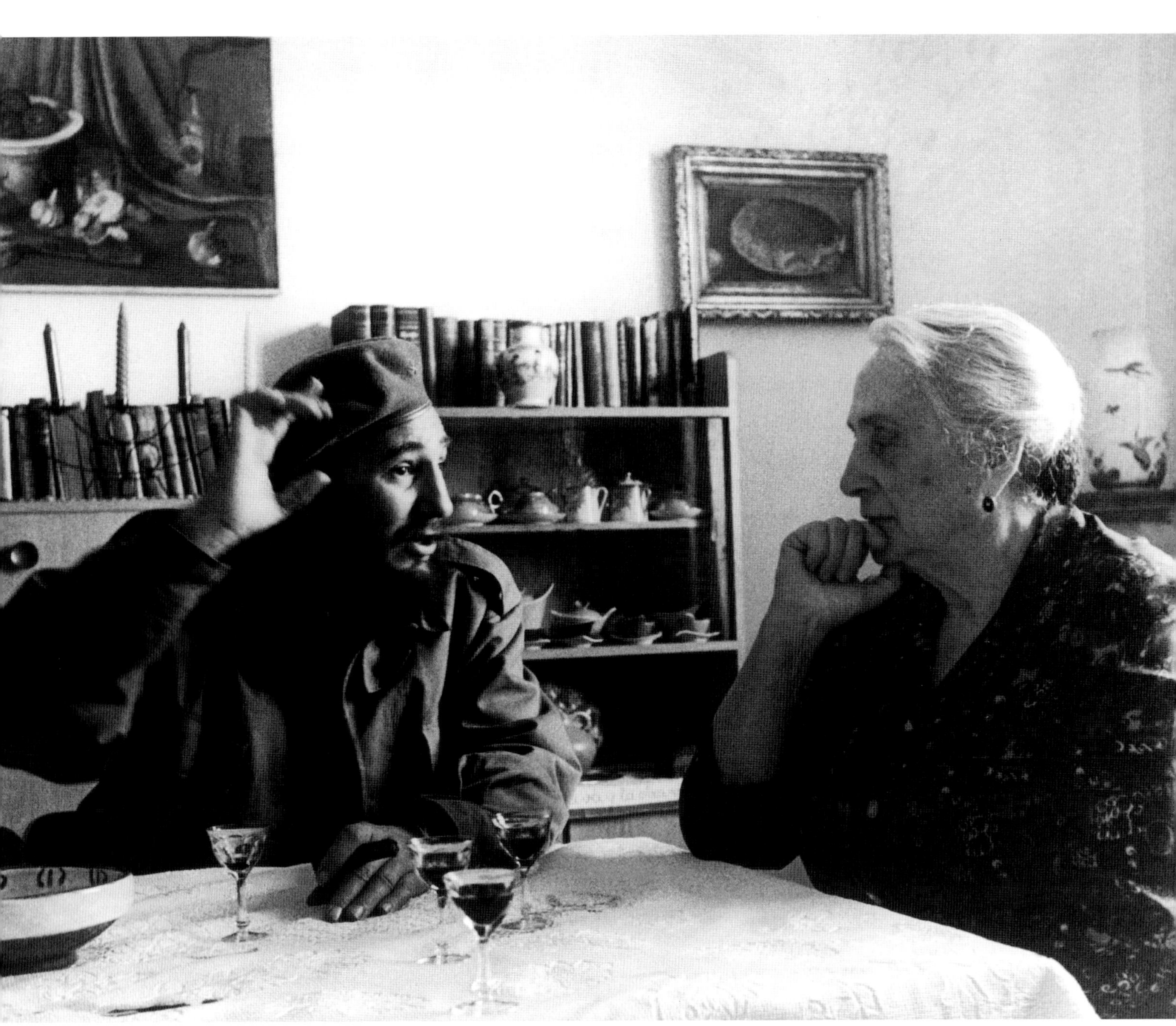

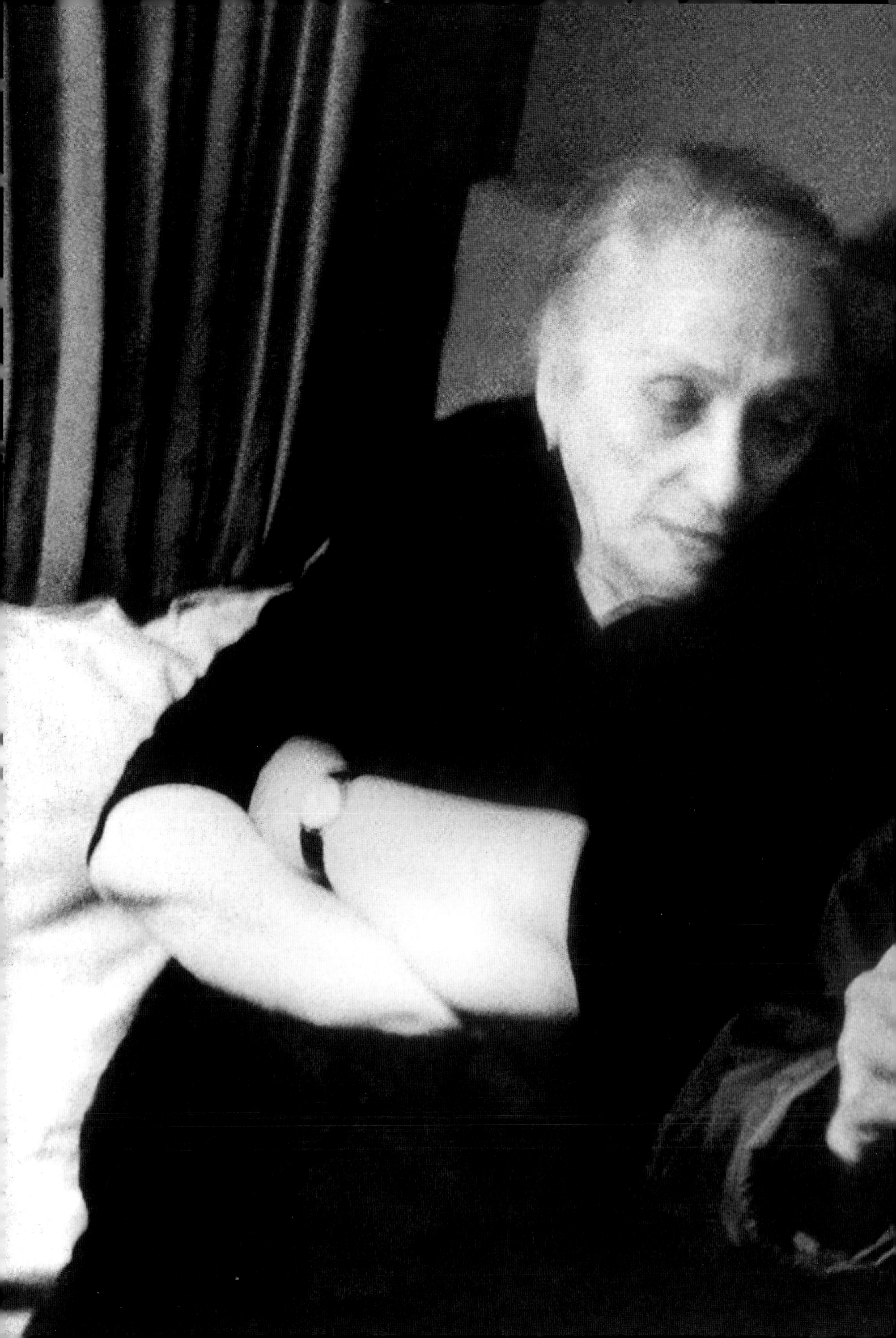

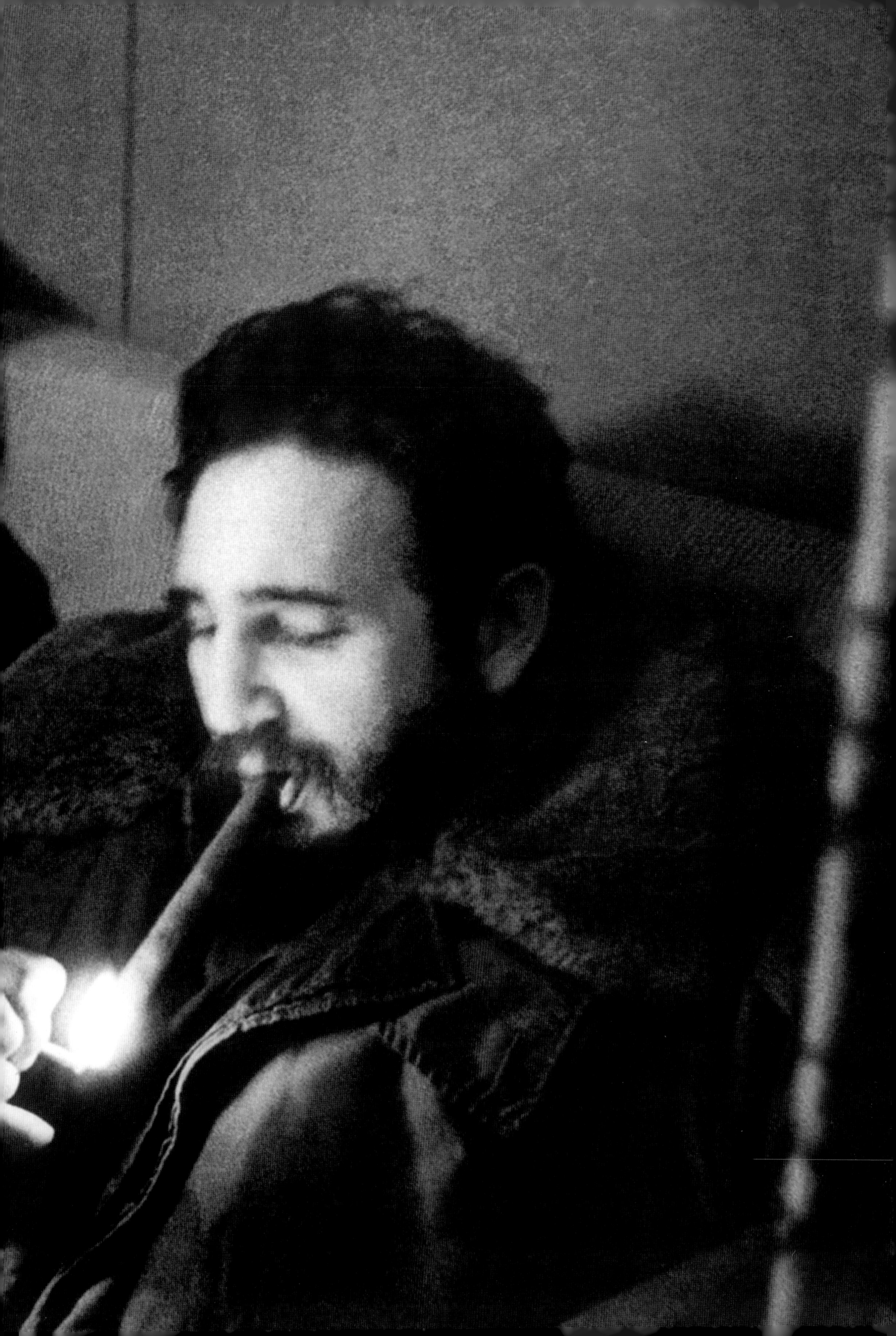

"Che was doing some tests with the Alzadora, a new machine for cutting sugarcane that he had designed with a French engineer. When I found him, his face blackened with sweat and dust and a bit puffed up with the cortisone he was taking at the time, he looked at me with a mixture of irony and surprise. 'Ah, you're here Korda. Where did you come from originally—the town or the countryside?' I replied: 'Me? From Havana, *comandante*.' He asked: 'And have you ever cut sugarcane?' and I had to reply 'Never!' He turned to one of his guards: 'Alfonso, find a machete for the compañero journalist.' And as he turned to me, he added: 'As for photos, try again next week.'"

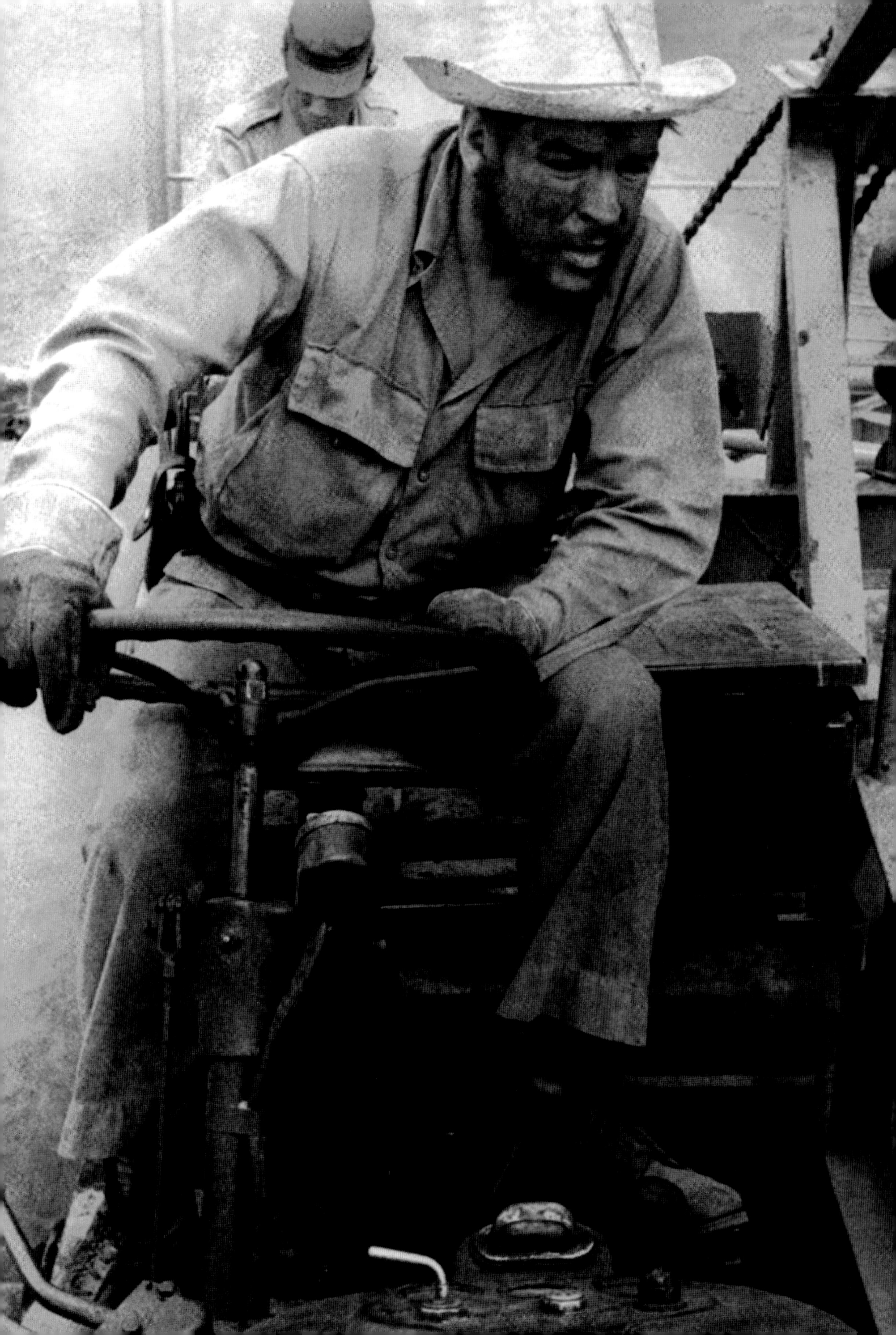

As a minister, Che saw voluntary labor as a sacred act for the revolution. On Sundays, he cut cane or loaded sugar bags. Like a crusader, he incarnated the New Man that was his dream: "At the risk of seeming ridiculous, let me say that the true revolutionary is guided by great feelings of love... Perhaps it is one of the great dramas of the leader that he or she must combine a passionate spirit with a cold intelligence and make painful decisions without flinching... In these

"It took me some time to understand this man, who brought together the strength of steel and the tenderness of a rose... who refused to be a savage, vowing to create a New Man..."

circumstances one must have a large dose of humanity, a large dose of a sense of justice and truth in order to avoid dogmatic extremes, cold scholasticism, or isolation from the masses." However, from December 1964, Che projected himself into the future: "When the moment comes, I am ready to give my life for the liberation of one of the Latin American countries, without asking anything in return..." In March 1965, he disappeared, but in fact he had chosen Africa. After a setback in the Congo where he tried to open a new guerrilla front, he turned to Bolivia. On October 8, 1967, he was captured by Bolivian army rangers and summarily executed the next day. His photo in death, with eyes open, would become the banner of revolt for a new generation. But another portrait would soon serve this purpose just as well: the photo taken by Korda seven years earlier. The students of Milan were the first to carry it high during their demonstrations, with the banner: "Che Lives!"

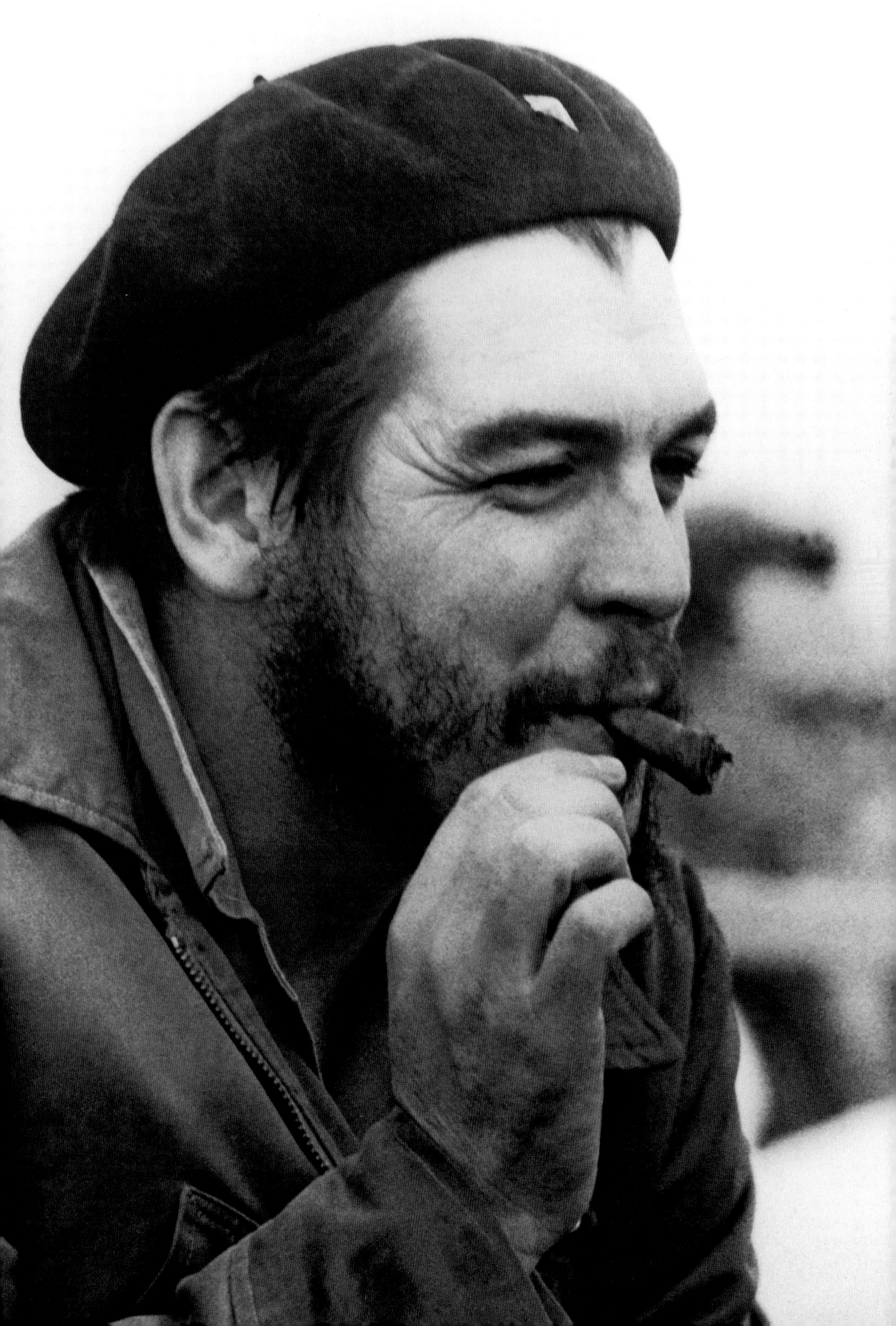

other ocean press titles

BOOKS BY CHE GUEVARA

SELF-PORTRAIT
A Photographic and Literary Memoir

THE MOTORCYCLE DIARIES
Notes on a Latin American Journey

REMINISCENCES OF THE
CUBAN REVOLUTIONARY WAR
Authorized Edition

THE BOLIVIAN DIARY
Authorized Edition

CHE GUEVARA READER
Writings on Politics and Revolution

GUERRILLA WARFARE
Authorized Edition

BOOKS ABOUT CHE GUEVARA

CHE: A MEMOIR BY FIDEL CASTRO
By Fidel Castro

CHE AND THE LATIN AMERICAN REVOLUTION
By Manuel "Barbarroja" Piñeiro

BOOKS ON CUBA AND LATIN AMERICA

AMERICA, MY BROTHER, MY BLOOD
Oswaldo Guayasamín and Pablo Neruda

CUBAN REVOLUTION READER
Edited by Julio García Luis

MY EARLY YEARS
By Fidel Castro

The book was finished without the support of Alberto Korda, who sadly passed away in 2001. But it is by Korda, dedicated to Korda, and in memory of Korda. For having helped us complete this project, we would like to give special thanks to Diana Díaz, who now has the difficult task of managing Korda's collection. Thanks to Pedro Álvarez Tabío, Fernando González Alfonso, and Elbia Fernández Soriano of the Historical Archives of the Cuban Council of State in Havana; thanks also to Rafael Acosta de Ariba, Rey Almira, Olivier Binst, Gérard Bonal, Eumelio Caballero, Christophe Cachera, Pierre and Estelle Champenois, Patricio Estay, Marc Grinsztajn, Hugo and Anael Guffanti, Céline Juanchich, Jean-Lin Lepoutre, Jean Lévy, Mabel Llevat Soy, Norka, Jacques Philibert, Jaime Sarusky, Lourdes Socarras, Vincent Touze, Yolanda Wood, Inaki Zabala.

C.L. and A.S.L.

For the translation, special thanks to Pierre Riant, Nancy Atkin, and all the staff at Ocean Press.

N.M.

PUBLISHED BY OCEAN PRESS

Australia: GPO Box 3279, Melbourne, Victoria 3051
Tel: (61-3) 9326 4280 Fax: (61-3) 9329 5040
E-mail: info@oceanbooks.com.au

USA: PO Box 1186, Old Chelsea Station, New York, NY 10113-1186
Tel/Fax: (1-212) 260 3690

OCEAN PRESS DISTRIBUTORS

USA and Canada: *Consortium Book Sales and Distribution*
Tel: 1-800-283-3572 www.cbsd.com

Australia and New Zealand: *Palgrave Macmillan*
E-mail: customer.service@macmillan.com.au

UK and Europe: *Turnaround Publisher Services*
E-mail: orders@turnaround-uk.com

Cuba and Latin America: *Ocean Press*
E-mail: oceanhav@enet.cu

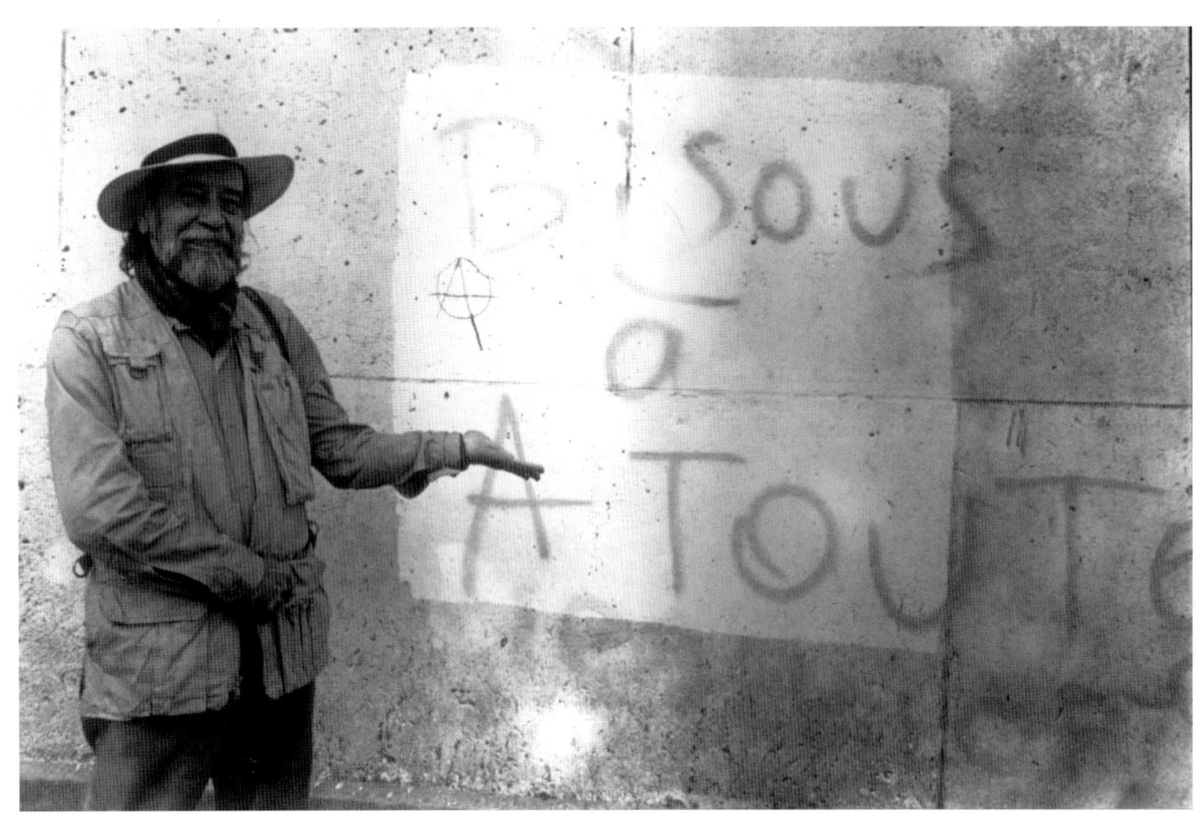

"A kiss to the girls"
Photograph of
Alberto Korda
by Patricio Estay.

Published by Ocean Press

info@oceanbooks.com.au
www.oceanbooks.com.au